Acclaim for *Beyond Prisons*

"*Beyond Prisons* **not only describes the evils of imprisonment, it sets forth a new justice paradigm.** ... Restorative justice, peace building, and reconciliation are the hallmarks of this new justice system. The Rev. Martin Luther King once proclaimed, 'I have a dream. . . .' Moving an entire government and society . . . may appear as a foolish dream to some. To others, however, . . . the dream of a new system which will be morally 'right and good' cannot be ignored."

—Paul E. Rogers
President, American Correctional Chaplains Association

"As the church struggles with the concept of 'prophetic *diakonia*,' how we relate to over two million of our incarcerated sisters and brothers is one of the greatest challenges to the faith community today. *Beyond Prisons* **is a 'must read'** for all who envision a criminal justice system that promotes rehabilitation, healing, reconciliation, and justice."

—Loretta Horton
Director for Poverty Ministries Networking, Evangelical Lutheran Church in America

D0180413

BEYOND PRISONS

A New Interfaith Paradigm
for Our Failed Prison System

Laura Magnani
Harmon L. Wray

Fortress Press   Minneapolis

BEYOND PRISONS
A New Interfaith Paradigm for Our Failed Prison System

The Society of Friends (Quakers) founded the American Friends Service Committee in 1917. The AFSC carries out service, development, and peace programs throughout the world, including a focus in criminal justice and new visions of justice. More information can be found online at www.afsc.org.

Cover photo: © Royalty-free/Corbis
Cover design: Brad Norr Design
Book design: Jill Carroll Lafferty

Marilyn Buck, "Clandestine Kisses," *Rescue the Word: Poems* (San Francisco, Calif.: Friends of Marilyn Buck, 2001). Used by permission.

Author photos: Harmon Wray, © Ashley Hunt; Laura Magnani, © Dawn Marie Wadle. Used by permission.

Library of Congress Cataloging-in-Publication Data

Magnani, Laura, 1949-
  Beyond prisons : a new interfaith paradigm for our failed prison system : a report by the American Friends Service Committee, Criminal Justice Task Force / by Laura Magnani, Harmon L. Wray.
    p. cm.
  Includes bibliographical references.
  ISBN 0-8006-3832-8 (alk. paper)
  1. Criminal justice, Administration of—Moral and ethical aspects—United States. 2. Prisons—United States. 3. Corrections—United States. I. Wray, Harmon L. II. American Friends Service Committee. Criminal Justice Task Force. III. Title.
  HV9950.M24 2006
  364.60973—dc22
                            2005037388

CONTENTS

Acknowledgments   vii

INTRODUCTION: A NEW MORALITY   I

Confession and Healing Justice, 3 / Definitions: More than
Mere Words, 6 / Outline of the Book, 17

I   HISTORY OF A FAILED SYSTEM   18

The Philadelphia Experiment, 18 / The Penitentiary System—
Religious Roots, 22 / The Penitentiary System—Philosophical
Roots, 24 / The Panopticon, 24 / The Development of the
Penitentiary System, 26

2   THE DYNAMICS OF CRIME AND PUNISHMENT
    IN AMERICA   30

The Problem, 30 / The Intersection of Race and Class, 33 /
Practicing White Supremacy, 33 / The Legacy of Economic
Dominance: Class, 37

3   IN OUR BACKYARDS:
    THE PENAL SYSTEM AT THE LOCAL LEVEL   43

Policing, 44 / In the Courthouse: The U.S. Adversarial Legal
System, 48 / The Pre-trial Process, 53 / County Jails, 54 /
Probation and Community Corrections, 57 / Taking Local
Communities Seriously, 59

4   SENTENCING: THE COLD HEART
    OF THE PENAL SYSTEM   62

The California Example, 63 / Federal Sentencing Policy, 65 /
Carrying Out the Drug War, 66 / Three Strikes, 67 / The Death
Penalty, 69 / Throwing Away the Key: Life without Mercy,
76 / Parole: The Terminating Program in the Rehabilitative
Model, 77 / Extra Punishment for Sex Offenders, 81 / Criminal
Records: The Permanent Punishment, 84

5 CAGES: STATE AND FEDERAL PRISONS TODAY   88

The Corporatization of Punishment, 88 / Private Prisons and
Accountability, 94 / Prison Guards, 95 / The Super-max and
Other Forms of Torture, 97 / Manufacturing Madness, 100 /
Prison Gang Policies: A Threat to Our Security, 102 / Political
Prisoners, 106 / Immigrants in the Criminal Justice System,
108 / Sexism, 113 / Women, 115 / Sexual Relations and Prison
Rape, 117 / Transgender Prisoners, 119 / Prison and Disability,
120 / The Mentally Ill, 122 / Health Care, 127 / Spanning
Generations: Impact of Prisons on Families, 128 / Prison
Ministry, 132

6 YOUTH, POVERTY, AND DELINQUENCY   137

History of the Juvenile Justice System, 139 / The Language of
Demonization, 140 / Criminalization of Youth, 142 / Creating
Gangs, 143 / Zero Tolerance, 144

7 AN ALTERNATIVE VISION OF JUSTICE   148

Survivors, 148 / Punishment, 150 / Forgiveness, 154 / Breaking
the Cycle, 155

8 SEARCHING FOR A NEW JUSTICE PARADIGM   159

Can Prisons Rehabilitate? 159 / From Prison Abolition to a
New Paradigm, 161 / Reform vs. Abolition, 162 / Alternatives,
163 / Restorative/Peace-building Justice, 164 / Problems with
Restorative Justice, 166 / Examples of Peace-building Justice,
168 / AFSC's Twelve-point Plan, 173 / Conclusion, 186

Notes   189

Bibliography   193

Index   202

ACKNOWLEDGMENTS

The number of people who have contributed to this project is long, but their contributions have been considerable so we want to linger over these names to do them full justice. First and foremost we thank Patricia R. Stewart for her vision, her persistence, her patience, and her support. Without Pat the book would not have been written.

Second, we acknowledge the significant contributions of Jamie Bissonnette, American Friends Service Committee (AFSC) staffer in the Cambridge office. We wanted to list Jamie as a co-author, which she clearly has been, but she declined the offer in the end. Jamie's deep analysis of social, racial, and economic issues is evident throughout the book and enabled all of us to represent the underside of history in ways we would not have accomplished without her commitment. Many other staff of AFSC made significant contributions, either to the text itself or to the thinking behind the text: Jana Schroeder, Bonnie Kerness, Masai Ehehosi, Kazi Toure, Kay Whitlock, Caroline Isaacs, Eric Moon, Rachel Kamel, Joyce Miller, Pat Clark, Tonya McClary, and the late Jan Marinissen. We also had the privilege of working with Lynn Damme, who edited the entire manuscript before we sent it out to publishers. Our editors at Fortress have also been wonderful, especially Michael West, Neil Elliott, and Abby Hartman.

A web of committees governs the AFSC, and Regional Criminal Justice Committees throughout the country had input on many drafts of this manuscript. But the greatest contributions by committees came from the national Criminal Justice Task Force, in whose name the document is written. We would like to express particular gratitude to Michael Schell, Minerva Glidden, Don Reeves, and Connie Curry. The national Board Executive Committee also spent many hours reviewing the document and sending recommendations, particularly the chair of the National AFSC Board, Paul Lacey, and AFSC general secretary Mary Ellen McNish.

A number of prisoner readers, including Hasani Burleson and Shellery Moore, have been invaluable. Marilyn Buck contributed a powerful poem, "Clandestine Kisses," in chapter 5, and Mumia Abu-Jamal helped reveal the impact of religion in matters of social policy.

Finally, we thank our families for their patience, guidance, and endurance in the years it took to birth this document. Laura thanks Joe, Zachary, Ann, and Elaine especially—realizing that her family is much broader than these four—and many other loved ones who have held her hand throughout. Harmon is very grateful to his beloved partner, Judy Parks, for her many years of support and challenge and her deep wisdom about human beings; his beloved mother, Celeste Wray, a weekly visitor of imprisoned persons for sixteen years; and a host of colleagues—some free and some incarcerated—in the struggle for a justice more healing and less punitive.

INTRODUCTION:
A NEW MORALITY

People demanding punitive justice are ignoring the great justice a new morality could bring—a shared morality freed from colonialism, oppression, and greed.

—Rev. Frank Chikane, South African Council of Churches

It is time for a new morality in the United States.

This new morality must be based on achieving balance—balance in relationships, balance economically, balance with nature and the forces outside ourselves. Nature teaches a great deal about how to cleanse and how to restore. Indeed, this drive toward wholeness is much more natural than the perpetuation of violence and brokenness to which we have become so attached. Judgment and punishment, as First Nations peoples—and Jesus's Sermon on the Mount (Matthew 5–7)—show us, belong to the Creator. It cannot define how we relate to one another.

Beyond Prisons is an attempt to articulate a new morality in terms of this balance and to redefine our relationships beyond notions of judgment and punishment. In this book, the Criminal Justice Task Force of the American Friends Service Committee (AFSC), a Quaker-based organization rooted in the Religious Society of Friends, brings its decades of experience inside and outside of prisons to bear on the issues of crime and punishment.[1] By maintaining the focus on problems caused by both the penal system and the increasing numbers of people in our prisons, the AFSC endeavors to envision a world without prisons.

Though rooted in Quaker understandings, this book takes an interfaith approach as we analyze the signs and evidence of weakness in our national culture of punishment and articulate a vision gained by constructing a new justice paradigm and a culture of peace. We speak of a new paradigm because the approach we are calling for cannot be added on to the existing retributive system. All things must be made new; the paradigm we envision cannot be driven by fear. The real work lying before us is spiritual and calls us to nothing less than fundamental change. The real work takes us beyond prisons to a new morality, and ultimately to a new reality.

The AFSC's concern for both crime survivors and people convicted of or accused of crimes in this society is rooted in the Quaker opposition to violence and injustice—and the Quaker principle that there is that of God in every person. The AFSC views each individual as a person of worth who should be treated humanely, with dignity and respect, regardless of his or her circumstances in life or how offensive his or her behavior has been to others. Cruelty and abuse in reaction to a person's behavior often eclipse and compound the wrong of the original act. The AFSC seeks to achieve meaningful communication with all people—those who victimize others, those who are victims, those who oppress, and those who are oppressed—in the expectation that the measure of goodness and truth in each individual, however latent or invisible, seeks expression and can respond.

History is written from the standpoint of the victors; the underside—"the losers"—remains hidden. Prisons were constructed to hide and to separate. Although the realities and failures of the U.S. criminal justice system have been well documented, the myth that punishment is an essential element of justice persists. As we will demonstrate, it persists because prisons serve the power structure—the status quo—as it stands. The answer to the question "Do prisons work?" changes depending on one's perspective on the purpose prisons are meant to fulfill. If the purpose of prisons is to keep some people down and to deflect attention away from underlying causes, the answer is yes. If the goal, however, is to heal brokenness and build community, the answer is no.

Although redemption and rehabilitation were embedded in the original intention behind the penitentiary, very little room is left today for captives of the system to change for the better. To be sure, thousands of individuals have done so on their own, overcoming the cruelty and isolation to which they have been subjected. But they are the saints—the strong and courageous few.

For the most part, the criminal justice system breeds more violence, more racism, deeper hatreds. It makes people less able to participate in the economic system, to function fully on the outside, or to develop healthy relationships. It utterly ignores the needs of survivors of crime. It never even asks what healing or wholeness could look like. Healing cannot occur superficially, as history has shown us again and again. Healing will require us to address the extreme power imbalances that have allowed some people, and one class, to remain at the top at the expense of other races and classes.

Recognizing the privilege that most mainline Protestants, including Quakers, have had is an important first step in the healing process. One dimension of this step in the move toward a healing model of justice, as opposed to the revenge model now practiced in so many parts of the world, is confession. Can we honestly admit when we have failed? And who would be included among the "we" of that question?

Confession and Healing Justice

Healing justice begins with confession—with recognizing when we have participated in wrongdoing, owning up to it, and being held accountable. Historically, Quakers, or Friends, have been opposed to war and slavery. They have a history of dissent from prevailing practices that deny the equality and value of each person. In the United States, they have long been concerned with improving conditions in mental hospitals and prisons, alleviating the suffering of the poor, and working for racial equality (AFSC 2004, 1).

Nevertheless, Friends have been both a part of the problem and a part of the solution when it comes to criminal justice. For centuries Quakers have pioneered many reforms and innovations in penology, from their involvement in the beginnings of the penitentiary system to the present day. Yet, rather than being among the first critics of the penitentiary experiment when its intended benefits did not materialize, Quakers instead were among those who advocated building a bigger and often more repressive version. They supported the use of the iron gag to enforce the discipline of total silence—a device that can only be seen today as an instrument of torture. As a Quaker organization we need to own our role in such acts, to set the record straight, and to sound the alarm at the injustice and torture we see throughout the prison system. Other mainline Protestant denominations undoubtedly have similar histories of complicity in injustice to confess.

Current penal practices in the United States bring both these Quaker failings and the Quaker concern for human rights into high relief. During the civil rights movement and the peace movement against the Vietnam War, the Rev. Dr. Martin Luther King, Jr. taught us that the bombs we drop overseas explode in our own cities. There was hope at the demise of the Cold War that the Military Industrial Complex would be dismantled. Instead, it has expanded to many more fronts—including the domestic front, where it is paralleled by the "Prison Industrial Complex" (PIC) (see chapter 5), where criminal justice policies and economic interests are so intertwined they feed upon each other until economic factors become dominant.

Engaging in brutal, even deadly crimes and repression is all too human. It is not hard to cross the line from a form of enforcement that is thought to be legitimate to one that becomes torture, as we have observed in the controversies over the treatment of prisoners in the U.S. government's "war against terrorism" and the Iraq war. The United States has been crossing this line over and over again in the name of fighting terrorism—claiming that well-meaning people "like us" couldn't possibly commit torture because our motives are good. Interrogation of a suspect is meant to uncover evidence. Applying greater and greater pressure to the suspect, if the desired "information" isn't forthcoming, seems like just a natural progression, a change of degrees. Even if the pressure moves toward humiliation, or involves physical pain, or other methods of "breaking down" a stubborn subject, this can be excused if the perpetrators had good intentions. But the time for such excuses has passed. Evidence of torture at Abu Ghraib, Guantánamo Bay, and secret CIA-run prisons around the world is mounting and the public is justifiably outraged. The acts being committed in these places seem to us too widespread to be the isolated actions of a few low-level soldiers. They were apparently carefully calculated at the highest levels of government.

The extermination of millions of people under Nazi Germany involved many ordinary people swept up in a system, following orders, pursuing "good intentions"—people who had fallen asleep. All of us are susceptible to abusing power, not just professionals such as district attorneys or guards or policy makers. Therefore, rather than demonize any particular group, our goal is to point out the dangers that lurk in structures intended for violence and oppression.

Who can take responsibility for a punishment system that has functioned as a tool to support the legacy of colonialism, racism, and imperialism that is so deeply rooted in U.S. culture? For healing justice to become the dominant system would require a serious recognition of this legacy and the implementation of a process for truth telling, acknowledgment, and reparations—as we say, a new morality.

The domestic "war on crime" calls for a domestic peace agenda. Quakers have always held that war is contrary to the love and respect they hold for all people. In 1661, Quakers testified to their commitment to peace:

> We utterly deny all outward wars and strife, and fightings with outward weapons, for any end, or under any pretense whatsoever; this is our testimony to the whole world. (Declaration to Charles I)

Since the Quaker peace testimony is not only opposition to active participation in war, but also a positive affirmation of the power of good to overcome evil, the AFSC has been led to work in prisons and in poor and working-class communities from which many prisoners come. The AFSC calls for peace that is based on truth, repentance, justice, and love: truth about institutions of oppression, as well as truth about harm to individuals; repentance of oppressors and perpetrators; radical justice that comes from the ground up; and love that births compassion. Repentance is critical. It entails specific action by those who have done harm: acknowledgment of the harm, assumption of responsibility for doing the harm, and agreement that change must take place to ensure that further harm will not be done.

How we deal with rifts in the social compact defines who we are as a nation, where our priorities lie, and how we relate to one another across class, cultural, and racial lines. Punishment, by its very nature, causes harm. AFSC criminal justice programs focus on the impact of the "culture of punishment" that is prevalent in the United States. We cannot punish our way to a healthy society.

Definitions: More than Mere Words

Criminal justice is more than mere words; it is patterns of behavior. The patterns imply ideas, ideologies, values, attitudes, but these are not the ones expressed in the higher culture, the official stories, the public propaganda. Police brutality, plea bargaining, and the third degree are just as much a part of the fabric as decisions of the Supreme Court; and so, too, are thousands of unrecorded, tiny acts of minor clemency and petty tyranny at the level of the streets, station houses, courtrooms, and jails.

—Friedman 1993, 56

The terms used by all of us, daily, to describe the criminal justice system are often bandied about without agreement as to their meanings. To frame the analysis that comes in the rest of this book, we offer our own set of definitions for words like *safety* and *crime*, some ideas about the responsibilities of government, and finally, our understanding of justice, relying on wisdom from a variety of faith traditions as well as on our own experience.

Safety

Much of modern criminal justice practice is derived from notions about what will increase public safety. Much of the repression done by the criminal justice system is done in the name of safety, just as "national security" is used as a rationale for militarization. We have been taught to equate safety with physical protection. Our homes will be safe if we have a security system; our cars will be safe if they are alarmed and have a device in place locking the wheel; our schools will be safe if we have metal detectors and security officers; and, against all evidence, our communities will be safe if we have more police. Some communities define their safety by the quantity of law enforcers who patrol their borders and detain those who do not belong.

It is difficult to overstate the role of fear in driving public policy on crime and punishment. People want to feel safe. Many communities feel as if they are in a "war zone" because of the prevalence of guns, gun violence, and drug transactions. Many also have a sense of being in an "occupied territory" because of police presence. There is good reason to fear violence and to insist on living conditions free of violence.

What does safety look like when equitable relationships exist? How can we make communities truly safe? What is law enforcement in this context? What roles should law enforcers play?

Safety prevails when people have both security as physical protection, and a sense of well-being that encompasses physical, emotional, and economic spheres. For example, children are not safe if they are free from physical abuse but emotionally neglected. Adults are not safe if they are free from physical and emotional abuse but are jobless or homeless or hungry. Safety requires a sense of community—that is, the ongoing presence of caring, attentive people to whom we are mutually accountable. It also requires sufficient access to resources to ensure freedom from hunger, joblessness, homelessness, and inadequate health care.

Law enforcement that supports the achievement of this kind of safety must rely on understandings of government and safety as defined above. True public-safety initiatives will intervene on behalf of struggling families, directing them to services and resources that will restore them to balance. These initiatives will rescue children in abusive homes and find caring places for them until their families of origin are stabilized. They will simultaneously address the deficits of those families. In cases where crimes of violence occur and perpetrators are identified, these public-safety initiatives will focus on breaking the cycle of violence, and criminal sanctions will be measured against such a standard. True public-safety initiatives will focus on removing the root causes of crime and on addressing poverty.

Is public safety reliant on good policing? Historically, the job of the police has been to prevent crime, keep the peace, and capture criminals. Today, at the very least, the purpose of the police should be to keep the peace and protect the most vulnerable. In providing this protection, the police should strive to function in a noncoercive manner. The "justifiable" use of lethal force should be named as the violence that it is. A standard of least-restrictive alternatives to any use of force should be applied in all police protocols.

Crime

A crime is evidence that there is something wrong with relationships. An event must be seen in the context of what created it.

—Yazzie 2000

The AFSC Criminal Justice Task Force does not accept the common usage of the term *crime*. Crime is not solely the violation of legal codes; it encompasses behavior that violates human rights. But beyond the legal understandings, crime shatters relationships—both social (including political and economic) and interpersonal. Substance abuse and prostitution, activities defined as against the law, certainly impact the lives and the rights of others but could be addressed more effectively outside the criminal justice system. Lee Griffith questions the definition of crime, saying it is a relative matter that changes with the disposition of legislative bodies. Homicide is typically considered a crime—unless the perpetrator acted in self-defense, by reason of insanity, or "in the line of duty" as a member of a police force, a legal execution team, or a military body. Indeed, soldiers might be criminally liable for refusing to kill on order, or for refusing to register with selective service. It is considered criminal behavior to lie under oath, but otherwise lying is lawful for everyone from presidents to common folk. It is illegal to speak about classified documents, and it is illegal not to speak before grand juries—unless the speaking would involve self-incrimination, in which case it becomes legal not to speak (unless one has been granted immunity from prosecution, in which case it becomes illegal not to speak!). In short, everything from killing (or refusing to kill) to speaking (or refusing to speak) is or is not a crime, depending on the widest range of circumstances. So divorced is civil law from moral reflection that we barely blink when presidents somberly intone that we have to stop violence in America, while as a nation we spend thousands of dollars a minute building bombs (Griffith 1993, 30).

In American colonial times, crime was tied up with definitions of sin. Today, the fact that crime is thought to be strictly a legal concept obscures the extent to which our criminal law continues to be rooted in moralistic biases about unacceptable individual behavior rather than in consistent concern about how some violate others. As Stanford University law professor Lawrence Friedman notes, "Behind every legal judgment of criminality is more powerful social judgment"

(Friedman 1993, 4). The government must pass a law to declare a particular act a crime. In many ways, the law creates the crime that it punishes. For example, in many feudal societies, hunting game on the landowner's property was considered a legitimate way to put food on the table—until lawmakers decided it was "poaching." All crimes are "acts that society, or at least some dominant elements in society, sees as a threat" (Parenti 2000:83). In the aftermath of Hurricane Katrina in 2005, a majority of the people who, in their efforts to survive, took food off the shelves of decimated grocery stores were people of color; they were routinely called "looters" and charged with crimes. Anglo-Europeans engaging in the same acts were called "resourceful." The criminalization of poverty was played out before our eyes on the evening news.

This is not to imply that certain acts, especially acts of violence, do not cause real harm and do not need to be stopped. Though the law often represents the interests of the dominant class, there are common shared interests for safety and well-being that must be honored and respected. Clearly, in order for any society to function, acts such as murder, rape, kidnapping, and armed robbery—along with corporate and government crime—must be proscribed and held to a minimum. Our concern, however, is with the slippery slope we can find ourselves on as soon as we accept existing conventional understandings of crime as having sacrosanct status.

In picking out whom to punish, our criminal justice system deals most harshly with those already victimized by basic social, economic, and political injustices. While behavior that could be considered criminal permeates all levels of our society, wealthy and middle-class people who engage in criminal activity tend to receive little or no penalty, while people of color, the poor, and other exploited people engaged in similar activities are given harsh sentences. Youth from poor communities are routinely charged with crime and go to prison, while youth from middle-class communities are often given a warning and sent back to school. The penal system too easily becomes the repressive arm of the state that reinforces the oppression of the exploited. Instead of correcting the problems it is intended to relieve, the justice system itself in many ways has become a monstrous crime against humanity. Selective enforcement of laws is all too human. Each of us inevitably brings our own assumptions and prejudices to the decisions we make each day. Still, law enforcement officers, prosecutors, judges, and juries have broad-ranging discretion that has a permanent impact on the futures of others.

Selective enforcement allows those in power to use "criminality" as a label to condemn those on the margins of society whom they wish to control. The label of "criminal" is a permanent one today in the United States. A conviction, no matter how old, may successfully keep a person from ever obtaining viable employment, decent housing, or certain constitutional rights such as voting. Criminalization has become a tool of social control. It is more "politically correct" than outright expressions of racism or classism, but it accomplishes the same purpose. It is possible only when people are convinced that criminal behavior is solely a result of individual weakness or inherent badness rather than the direct outgrowth of social inequality, poverty, racism, deteriorating education, and decaying communities. It is easy to track the growth over the past thirty years of the myth of the "criminal type" and the ways in which those in power have manipulated the inherent racism and classism in our society to cast poor people and people of color as "criminally inclined."

We reject the concept of criminality that supports the myth of a criminal type—a concept that grows in part out of ignorance and fears rooted in biases and prejudices. This concept of criminality represents a gross distortion of the nature of those caught up in the criminal justice system and provides a simplistic explanation of highly complex social problems. It tends to project distinctive images of good people as opposed to bad people, and victims as opposed to villains. These misunderstandings result in the perpetuation of the criminal stereotype, although behavior defined as crime occurs at all levels of society.

The Role of Government

Government's primary function is to ensure the common good—to provide an economic and social framework within which people can meet their basic human needs for food, housing, health, and education, and within which all people can live in peace. According to the South African Kairos Document, "To promote the common good is to govern in the interests of, and for the benefit of, all the people" (Kairos Theologians 1986, 18). The language in the preamble of the U.S. Constitution expresses similar values: "establish justice . . . promote the general welfare." Yet, as this book will demonstrate, concepts of the general welfare vary widely and justice is denied to many. Government must provide a structure that will allow for all people to experience justice.

Further, government must establish mechanisms that allow people to live with dignity—to trade their skills for the resources necessary to sustain themselves, their families, and their communities. Government must play a balancing role on behalf of the whole society. Governments must not align themselves with the economically powerful, but rather restrain profit-making enterprises that benefit the few at the expense of the many. Communities where the common good is ensured can be healthy and safe communities.

Too often the social policies of the United States government benefit the rich at the expense of the poor. Law protects power and property; it safeguards wealth; and, by the same token, it perpetuates the subordinate status of the people on the bottom (Friedman 1993, 84).

This is particularly the case with the penal system. This system has penetrated all aspects of the lives of the poor. While wealth and material success are valued by our culture, the poor are feared. It is not hard to see, therefore, why most Americans have shown little concern for the increasing numbers of poor citizens in U.S. prisons.[2] As a nation, the United States has encouraged this oppression. Those who dissent have been neutralized. "Neutrality enables the status quo of oppression (and therefore violence) to continue. It is a way of giving tacit support to the oppressor" (Friedman 1993, 13).

This crisis demands a bold, incisive, prophetic response to these social policies. Government must be held accountable, especially when governments align themselves with the rich and powerful at the expense of the poor. The AFSC is called to articulate the demand for justice that is the birthright of all people.

Justice

As a faith-based, Quaker organization, the AFSC is situated within the Judeo-Christian tradition. Special attention is given to this theological tradition because it is often used to underpin some of the most oppressive penal policies in the United States.

When justice is spoken of in the context of Western, Judeo-Christian thought, the following quotation is often cited:

The Spirit of the Lord is upon me,
> because he has anointed me to bring good news to the poor.
He has sent me to proclaim release to the captives,
> and recovery of sight to the blind,
>> to let the oppressed go free,
to proclaim the year of the Lord's favor. (Luke 4:18-19)

This is the first recorded sermon of Jesus, quoting the prophet Isaiah (Isaiah 61:1) in his hometown synagogue in Nazareth to make it clear that he has taken up the cause of the poor and the oppressed. He tells the poor, as Isaiah did, that he has been anointed by God to preach to the poor. The good news (that is, the gospel) he preaches is one of liberation. As a poor person himself, he announces that he has been sent by God to "proclaim the year of the Lord's favor." Later in the same sermon, he calls the rich and powerful to repentance. Jesus preached a radical justice, a justice that comes from below and is determined by the people. This was not a justice of reform that would be determined by the state. Reform justice leaves structures and institutions intact. Radical justice redistributes resources among the people and creates space for the people both to define the changes that are required and to demand that they be implemented.

"The year of the Lord's favor" of which Jesus spoke is a direct reference to the concrete social programs of the "Sabbath" and the "Jubilee" years found in Leviticus 25. This radically egalitarian social program was deeply rooted in ancient Middle Eastern cultures and included the redistribution of wealth for the poor through cancellation of all debt, food for the hungry, clothes for the naked, land for the landless, and freedom for those who were enslaved and in prison. This was not symbolic language. It is central to the Hebrew Scripture, reappears throughout the ages in different forms, and is again central to Gospel teachings.

There is a tendency among most of us to dismiss this radical message on the grounds that it was only practiced inconsistently. Biblical scholar and theologian Ched Myers reminds us: "If we are going to dismiss the Jubilee because Israel practiced it only inconsistently, we should also ignore the Sermon on the Mount because Christians have rarely embodied Jesus' instruction to love our enemies."[3]

These social programs of the Year of the Lord symbolized the ruler's intent to govern for the common good of all citizens. If we accept that the Hebrews were descended from the ancient Habiru who were enslaved in Egypt, we may imagine that the Hebrews had knowledge and, perhaps, experience of this practice from their period of enslavement in Egypt.

> A ceremonial hymn such as that from the enthronement of Rameses IV in Egypt (ca. 1167 B.C.E.) is illustrative: "Oh happy day. . . . Those who had been hungry were fed. . . . Those who had been naked were clad. . . . Those who were in prison were set free." (Griffith 1993, 109)

The concept of radical justice was deeply embedded in Hebrew theology from the beginning. Again and again, throughout Hebrew Scripture, God appears as the liberator of the oppressed.

True justice is the enactment of the Sabbath year. The Hebrew word is *tsedekah*. *Tsedekah* is sometimes referred to as *shalom* justice, or peace-building justice. It is a true justice because it demands a radical change in the resources available to all people and in the structures of society. The Year of the Lord, if practiced, could introduce a true and lasting justice, creating right relationships between individuals and their communities, and putting structures in place to support and sustain this balance. This justice implies covenanted commitment among people, and between people and their government. This justice is focused on the community and the commitments and relationships that exist between and among us as people.

The AFSC's experience has caused it to question a justice of reform that leaves structures and institutions intact. True justice demands a radical change in the way resources are made available to all citizens, and a change in the structures of society. The goal would be a peace-building justice. This justice implies covenanted commitment among people, and between people and their government. This justice is not focused on the individual; it is about all of us.

Friends use the expression "rightly ordered," which can be understood in theological terms as that order which is in alignment with the Divine. In secular terms, "rightly ordered" can be understood as something that is organized to sustain and enhance life—something that is in balance. The new morality we seek demands a reordering of priorities in a way that enhances life and is just for everyone. Economic justice—a redistribution of wealth such that basic needs are met—must be at the heart of this new morality. Without economic justice, individuals will resort to violence, and all efforts to curb violence will focus on individuals instead of on systemic imbalance.

What does peace-building justice mean in relation to the punishment inflicted by the modern penal system? As Lee Griffith, a Christian social activist and author of several books challenging the moral underpinnings of institutions of our time, notes, "Any ideology that demands the intentional increase in suffering rather than its diminution can hardly lay claim to justice" (Griffith 1993, 97). Punishment, like crime, may be understood as the deliberate infliction of pain and suffering upon human beings. Based on that understanding, we can say unhesitatingly that our current criminal justice system intentionally increases suffering. Those convicted of crime are not only removed from their communities, they are placed in institutions designed to incapacitate and punish them. Policymakers who advocate mandatory life sentences to replace the death penalty are settling for "death by incarceration." Peace-building justice seeks peaceful settlement of conflicts in ways that take seriously the harm suffered, address needs for accountability, and move toward healing and wholeness.

In accepting the definition of crime as behavior that violates human rights—in essence, behavior that harms individuals and communities—we believe that our response to those who behave in criminal fashion must refrain from harming them. This perspective inescapably leads us to reexamine the criminal justice system, to ask who are the harmers, and to create new institutions and structures that address the violation of human rights.

The modern penal system appears to have abandoned the possibility of redemption. The few rehabilitative programs that once existed in prisons (higher education, intensive drug treatment, family reunification, and vocational training) have been cut from most prisons over the past thirty years. At the same time, people are going to prison for offenses that thirty years ago would have resulted in misdemeanor charges, probation, or some other community-based sentence.

Present prison policy demonstrates that we do not believe that prisoners can repent, show remorse, and work toward healing themselves and their relationships. When the weakest or most impoverished among us does not experience the support or sustaining balance of a healthy society, we are not a just society. Just as when survivors of serious crime are unheard, marginalized, or exploited, when offenders

suffer the unending isolation of our prisons we can hardly lay claim to justice. Justice implies covenanted commitment in which we enter into promises with one another. Yet covenants will sometimes be broken. We are all breakers of rules, laws, and covenants. When a covenant is broken, justice demands repentance. The wrong must be righted. Finally, the covenant can be restored. After that, the offender is set free to enter into covenant again. This formulation applies equally to those in power who promote unjust policies as it does to an offender on the streets. When governmental policies and decisions or policies of corporations harm communities, those in power must repent, the wrong must be righted, and the government or corporation must restore its covenant with those it has harmed. The expectation is that once the individual, the government, or the corporate entity repents, and along with the broader community rights the wrong, the individual or other entity will be free to reestablish right relationships with their communities. Forgiveness can be accomplished through acknowledgment, repentance, reparation, and reintegration into society.

This covenanted commitment was best articulated in the documents that led to the South African Constitution, written after the end of forty years of brutal repression under apartheid. The adoption of this constitution lays the secure foundation for the people of South Africa to transcend the divisions and strife of the past, which generated gross violations of human rights; the transgression of humanitarian principles in violent conflicts; and a legacy of hatred, fear, guilt, and revenge. These can now be addressed on the basis that there is a need for understanding but not for vengeance, a need for reparation but not for retaliation, a need for *ubuntu* (the African philosophy of humanism) but not for victimization.

The need for *ubuntu* is urgently demonstrated in the United States especially, where we have imprisoned over two million of our brothers and sisters and put in place structures and institutions that continue to punish them for the entirety of their lives. Our comfort with punishment should alarm us and make us ask ourselves profound questions about who we are as a people.

In the Buddhist tradition, understandings that move beyond punishment are based in compassion. "Here there can be no domination of self over other or other over self. Instead, all beings, including each one of us, enemy and friend alike, exist in patterns of mutuality, inter-connectedness, and co-responsibility and, ultimately in nonduality. . . . It is from this base that authentic harmlessness and helpfulness awaken" (Halifax 1993, 201). In examining Buddhist beliefs about the death penalty and punishment more generally, one could begin with the precepts, the most basic set of training rules in the teachings.

The first precept is to abstain from taking life. This advice is rein-forced in other important texts in Buddhism, including the final chap-ter of the *Dhammapada*, which says, "Him I call a Brahmin who has put aside weapons and renounced violence toward all creatures. He neither kills nor helps others to kill" (Easwaran 1985, 197). And there are other teachings that question the appropriateness of punishment itself (Horigan 1999). Punishment affects those who impose it as well as those being directly punished.

According to Buddhist teaching, we all possess the Buddha nature, so the task of rehabilitation is to help someone come into communion with his or her Buddha nature. As in the Quaker belief in that of God in everyone, this potential in each of us can be ignited and nurtured. Our task in healing justice, therefore, is to work for systems and pro-cesses that make such change possible.

Death row prisoner and journalist Mumia Abu-Jamal follows the teachings of John Africa, founder of the MOVE organization in Philadelphia. He has written about the different roles religion has played in either supporting or opposing repressive policies:

> Religion has often been less a force for liberation than a tool of oppression—an impetus for civil unrest, warfare and genocide. . . .

> If religion has had no impact on the shedding of blood (has it done anything other than aid and abet it?) then why the need for it? . . .

> We live in a world of megadeath, on land reddened by its original peoples' blood, and saddened with the tears of unwilling captives. We missionize and maim, westernize and rob, torture and starve our fellow humans around the globe. We kill each other, but not only that, we abuse the Earth, our common mother. . . .

> We are in need of a religion of Life that sees the world in more than merely utilitarian terms. A religion that reveres all life as valuable in itself; that sees Earth as an extension of self, and if wounded, as an injury to self. (Abu-Jamal 2003)

Outline of the Book

Having given this overview of the understandings and definitions that inform this book's agenda, we begin our book with a historical examination of what gave rise to the prison system. Using a socioeconomic lens, we devote the following six chapters to an extensive exposé of the system as it has evolved in the last two hundred years, with special attention to the system as it is today. The questions we ask are: Who benefits from the system as it is? Who pays the price? What are the results? What alternatives are possible?

As the book moves from its comprehensive analysis of the criminal justice system as it exists to an examination of the underlying assumptions and possible new directions, it draws from the American Friends Service Committee's fifty-plus years of experience with the criminal justice system, particularly its concern for the people most affected—victims of crime, the imprisoned, and their families. In addition, it examines a variety of other faith traditions that could be a source of hope, such as Jewish and Christian teachings, Native American teachings, and Buddhism. All these sources offer different insights and directions for healing, and question whether true justice can come from punishment.

Our closing chapters begin to ask the big questions and to define the terms of the discussion in new ways. As long as the economic system continues to reward greed and exploitation, the vast majority of people will not have enough to eat or safe places to sleep, or access to education and health care. As long as we are caught in the revenge loop, there will be no hope for change. As long as institutions like prisons and courts continue to reinforce racial separation and enforce economic inequality, there will be no room for justice.

1: HISTORY OF A FAILED SYSTEM

In order to understand how it came to pass that the United States incarcerates over two million people, we must return to the nation's roots. The roots of this country's institutions are in the Christian establishment, which is mostly white, and its beliefs about right and wrong, worthy and unworthy. In this context, prisons have always served a dual function for those in power: economic gain and social control.

The Philadelphia Experiment

During the colonial period, the British legal system had been replicated in the American colonies. This was a common-law system that placed a great deal of emphasis on the spoken word. It relied upon the judgment of a grand jury drawn from the public to indict an individual. Public shame was a very important factor in colonial punishment. The goal was to teach a swift lesson and evoke repentance. Public whipping, especially for servants and slaves, was thus common. By far the most common punishments, however, were fines and restitution. The wealthy

> *For a century and a half the prison had always been offered as its own remedy: the reactivation of the penitentiary techniques as the only means of overcoming their perpetual failure; the realization of the corrective project as the only method of overcoming the impossibility of implementing it.*
>
> —Foucault 1995, 268

were permitted to put up security as a guarantee of good behavior. For more serious crimes, convicts were mutilated, branded, or hanged. Thirteen crimes carried the death penalty. Largely missing from this roster of consequences was imprisonment. There were, for instance, only nineteen cases of imprisonment for crime in New York between 1691 and 1776 (Friedman 1993, 48). It stands to reason that in a society where there was a shortage of laborers, there would be a reluctance to imprison able-bodied adults, except for failure to pay outstanding debts. In the young capitalist colonies, debtors were a drain on both farmers and merchants and were punished to deter others.

In colonial times, prisons were basically debtors' prisons. The legal system was arranged in such a way that it was both complex and expensive to gain one's freedom after being convicted of debt-related offenses. The Pennsylvania Constitution of 1776 reformed the laws of imprisonment for debt, but these laws were not implemented until 1787, after the Revolutionary War. Between 1780 and 1790, the number of debtors in jail in Philadelphia (the birthplace of the modern penitentiary) continued to be greater than the number of what we would today consider criminals. In 1785, half of the 151 persons confined to the Philadelphia jail were debtors. These debts were often small. Even individuals who were declared not guilty of the charge of debt were still required to pay their court fees before they could be released. This was often beyond their means.

The post-revolutionary period in the United States, 1780–1800, saw the continuation of the revolutionary spirit into a time of great experimentation. All relationships and institutions were being reexamined. The form of republicanism that was being developed was paternalistic, and public debate and

> *Of that half, not more than fifteen could support themselves. The other sixty were so miserably poor, that they must perish with hunger and cold, unless fed and clothed by the charitable inhabitants of the city!*
>
> —Alexander 1980

policy decisions were almost exclusively in the hands of the landed elite.

During this time, the new nation's population grew dramatically, as did the number of impoverished people. Many of the poor settling into the Philadelphia area were Irish and French immigrants. There was also a small, free black population encompassing about 1 percent of the city's inhabitants. Some public officials characterized the poor as "bloody Jacobins thirsting to subvert order and stability" (Alexander 1980, 27). There was much public debate about the amount of democratic participation the poor should be allowed. Benjamin Rush, a Philadelphia doctor, in letters to his friends referred to the idea that participation in civic affairs should be open to all as a "mobocracy. . . . Where all laws breathe the spirit of town meetings and porter shops [to satisfy] common people" (Alexander 1980, 37).

The elite believed the poor to be of two types: the industrious poor and the criminal poor. A campaign to turn the criminal poor into the industrious poor was seen to be crucial to maintaining social order and stability. Crime was thought to originate with the "worst evils associated with idle, vicious poverty" (Alexander 1980, 80).

The conditions in the Philadelphia jail were deplorable. Prisoners and their families had to provide for all their needs as well as try to pay off their debts. The drive toward creation of the penitentiary began, in large part, in response to the horrible conditions of the dungeon-style jails and the cruelty of public punishments. The humiliation of these punishments, and the violence they inspired in the people who observed them, caused the city fathers to begin searching for alternatives. The law that required chaining convicts to wheelbarrows and putting them to work in the streets was overturned. Hard, public labor for imprisoned debtors was abandoned in favor of labor within the walls of the jail.

It was within this historical context that the 1790 Penal Code was passed in Pennsylvania. The ruling elite's fear of disorder should the poor gain political power, coupled with discomfort over the barbaric and often public punishments of the colonial period, led to new experiments in dealing with criminals. Prisoners would now be sentenced to unremitting solitude coupled with laborious employment in the prison in hopes of reforming them and deterring potential criminals.

The Philadelphia Society for Alleviating the Miseries of Public Prisons was the first interdenominational Protestant organization in the United States. Chaired for almost a half-century by Anglican Bishop William White, its membership was about 50 percent Quaker. In 1790, this group prevailed upon the Pennsylvania legislature to convert Philadelphia's Walnut Street Jail to include a new unit—one designed for those criminals considered to be the worst to be segregated from other prisoners and from one another in single cells.

The establishment of this new housing unit for those prisoners deemed to be the hardest cases, and the institution of a regimen for individual prisoner reform, constitutes the first attempt to classify prisoners, and represents the beginning of the penitentiary movement in the United States. Other elements of the experiment included a clean, sanitary physical environment; regularized work; trained, paid jail staff; total separation of prisoners from their families and friends; enforced solitude and silence; and human contact severely limited to a few carefully chosen inspectors and jail staff. Prisoners were intended to work all day in their individual cells in the new unit at Walnut Street, but overcrowding prevented this.

> *Cells, six feet by eight feet square and nine feet high, were to be built in the yard and separated from the common yard by walls high enough to prevent all external communication. These cells would house the more hardened and atrocious offenders. This action reaffirmed the legislators' efforts to reclaim persons who still had remaining seeds of virtue and goodness.*
>
> —Alexander 1980

Who were these prisoners? The inhabitants of the Philadelphia jail were poor immigrants and blacks. Of those convicted in the Mayor's Court in 1796, 70 percent were born outside the American colonies, 31.7 percent in Ireland. Persons of African descent constituted 31.8 percent of the prisoners. From 1794 to 1804, black people constituted only 1 percent of the city's population, but they averaged 28.5 percent of the Walnut Street Jail residents. By the time prisoners were moved from the jail to Pennsylvania's newly built Eastern State Penitentiary in 1830, Walnut Street's black population outnumbered the white (Magnani 1990, 53).

The Philadelphia and Pennsylvania experience was in many ways an instructive microcosm of the course that the development of the penitentiary system took in many of the American colonies and much of the new nation. From the beginning, prisons in the New World were expected to contain unemployed, unskilled laborers. They were expected to reform these wayward individuals and turn them into good workers who could return to society and take their places in the ranks of laborers among the industrious poor.

The Philadelphia Society for Alleviating the Miseries of Public Prisons soon became the Pennsylvania Prison Society, and its mostly well-heeled Protestant church folk acted as inspectors of the Walnut Street Jail and as official visitors to the prisoners there. Seeing their role as reforming both "lost" individual prisoners and cruel or ineffective governmental penal policies, these official jail inspectors and visitors reported back to the legislature as well as to the Pennsylvania Prison Society membership. There was a real conflict between their duties as inspectors and their strong investment in, and allegiance to, the success of their penal experiment. The members of the society never questioned whether enforced, perpetual solitude was leading to madness, or whether released prisoners were returning to a life of crime. The mental torture represented by the silent system went unacknowledged.

Within a decade, the Walnut Street Jail experiment was a failure in almost every respect. The sixteen tiny "single" cells ultimately held three prisoners each; silence and cleanliness could not be maintained; and, although the legislature paid the jail staff, their training was questionable. The experiment, however, did not end with this obvious failure, as the Pennsylvania Prison Society and Pennsylvania's ruling class saw the building of a bigger and better penitentiary as the solution. Eastern State Penitentiary became the successor to the Walnut Street Jail. It represents the beginning, in practice, of what became known as the "segregate" style of prison labor in the new penitentiary. With no real evidence to back the claim that incarceration as a sanction would "reform" people, the practice of imprisoning criminals and the poor was declared successful.

The Penitentiary System—Religious Roots

In examining the genesis of the modern penal system more than two hundred years after the first penitentiary was constructed, it is important to study the historical and intellectual underpinnings of the American penal system. There were two strands of influence on its development: the religious understanding of the relationship between punishment and penitence, and the intellectual climate of the Enlightenment period.

It is impossible to overstate the religious fervor that accompanied the penitentiary movement. The word *penitentiary* derives from the word *penitent*, and both derive from roots they share with the words *pain, penal*, and *punish*. Elements of the Christian monastic tradition were incorporated into the design of these prisons. Benedictine monks a century earlier had declared the use of monasteries as religious prisons to be evil—seeing forced silence and isolation to make people "insane or hardened or desperate" (Magnani 1990, 41). It is ironic that the framers of the penitentiary were at once borrowing from monastic tradition and ignoring the lessons of the long-abandoned practice of having monasteries accept prisoners while at the same time they ended up incarcerating a disproportionate number of Catholics.

Quakers are often credited with, and blamed for, developing the penitentiary system. Their influence was substantial, both in the United States and in Britain. Even though Quakers had withdrawn from holding public office in the United States, they remained concerned and involved in engineering the new democracy. Wealthy Quaker landowners shared the ruling elite's belief that the working class and the poor were not ready to participate in the new democracy, and that there was a need to reform the vice-ridden poor.

In 1797–98 a Philadelphia tavern keeper, Israel Israel, ran for the Pennsylvania state legislature. His election would have been the first time a member of the working class held public office. He enjoyed much public support because he had worked with the poor during an outbreak of yellow fever when all who could afford to flee abandoned the city of Philadelphia. Israel won the first election, but the legislature declared the election invalid and demanded another vote. Quakers, who usually did not vote, turned out this time to oppose Israel at the polls. Quaker farmers even denied transportation to the polls for their workers who supported Israel's candidacy. The Quakers, voting as a bloc, handed the close election to the ruling-class candidate (Magnani 1990, 37–42).

At the same time, the intentions of many Quakers were clearly rooted in compassion for the downtrodden. A number of Quakers saw a particular role for themselves in the creation of a penal system that addressed poverty and vice in a humane way, and transformed criminals into the industrious laborers the new republic needed. The involvement of Quakers with the Philadelphia jail began in 1770 after a prisoner, unable to get food or firewood, perished. Quakers organized the Society for Assisting Distressed Prisoners in 1776 to provide relief to indigent prisoners and to ensure that prisoners did not die. Another motivation for Quaker involvement in prison ministry and reform was their own direct experience of imprisonment, dating back to the religious persecution of Friends in Britain and the colonies. This legacy gave some Friends a glimpse of the abuses possible in both the court and punishment systems.

The Penitentiary System—Philosophical Roots

The philosophical roots of the penitentiary can be traced to philosophers John Locke, Cesare Beccaria, and Jeremy Bentham. Intellectual developments on both sides of the Atlantic paralleled one another, and there was substantial overlap between the goals of religious reformers and the experiments that the educated elite sought to implement. We can see this convergence of Protestant and Enlightenment thought, for example, in a 1787 meeting at Benjamin Franklin's home of a group called the Society for Political Inquiries. The first paper read at this gathering of the local elite, by Dr. Benjamin Rush, was a reform-oriented critique of physically brutal and humiliating punishments entitled "An Enquiry into the Effects of Public Punishments upon Criminals, and upon Society." The paper laid out a vision of what Rush considered to be a better penal course, which found its way into the design of the Walnut Street Jail experiment.

The excitement of these new penal ideals was also reflected in English and American literature of the time. British novelists like Daniel Defoe in *Moll Flanders* and *Robinson Crusoe* began vividly describing prison conditions, and imagining the virtues of solitude and the reformation of inner thought. In *Moll Flanders,* the narrator describes her plight in London's Newgate Prison:

> I degenerated into Stone; I turn'd first Stupid and Senseless, then Brutish and thoughtless, and at last raving Mad as any of them were; and in short I became as naturally pleas'd and easie with the Place, as if indeed I had been Born there. (Defoe 1991, 204)

The Panopticon

> Morals reformed—health preserved—industry invigorated—instruction diffused—public burthens lightened—*Economy seated, as it were, upon a rock—the gordian knot of the Poor-Laws not cut, but untied—all by a simple idea in architecture!*
>
> —Bentham, Preface to *Panopticon* (Foucault 1995, 207)

As the educated elite in the United States began to envision a new prison system, similar efforts were under way in Britain. The British penitentiary movement was led by John Howard, who had documented prison conditions throughout Europe, and by the philosopher Jeremy Bentham, who developed the "Panopticon" design for penitentiaries. No concept or movement more clearly illustrates the use of prisons as complete social control than the Panopticon. It effectively blended the use of physical surroundings, technology (to the extent available at the time), and psychological manipulation to ensure conformity in prisoners.

The Panopticon prison design was meant to reverse the principles of the dungeon. It featured cellblocks stretching out like spokes on a wheel, with the guard tower, or control room, as the hub, or center, of the wheel. The major effect of the Panopticon was to "induce in the inmate a state of conscious and permanent visibility" (Foucault 1995, 201). Through constant surveillance, the prisoner was left insecure and fearful of doing wrong. The prisoner was rendered powerless and, in that state of powerlessness, receptive to reform.

In his writings, Bentham lauded the Panopticon as a "privileged place for experiments on men" and encouraged the application of Panopticon principles to schools, orphanages, hospitals, and mental institutions: "Its great excellence consists in the great strength it is capable of giving to *any* institution it may be thought proper to apply to" (quoted in Foucault 1995, 206). Through severely limiting contact with the outside world, imposing total silence, and enforcing regimentation of schedules and movement, prison designers and officials attempted to force the prisoner to revise his or her thinking to conform to the "wholesome" expectations of the dominant culture. Just as randomness had been the rule in the old prisons and

If it were possible to find a method of becoming master of everything which might happen to a certain number of men, to dispose of everything around them so as to produce on them the desired impression to make certain of their actions, of their connections, and of all the circumstances of their lives, so that nothing could escape, nor could oppose the desired effect, it cannot be doubted that a method of this kind would be a very powerful and very useful instrument which governments might apply to various objects of the utmost importance.

—Bentham, *Panopticon* (Foucault 1995)

in the lives of the poor, the lives of the incarcerated, impoverished, and institutionalized would be ordered with geometric precision and predictability.

The Panopticon prison design endures to the present day. In the modern prison, the ideal of constant surveillance has found a new technology in the use of video monitors throughout the institution. The idea of total control over human lives as a way of forcing people to conform in precise ways the authorities intend is still seen as a viable philosophy in mainstream "corrections" thinking.

The Development of the Penitentiary System

One inveighs against the slave trade. But are not prisoners sold, like the slaves, by entrepreneurs and bought by manufacturers. . . . Is this how we teach our prisoners honesty? Are they not still more demoralized by these examples of abominable exploitation?

—Worker imprisoned for joining a workers' association, 1837

In 1817, the Auburn State Penitentiary was completed in New York. In 1819, a local citizen was given a contract to operate a factory within it. Even though these factories were never profitable for the state, this arrangement was replicated in other penitentiaries. Also popular was the convict leasing system. Prisoners in New York, for example, were leased to private bidders who paid a fee for their labor and who became responsible for housing, feeding, and working their prisoners/laborers. The private citizens who ran factories in prisons and leased the labor of convicts did profit from these arrangements.

The opening of Auburn was followed by the construction of the Massachusetts State Prison in Charlestown, which was soon renovated in the style of Auburn. The Auburn style differed from the Pennsylvania style in that in the newer facility prisoners worked in silence in congregate settings during the day rather than in solitude in their cells. The two styles became known as the congregate and the segregate styles. All penitentiaries were committed to silence, solitary confinement, discipline, and regimentation. On entry to the penitentiary, prisoners were stripped of their identity, their right to express themselves, and all creativity.

Eastern, or Cherry Hill, Penitentiary in Pennsylvania followed Charlestown. Cherry Hill was characterized by utter solitude. Prisoners were alone day and night and wore hoods over their heads when they were removed from their cells. Writing about Cherry Hill in 1833, Gustave de Beaumont and Alexis de Tocqueville liken the silence of prison to the silence

> of death. We have often trod, during the night, those monotonous and dim galleries, where a lamp is always burning: we felt as if we traversed catacombs; there were a thousand living beings, and yet it was a desert solitude. (De Beaumont and de Tocqueville 1833)

Soon it became apparent that without real human fellowship and communication, prisoners went mad. In New York, one prisoner tried to commit suicide by throwing himself from the fourth-floor gallery to the pavement. Another beat and mangled his head against the walls of his cell until he destroyed one of his eyes. At Pennsylvania's Eastern State Prison, the rule of silence was so well enforced that "for several years, there has not been any case reported of a prisoner talking after he was locked up" (Friedman 1993, 79). In order to ensure compliance, Pennsylvania employed the iron gag, essentially a muzzle made of iron wrapped around the prisoner's head. Other punishments for breaking the regimen included the whip, the ball and chain, and the cold shower.

These early penitentiaries were viewed as "a grand theater, for the trial of all new plans in hygiene and education, in physical and moral reform" (Rothman 1971, 81). Prisons were conceived as "democratically controlled, constantly accessible to the great tribunal committee of the world" (Foucault 1995, 207). Most penitentiaries held regular tours. A European's visit to the United States was not complete without a tour of one of the great penitentiaries. Visitors viewed the prison inhabitants locked in their cells, in much the same way that animals would be viewed in their cages in a zoo. Visitors came and went, unnoticed by the prisoners, through underground tunnels that took them to the observation towers where the windows were outfitted with Venetian blinds so that prisoners would not be able to tell who was observing them or when they were being observed. One such visitor was author Charles Dickens, who returned to Britain and wrote his reactions in the book *American Notes*:

> In its intention I am well convinced that it is kind, humane, and meant for reformation; but I am persuaded that those who devised

the system and those benevolent gentlemen who carry it into execution do not know what it is they are doing. . . . I hold this slow and delicate tampering with the mysteries of the brain to be immeasurably worse than any torture of the body and because its ghastly signs and tokens are not so palpable to the eye and sense of touch as scars upon the flesh, because its wounds are not on the surface, and it extorts few cries that human ears can hear, therefore I denounce it as a secret punishment which slumbering humanity is not roused to stay. (Dickens 1996, 115)

The idea of the grim, austere penitentiary won many supporters, and the system was adopted throughout the northern and midwestern states, as well as throughout Europe. Often penitentiaries were modified soon after they were built. The silent system disappeared first; in Massachusetts it was gone by 1850. In order for silence to be maintained, single cells were necessary, which came to be seen as an "expensive luxury" (Friedman 1993, 157). Soon, there were two or three prisoners to a cell. By the time of the Civil War, the penitentiary system was in shambles, yet the ideology of the penitentiary has endured.

The creation of the penitentiary, along with the development of other institutions like hospitals and asylums for the mentally ill, must be seen as an effort to establish mechanisms of control over those who were seen as not fitting in. These institutions had many features in common, especially the belief that external order and regimentation would produce internal order and discipline. The fact that this reordering process also constituted a form of cultural annihilation—as a result of the total isolation and separation from family—must be seen as an intended consequence.

Understanding the use of imprisonment in its social and historical context provides a clearer view of the deep cultural beliefs that are still at work in this country's discussion of crime and punishment. Prisons are still filled with the "unworthy poor"—cast as criminal, lazy, and incapable of rehabilitation. Criminal behavior is still cast as a personal (perhaps even spiritual) failing. Prisons still serve the purpose of containing immigrants, people of color, poor whites, and the "deviant." At the same time, it is astonishing how special interests—from those who, like Bentham, design and build the latest in punishment technology; to those who benefit from fruits of prison labor; to corporations that promote private prisons—are still able to profit from this arrangement. Prisons are being cast as the recession-proof moneymaker, revealing the faith that there will always be populations to control and an endless supply of prisoners.

2: THE DYNAMICS OF CRIME AND PUNISHMENT IN AMERICA

The Problem

For the last three decades, the prison and jail population in the United States has more than sextupled, from just 330,000 in 1972 to 2.1 million in 2001. The increase in the number of prison and jail prisoners since 1990 is considerably greater than the total number of prisoners imprisoned in 1980 (501,886). The rate of imprisonment (number of prisoners per 100,000 population) in the United States is five to ten times higher than that of most industrialized nations—696 per 100,000 by the year 2001 (Harrison and Beck 2002).

One can map the concurrent evolution of the criminal justice system and the deterioration of the social safety net and of civil rights. There is often a direct trade-off, both financially and socially, between social programs and prisons. This happens regardless of which comes first. For example, as we detail below, the trend toward deinstitutionalization of the mentally ill in the 1970s was its own social movement designed to take people out of the dreadful conditions in mental asylums and place them in community treatment centers. The money to realize the second half of the vision never materialized, however, and many of the mentally ill were left on the streets and subsequently arrested. As a result, jails and prisons have become the primary sites for many people to receive mental health services. On the flip side, today many states are having trouble paying for the incarceration binge they indulged in during the "tough on crime" 1990s. As a result, prisons compete with other social programs, such as the improvement of public schools, for decreasing funds. Prisons, unfortunately, are winning. The longer people languish in jails and prisons, the more they experience firsthand the results of modern U.S. penal policy: drastic cutbacks in education and jobs programs, fewer recreation opportunities, reduced visiting time, reduced quality of visits (the trend is toward noncontact visits at all security levels), over-classification (prisoners are being held at higher security levels than warranted by their disciplinary records), and vastly more physical restriction. The introduction of "super-max" prisons—institutions devoted to solitary confinement for twenty-three to twenty-four hours per day—further degrades the daily imprisonment experience. All aspects of increasing harshness, whether in terms of length of stay or conditions imposed on specific prisoners, fall most heavily on people of color and mentally ill prisoners. For example, people of color make up 80 to 90 percent of the super-max prison population, and some therapists who work these prisons estimate that as many as 60 percent of their prisoners struggle with mental illness.

Recently enacted sentencing policies, like those contained in "three-strike" laws, utilize prior criminal histories in determining sentences, guaranteeing that disparities in past criminal justice policies will be compounded in the future. Mandatory sentences, which remove discretion from judges by placing specific sentencing requirements into the law, have proven to be ineffective and used in racially discriminatory ways. Not only are the numbers of prisoners increasing as a direct result of these policies, the average length of time served in prison has risen steeply in the same time period. As we will discuss later, drug policies, anti-immigration policies, racism within the criminal justice system, and a deteriorating economic climate for unskilled laborers all contribute to these trends.

The present bankrupt system renders justice to no one—not to those caught up in the criminal justice system as offenders, nor to those who are victimized by crime, nor to those who support the system and rely on its ability to protect them and to administer justice. Those populations in the community most vulnerable to crime not only suffer constant threats to their security and lack adequate redress, they see little choice but to support solutions that, as we explain below, actually compound their jeopardy. All these groups should be supported and helped to see their common stake in a more humane social order.

The actual functions of the criminal justice system are unstated, unacknowledged, and even illicit. Any criminal justice system reflects the values of those who hold power in society. Thus, "criminal law becomes a political instrument, formulated and enforced by those with status and power against those who predominantly are status-poor and powerless" (AFSC 1971, 101).

Even though the founding fathers went to unprecedented lengths to protect the exercise of political freedoms through the Constitution, the Bill of Rights, and the Fourteenth Amendment, as Judge Leon Higginbotham noted in 1970,

> We must also recognize that from its very origin in 1787 our Constitution was in part a racist document. For at least 78 years through the full force of law it sanctioned racism and its devastating brutality. . . . I cite this history because we will never be able to communicate to the thousands of black men locked up in our prisons today unless we first honestly look at our past history. We will not be able to solve today's racial problems either in our prisons or on the outside merely by suggesting that some of the black men who are angry are a few isolated hard-core militants. Perhaps we make the first step of the long hard journey ahead by our honesty and willingness to admit that our nation has caused much rage, that our nation has often been grossly unjust in the treatment of blacks and that we may have an obligation to work swiftly to eradicate the many consequences of that injustice, rather than to keep pretending that the problem never existed.[1]

We can hardly afford such pretense when, in 2001, African American men were locked up in prisons and jails at a rate of more than eight times the incarceration of black men in apartheid South Africa in 1993 (Wagner 2003). By and large, our prisons are reserved for those with dark skin, little money, or unconventional lifestyles. The powerful manage, most of the time, to escape the sanctions of the criminal justice system. Either they have the means to hire good defense lawyers or they are able to make a better impression on juries and judges. At another level, Jeffrey Reiman demonstrates in his *The Rich Get Richer and the Poor Get Prison* that violations of environmental, workplace safety, and other laws by corporations and hospitals are seldom prosecuted as crimes and punished by incarceration, though they kill and maim far more persons and rob and damage far more property than street crime committed by poor people (Reiman 2004, chapter 2).

The Intersection of Race and Class

When we look at prisons, we invariably must look at issues of race and class. In criminal justice issues, as in other areas of public policy, race and class intersect and create a complicated web of relationships. Uniformly, prisoners are working-class and poor people, regardless of race or ethnicity. Yet people of color are disproportionately represented in U.S. prisons.

The racism and classism that are deeply rooted in our society are also the foundation of the prison system in the United States. This helps explain why as a nation we are largely untroubled by the fact that 12 percent of black men between the ages of twenty-five and twenty-nine are imprisoned (Harrison and Beck 2005). After release, these men will suffer lifelong disenfranchisement and other civil disabilities, severely curtailing their ability to participate as citizens and their right to apply for work, thus diminishing the well-being of their families and their communities. Even though poor whites are also deeply affected by prison, there is little solidarity across color lines. White prisoners are more likely to receive shorter sentences, to have increased access to programming and resources, and to be released earlier on parole. They are less likely to be unfairly identified as gang members. Once paroled, they have an easier transition into their communities of origin. If we are sincere about ending the evils of the criminal justice system in our society, we must address the issues of racism and classism.

Practicing White Supremacy

Imprisoning indigenous people and people of color is not unique to the United States. In virtually every country in the world throughout history, people perceived as "outsiders"—even First Nations people who were perceived as inferior or barbaric—are feared and frequently put under some kind of control. What is particularly disturbing, however, is that racism, bias, and xenophobia are increasing, as the statistics we cite throughout this book demonstrate.

This structure of racism has existed in the criminal justice system in North America since the settlement of the continent by Europeans. Racism preceded the introduction of slavery to the continent. It began with the attempted enslavement and the eventual genocide of Native Peoples. Those who survived were forcefully removed from their traditional lands and the creation of reservations (which later became the prototype for South Africa's "homelands" structure). This was followed by the bureaucratic elimination of Native Peoples from federally kept rolls of citizens through the declaration of Native Nations as sovereign nations. Citizenship rights were thereby denied them, while occupation of their lands continued. This process of elimination continues today when Native Nations are removed from the Bureau of Indian Affairs's roll of recognized tribes. New institutions were created to formalize racism toward Native Americans with the formation of the Bureau of Indian Affairs. The Bureau of Indian Affairs and mission schools stole children from their families, leaving whole villages empty of children. After arrival in these schools, Native children's hair was cut, they were forbidden to communicate with their families, their languages were prohibited, their traditional foods were unavailable, and their indigenous cultures were denied. Many were abused physically and sexually. The results of this racism toward Native Peoples are evident today in their persistently high levels of poverty, addiction, and imprisonment.

> *The justice system functions to maintain a racist relationship between the black, brown, red, and yellow minorities in America.*
>
> —AFSC 1971

Black Africans, who were stolen from their homelands, were also reduced to the status of real estate or livestock under the cruel system of chattel slavery. African slaves were legal nonentities in the eyes of the courts. Declared to be "three-fifths of a man" by the U.S. Constitution, the former slave and his or her children came to know the legal system only as an extension of the rule of the slave system.

Before the Civil War, the legal status of freedmen paralleled the slave's utter legal powerlessness, and states outside the South also passed freed Negro laws to lock in such powerlessness. The rise in both civil police systems and prison systems can be traced directly to initiatives to maintain the power imbalances created by slavery. With every wave of immigration and migration, the United States has replicated policies to maintain racial and economic inequalities.

Mexican Americans suffered from the hegemonic policies of U.S. "manifest destiny." From the late 1830s to the late 1840s, the United States conducted a brutal onslaught upon the Mexican people in order to gain possession of California. Mexican response to the arrival of Americans was described in the *American Review* as yielding to a "superior population, insensibly oozing into her territories, changing her customs and outliving, out-trading, exterminating her weaker blood" (Zinn 1980, 152). After defeat and the loss of over one-third of their lands, Mexicans who lived in Texas, California, New Mexico, and Nevada suffered broken treaties and virulent racism. Over the past 160 years, Mexican labor has been used to buttress the United States' economy, while leaving Mexican workers underpaid and unprotected by law.

Shortly after the Mexican-American War, Asians began to enter the country from the west as workers, suffering brutal working conditions while building railroads and doing agricultural work. As they stayed and sought to become citizens, immigration statutes in the form of "exclusion laws" were put in place that particularly targeted them. These had a deep impact upon people's ability to become citizens and to own property, and have only recently, and often inconsistently, been reversed. The internment of Japanese in concentration camps during World War II paralleled a number of aspects of European Fascism. One hundred ten thousand men, women, and children were arrested on the West Coast. Of these Japanese families, three-quarters were United States citizens. Japanese were kept in prison conditions, in the desert, for two to three years. In 1944, the United States Supreme Court upheld these forced evacuations on the grounds of military necessity (Zinn 1980, 407).

Each migration of Asians from different centuries tells a different story of class, race, and often imperialism—stories that are far beyond the scope of this book. The overall incarceration rate for Asian Americans is 99 per 100,000 but the numbers change dramatically when certain groups are singled out.

Today, African Americans are being imprisoned at a rate of 2,526 per 100,000 nationally (Prison Policy Initiative 2004), and at an even higher rate in many states. An African American male has a 28 percent chance of going to state or federal prison in the course of his life-time, compared to 6.6 percent of Hispanic males and 4.4 percent of white males (Harrison and Beck 2002). In many states, most notably

California, the fastest-growing segment of the state prison system is "Hispanic" (Mexican American and Latinos).

This thumbnail sketch of the legacy of racism in the United States sets the stage for recognizing the entrenched impact of the deep social divisions in United States culture. The role of the criminal justice system in enforcing separation and division among races can hardly be overstated. For example, the extraordinarily high rates of imprisonment and executions among blacks demonstrate a malignant pattern of racism that pervades our criminal justice system and affects all people of color. Another devastating effect of racism in the criminal justice system is the role it plays in disenfranchisement.

In our view, the total impact of the pattern just described can arguably be called genocidal. Our use of such grave language is quite deliberate. The United Nations International Convention on the Prevention and Punishment of the Crime of Genocide defines genocide as:

> Any of the following acts committed with intent to destroy, in whole or in part, a national, ethnic, racial or religious group as such:
>
> Killing members of the group;
>
> Causing serious bodily or mental harm to members of the group;
>
> Deliberately inflicting on the group conditions of life calculated to bring about its physical destruction in whole or part;
>
> Imposing measures intended to prevent births within the group;
>
> Forcibly transferring children of the group to another group. (United Nations 1948)

Another of the most devastating effects of racism in the criminal justice system is the role it plays in disenfranchisement:

> Almost all states have laws restricting the right to vote for convicted felons. Forty-[seven] states deny the right to vote to anyone who is imprisoned, thirty-two restrict voting privileges of offenders on probation and/or parole, and in fourteen states anyone ever convicted of a felony can lose the right to vote for life. . . . One in four black men are permanently disenfranchised in Alabama, Florida, Iowa, Mississippi, New Mexico, Virginia, and Wyoming. (Fellner and Mauer 1998)

The problems of racism will not be cured by specific, local interventions, although these interventions may change the lives of individuals. The problems of racism are systemic. Therefore, the solutions not only must be systemic, they must challenge our fundamental assumptions about public safety as well.

The Legacy of Economic Dominance: Class

That the judicial system was and is used to hinder the struggle of working-class people to organize and better their situation is undeniable. Labor's struggle for the right to organize is one of the bloodiest chapters in American history. Throughout the nineteenth and twentieth centuries, courts repeatedly took the side of industrialists. Judicial intervention was used in obtaining injunctions against strikers. Court injunctions against picketing in labor disputes are still common today.

Historically, local institutions of justice have been and continue to be used to protect the powerful. Middle-class felons charged with "white-collar crimes" are treated differently from working-class people. When the government acts in white-collar cases, it usually prefers administrative rather than criminal proceedings. Penalties, if any, are lower and usually consist of modest fines payable to the government. In those rare cases resulting in criminal prosecution and conviction, sentences are usually served in minimum security or under probation (Reiman 2004, chapter 2).

The poor are disproportionately represented in the criminal justice system as defendants and as prisoners, both pretrial and post-conviction. When arrested, poor people are dependent, in many states, on the often-limited resources of public defenders who are overworked and understaffed. Even though our criminal law rests on the presumption of innocence, our government generously funds law enforcement and prosecutors while apportioning scant resources to public defenders' offices. In some states, there is no public counsel at all, and indigent defendants are assigned private attorneys to defend them. These attorneys receive flat and typically low fees from the state, and are sometimes untrained in criminal law. The lack of resources available for the defense of indigent defendants deprives them of the amount of attention and quality of services purchased by more affluent people. While imprisoned, the poor must function as "slave labor"—working for low or no wages. With only limited wage-earning capacity, their families and neighborhoods remain poor and under-resourced. The criminal justice system creates a separate class: those who have been caught up in it. The criminal record, even an arrest without conviction, is a formidable barrier to constructive reentry and to positive participation in the community. Once branded, one becomes a permanent part of this disadvantaged class.

Prison Labor

If we look at the chain gangs, jails, and other penal institutions in the country and the state, we arrive at one of two conclusions. Either education and wealth are two of the strongest fortifications against the commission of crime, or there is a different measure of justice for the rich and the poor, white and black, the educated and the unlettered.

—*Raleigh* (North Carolina) *News and Observer,* December 27, 1930

Prisons have always reflected the relationship between wealth and power in a country. In the United States today, prisons still clearly reflect the racism and greed that have shaped the national identity.

The use of prisoner labor for corporate or public-sector profit results in prison labor conditions similar to those reported to exist in China. The United States government has regularly and properly condemned the Chinese government's practices. Prison labor programs, and the privatization of prison systems and programs, encourage prison authorities and the state to maximize the number of people in prison rather than focus on public safety. They further shift prison policies away from constructive programs that actually prepare a prisoner psychologically and practically for his or her return to the community.

The forced labor of prisoners has been a crucial factor in the development of prison policy and in the stabilization of the American economy from the very beginning of the U.S. prison system. From the start of the penitentiary movement, the idea that decreasing idleness through productive labor and quiet reflection upon one's crime in the privacy of one's cell was the best way to reform the prisoner, and the practice of leasing prison laborers to private bidders, became the legal and cultural platform upon which the United States' prison industry was built.

The United States has frequently relied upon a secondary labor force that is in bondage. Forced labor has always existed alongside of, and been recruited from the ranks of, free labor. In times of economic crisis (most notably the Reconstruction period after the Civil War; the period directly following the collapse of the stock market in 1929; and the current period, as we see great underemployment of minimum wage and low-skilled workers), the prison population has swelled and prisoners have been put to work. These upsurges in the prison population historically have not been followed by a proportional abatement in the number of those imprisoned when the economic crisis has subsided.

Before the abolition of slavery, there were few prisons and penitentiaries in the United States. All large penitentiaries were in northern states. Southern states had smaller prisons, populated almost entirely by white people, since slave owners conducted their own punishment of their slaves. The rapid expansion of state prison systems in the late nineteenth century had the effect of maintaining the power, racial, and economic relationships that existed under slavery. When slavery was abolished, the Slave Codes, which had regulated the behavior of slaves and all those of African descent, were rewritten as the Black Codes. The Black Codes had been used in northern states as early as 1790 to criminalize previously legal activities for African Americans and to regulate the activities of free people of African descent. Black men were arrested for "vagrancy" or "breaking curfew." In the South, after the Civil War, former slaves were sentenced to prison and then leased out by the prison to work for local plantation owners.

In the southern states, with the protection of the Thirteenth Amendment, the convict lease system expanded beyond the old slave plantations to include coal mining, railroad building, and other businesses rising in the "New South." In the 1880s, a fledgling labor movement took on the former slave states' exploitation of black and poor white prisoner labor and its effects of disemploying free labor and driving free-world wages down. After decades of political, sometimes violent, struggle, the convict lease system died out in most of the South by the early twentieth century.[2]

Just as sharecropping and tenant farming replaced slave labor, the convict lease system was replaced by a combination of chain gangs of prisoners (often under county jurisdictions) working on roads and other public works and state prison industries run by the governments. Since organized labor had successfully pushed through laws prohibiting states from marketing prison-made merchandise on the open market, many prisoners were put to work manufacturing products to be used only in and by state government—for example, office furniture, license plates, road signs, and work clothes and uniforms for prisoners and state workers. Others were employed in various farming, maintenance, food service, and laundry service work for the prisons themselves.

In 1979, the United States government repealed the interstate transport law that had forbidden interstate transport of prisoner-made goods. The Department of Justice implemented a national work program throughout the federal prison system. There, prisoners theoretically work for minimum wage, of which 80 percent is withheld for room, board, survivor compensation, medical fees, and educational costs.

In the 1970s and 1980s, the economy saw increased mobility of United States corporations and the growth of transnational corporations. Seeking greater profit, manufacturers continued their century-long pattern of first going to the southern states, where labor was unorganized. Later, many plants and jobs were moved to poorer nations, as companies continued to seek to maximize profits at the expense of labor. The flight of factories from manufacturing centers has left entire cities economically unstable. The ensuing poverty and economic vulnerability has resulted in dramatic increases in criminal activity, usually drug crimes and crimes against property, in urban communities. Some jobs are now returning to the United States—but to the prisons, which contract with private industry, instead of to the urban centers. Industrial programs in prisons subsidize private industry by providing free factory space, subsidies for the tooling of the factory, security, electricity, and guaranteed cheap labor. Thirty states now allow some type of legalized contracting of prison labor to private firms (Kicenski 2002, 4). Thus, prison labor has become an alternative to moving offshore for many corporations. Workers unemployed because of job flight—and their children—are now working these jobs in prison. Upon release, they will go home to the same poor and jobless communities, and they will be as vulnerable to crime as they were before they went to prison.

Penal Servitude

What we have is a billion-dollar manufacturing industry that legally utilizes slave labor, has little overhead, is unregulated by state and

*federal workplace safety or labor laws, provides no health insurance or
benefits and no sick pay for its employees, includes hazardous materials
in the construction of its products, forces customers to buy its products
under penalty of law, and prohibits its workers from organizing.*

—Kicenski 2002

Today, all forms of convict labor have returned in one form or another.
Minimum-wage laws usually do not cover prisoners. They do not
receive workers' compensation if they are injured while working.
Prison laborers are not protected by the Fair Labor Standards Act,
nor are they protected by the Occupational Safety and Health Act.
Prison laborers are not permitted to meet among themselves to try to
improve their working conditions. Average minimum wages for state
prison labor in this country are $.93 a day for nonindustry work; aver-
age maximum wages are $4.73 a day. The wages are much lower than
public- or private-sector minimum wages because the vast majority of
prisoners work in institutional prison jobs, not in jobs with private
industry. Private-industry state prison jobs pay anywhere from $.23
to $7.00 an hour, but the "take-home" portion of prison pay is only
about 20 percent of that amount (Singleton and Boushey 2002). This
is equivalent to the cost of *maquiladora* labor in the factories across the
border in Mexico, which pay extremely low wages and have notori-
ously poor working conditions. Due to the severe restrictions on the
rights of prison labor, it is not surprising that some industries are turning to the use of prison labor as an alternative to moving offshore.

Politicians and policymakers like to promote prison labor programs as job training, but products fabricated by prisoners are products not being produced by free workers. Thus, labor skills mastered
in prison do not necessarily translate into jobs upon release. Private
industries, for their part, use prison laborers to drive wages and benefits down and to wield power over their external work force. While
prison officials use prison labor as a management tool, prisoners use
it as their only legal way to earn any revenue. Statistics on the hiring
of former prisoners do not exist, but very few former prisoners report
being hired as a result of their prison work experience. In principle, a
fair and voluntary work program, paying meaningful wages for meaningful work, with reasonable opportunities to unionize, gain promo-
tions and raises, and learn job skills marketable on the outside upon
release, would serve both prisoners and society. But under the present

penal regime, prison-industry programs are about exploiting vulnerable people's labor for wealthy executives' and shareholders' profit, not about job training and preparation.

The Thirteenth Amendment to the United States Constitution reads: "Neither slavery nor involuntary servitude, except as punishment for crime whereof the party shall have been duly convicted, shall exist within the United States, or any place subject to their jurisdiction." We oppose slavery of all kinds—including the use of prisoner labor for profit—while supporting the creation of substantial job-training and skills-building programs.

3: IN OUR BACKYARDS:
THE PENAL SYSTEM AT
THE LOCAL LEVEL

The response to crime is mainly a State and local function. Very few crimes are under Federal jurisdiction. The responsibility to respond to most crime rests with State and local governments. Police protection is primarily a function of cities and towns. Corrections is primarily a function of State governments. Most justice personnel are employed at the local level.

—Bureau of Justice Statistics 2002

There is a tendency, in the public arena, to view the criminal justice system through the lens of the nightly news—with the latest crime spree or unsolved murder. Little attention is paid to what caused these dramatic events, or what happens to the people once they are caught and perhaps prosecuted. Though a fascination with catching "the bad guy" persists, the layers and layers of circumstances both before and after the incident go unnoticed or ignored. Indeed they lack drama unless the real consequences of economic injustice, racism, and classism are brought into focus. But even to name a bunch of "isms" runs the risk of sounding ideological alarms in the reader's mind at the point that we most need to capture the public's attention. This chapter attempts to lay out the problem within its social context so we do not ourselves become prisoners of the status quo, with too little information to challenge how things have always been, and too dim a vision of the world we want to create.

To paint a full picture of how the criminal justice system works, it is necessary to start at the local level where laws are implemented and enforced. Decisions made at the local level, though mirrors of the same assumptions and trends as elsewhere in the system, often put a distinctly parochial slant on the concept of "justice" as somehow blind and impartial. How particular jurisdictions treat a person varies dramatically. What rules apply to jail visitors trying to maintain contact with an incarcerated loved one differ enormously. Who sits in the judge's chair, jury box, sheriff's office, or prosecutor's office becomes decisive.

Most crime in the United States takes place at the local level and, for the most part, society's response to crime also occurs locally. Many convicted offenders are incarcerated in local county facilities. But the level of society's official response to crime is still not as local as most crime itself, which takes place in neighborhoods and communities and within subcultures that tend to be smaller than most governmental units and do not necessarily conform to jurisdictional and judicial-political boundaries.

Policing

Police forces in the United States were created to be civilian forces separate and distinct from military forces. This was done because citizens were outraged by the use of the National Guard against organized labor. They believed that civilian law enforcement could perform two tasks: protect citizens and their property and maintain peace and order. Although police forces clearly were created, in large part, to protect the rights of property owners, and although certain communities were routinely targeted for surveillance by police departments, the overall demeanor and purpose of the police were originally much more community-service oriented.

As grassroots movements grew in strength in the twentieth century, police forces proliferated. With the rise of the labor, civil rights, black power, farm workers, gay liberation, and anti-corporate globalization movements, an increased militarization of police forces has occurred.

Manifestations of this militarization are seen everywhere. Probation officers, security guards, and even meter readers in some jurisdictions now carry the weapons once carried by a small number of police officers assigned to certain specific situations. The city of Boston, famous for "community policing," has thirty-two types of police forces. Most cities are "protected" by traditional police, state police, highway patrol, county sheriffs, park rangers, prison guards, and a variety of private security companies. Universities often have their own police forces. As noted in the introduction, the primary root of this proliferation is fear, nurtured by false promises of "security."

The authority of these different agencies varies considerably, as do training and jurisdiction. The military is now the model for police forces, which receive, free of charge, decommissioned military equipment, such as high-tech guns and armored personnel carriers. The "civilian" demeanor has been dropped. In addition to engaging in military drilling and sharp-shooting practices, these forces routinely sport uniforms, automatic weapons, and other physical details that enhance their image of being intimidators to be reckoned with. The public's role in monitoring the authority of these forces has proven difficult to structure, institutionalize, or enforce.

In discussing the role of police, we hasten to draw a distinction between individuals and institutions. There are many good people who serve as police officers and genuinely work to improve lives in the community. However, the police as an institution have proven to be more a part of the problem than a part of the solution. Here we speak to the issues inherent in police cultures.

Increasingly, society is relying on police to solve many of its problems. Where parents, teachers, social workers, health-care professionals, union officials, and job foremen once addressed the majority of social problems, police are now turned to in many cases. This is particularly troubling when so many social programs, such as housing, welfare, education, and mental health care, have been cut back or eliminated. Often, funding for educational programs, youth intervention programs, and transitional programs assisting ex-prisoners in returning to their neighborhoods is channeled through the police, adding to an unprecedented level of surveillance and law enforcement.

As police are saddled with the conflicting tasks of social worker, educator, and law enforcer, they are given primarily military tools with which to respond—automatic weapons, cover of law, and immunity from prosecution in law or in practice. Poor public access, restrictive labor agreements, and debilitated or nonexistent citizen review boards hamper public scrutiny of police practices.

Police enforcement and presence are concentrated in communities of color and in poor communities. Many laws are slanted against these communities. Examples of this can be seen in the different penalties attached to the use of crack cocaine, commonly used by the poor, and powder cocaine, preferred by the middle class. People using crack receive a mandatory federal prison sentence of five years for using an amount of crack only 1/100th the amount of powder cocaine that it takes to trigger the same sentence. Another example is found in gang databases kept by most police departments. People of color are over-represented in profiles of gang members and are therefore scrutinized much more closely for arrest and prosecution. Racial profiling—training police to suspect people of crime in part because of their ethnic appearance—has been documented throughout the country. The most common and blatant incidents of this bias center around individual drivers stopped by the police.[1]

The AFSC joins other organizations and groups in aiming to eliminate the use of the criminal justice system as a tool for harassment and violation of basic human rights (AFSC 1978). The AFSC is opposed to law-enforcement officials using violence in fulfilling their responsibilities. The current standard for determining "unnecessary use of force" by courts and in investigations is very low. Juries have found shooting at unarmed suspects forty or more times to be "justifiable." Shooting unarmed prisoners on an exercise yard has been found to be legitimate. We oppose such frequent practices as intimidation; withholding of information; holding persons incommunicado; and illegal frisks, searches, or seizures. The spectrum of violence must be ended at all points. The AFSC Criminal Justice Task Force recommends gun control for the general populace and for most police and prison personnel because we are committed to making nonviolent problem solving the norm rather than the exception.

A trend toward "community policing" has been sweeping the country in recent years. Sometimes referred to as problem-oriented policing, this approach attempts to redirect police activity away from a crisis orientation (for instance, responding to 911 calls) to a prevention or problem-solving approach.

We question whether this role is one that law enforcement should play. When resources assigned for community building, public health, and education get channeled through the police, the community institutions that do this work are often weakened rather than enhanced.

The degree to which problem-oriented policing constitutes a partnership with people in the community varies widely from one community to another. Sometimes police departments claim to employ community-policing techniques when they merely deploy more foot or bicycle patrols, or institute a "community liaison" position. Such personnel have in their job description some responsibility for addressing citizen concerns.

> *The overall mission stretches beyond reactive crime control to include fear reduction, crime prevention, community building, and developing resistances against threats to the health and well-being of the community.*
>
> —Nicholl 1999, 28

These changes ignore the fundamental reality that police should derive authority from the community, not merely "allow" people to play a modest role. Similarly, police must be accountable to the community. Often, community-policing programs have been effective ways to co-opt neighborhoods—ending organizing against police abuse and derailing efforts toward self-determination.

For communities to claim their authority, they must solve their own problems. Resources need to be redirected to education, health, recreation, and social-service systems, and the hard work of conflict resolution must be practiced between people at the neighborhood level. Rather than relying on police as mediators, volunteers can be trained to help conflicting parties resolve differences. The community justice and restorative justice movements have shown that family conferencing, circle sentencing, and other group processes can provide mechanisms for communities to solve problems without undue reliance on threats and sanctions (Immarigeon 1999, 305–25; Pranis, Stuart, and Wedge 2003).

These processes are not easy or quick; they demand that people take the time necessary to build the relationships and develop the skills. Without a commitment to deep community building, we will continue to resort to uniformed authorities to solve our problems. The increasing presence and power of police will continue to have undesired and potentially fatal consequences.

Although it is difficult to reach a consensus on what "good policing" should look like (some advocate the elimination of police power completely), at the very least we can say that the purpose of the police should be to keep the peace and to protect the most vulnerable.

Noncoercive agencies should provide this protection. "Justifiable" use of force and lethal force should be examined as the violence that they are in closely applying a standard of least restrictive alternatives to all situations.

We strongly support independent citizen review boards, with realistic budgets and staffing, power to subpoena, and enforcement authority over police misconduct. If enforcement power does not rest with an independent body, full disclosure of factual findings by that group is compromised. We also advocate ombudsman positions for all lock-up facilities—local, state, and federal. As with citizen review boards, these overseers need broad investigative powers, full funding, and enforcement powers. They must be funded independently and be free of any conflicts of interests with correctional industries and correctional labor organizations. Moreover, to the greatest extent possible, they must be free from political pressures.

The problems with police are similar to the problems of prisons. As Lord Acton said in his 1887 letter to Bishop Mandell Creighton, "Power corrupts. Absolute power tends to corrupt absolutely." As long as such institutions exist, local constituencies subject to their authority must be able to hold them accountable. As long as they are hidden behind veils of secrecy and "security," there will be suspicion, distrust, and abuse.

In the Courthouse:
The U.S. Adversarial Legal System

The criminal justice system in most local jurisdictions in the United States is driven and dominated by the prosecutor's office. The 2,341 prosecutors' offices handling felony cases in state courts in 2001 employed more than 79,000 lawyers and other staff and operated with total budgets of more than $4.6 billion, an increase of 61 percent from 1994. In 2001, these offices closed more than 2.3 million felony cases (almost one for every one thousand residents) and about seven million misdemeanor cases. There were more than 32,000 instances of prosecutors proceeding against juvenile defendants in adult criminal court, a 23 percent increase from 1996. Most of the chief prosecutors are elected by the voters, and their median annual salary is $85,000. Almost a third of these chief prosecutors, mostly those in the larger districts (which represent 45 percent of the nation's population and whose prosecution budgets account for $2.9 billion of the overall $4.6 billion national budget for state prosecution), earn more than $100,000 a year. Twenty percent of the chief prosecutors in these large urban districts carry a firearm for personal safety (DeFrances 2001, 2002).

Framing the prosecutorial process as an adversarial drama or war game dominated by the state provides a different perspective upon the assumptions, procedures, and outcomes of the process that challenges conventional thinking. While this account may seem unfair at many points, that is in part to highlight how the normative process as it is commonly understood is itself often unfairly biased in favor of the state. Our criminal justice system, which rotates around the axis of guilt and punishment, defines crime as primarily an offense against the laws of the state. The state, in turn, as represented by law enforcement and the prosecution, assumes the power to arrest a likely offender and to process this person through this adversarial drama. The assumption is that truth will emerge when opposing sides do battle. In this theatrical process, the major actors—and definitely the actors who are in charge—are lawyers (judge, prosecutor, and defense counsel) who are supposed to function on behalf of the law, the people, and the defendant, respectively. There is, theoretically, a kind of symmetry and balance of power, symbolized by the scales of justice being held by the blindfolded woman, in which the scales are supposedly at the same level. This illusion is belied by the fact that in grand jury proceedings, often used to indict suspects, only the prosecutor may present evidence, with the defense not even permitted to be present. In addition, what transpires in these proceedings may not be shared with the defense or the public.

Through either a plea-bargaining process or a trial in open court, played according to rules the state establishes and the judge, acting as a referee, enforces, the opposing attorneys fight it out in a sort of war game. Eventually the accused is declared either guilty or not guilty. If the person is found, or pleads, guilty (guilty pleas represented 94 percent of felony convictions in U.S. state courts in 1998 [Durose, Levin, and Langan 2001]), then a sentence is imposed, usually by the judge (except in death penalty cases). This sentence, construed by all parties as retaliation by the state on behalf of society, may amount to simple probation or a relatively small fine; a punitive jail or prison term; ritual killing by the state (that is, the death penalty); or something in between. Examples of these intermediate sanctions, which are used only for a minority of those convicted of felonies, include large fines payable to the government; victim restitution (sometimes ordered, but seldom paid); intensive probation; community corrections; community service; and residential substance-abuse treatment.

The focus of the system is on the offender and his or her past behavior. The real victims of the crime, if there are any, are treated as marginal—as is the community, except insofar as they can be manipulated into lobbying for vengeance. The offender is treated as passive. The process is geared toward fixing blame, not solving problems. The process discourages both the defendant's repentance (except at the point of parole consideration) and the victim's forgiveness.

Accountability is defined strictly as the offender's passively taking his or her externally imposed punishment (which, to call it by its real name, is the intentional infliction of pain upon a human being by other human beings). But this function of inflicting pain is conveniently obscured, as "the criminal justice system," in the words of Renate Mohr, "was craftily designed as a series of discrete, self-contained compartments. He who lays the charge, he who bargains the charge, he who pronounces the sentence, and he who administers that sentence are all different people" (Mohr 1987). Participants are persuaded that they

> need not, indeed ought not . . . concern themselves any further
> with the pains of the punishment they have imposed on another
> human being. And so the process ensures that violence may be done
> to others on a daily basis without any one person having to take
> responsibility. (Zehr 1995, 74)

The whole process encourages competitive and individualistic values, assumes a win-lose outcome, and tends to ignore the social, economic, political, cultural, and moral context of the crime and the appropriate response to it. It is based on a commitment to retribution by the state against the offender, not on the principle of restitution of the victim by the offender. It is also based on the assumption of a balance of power between prosecution and defense. In order to participate fully in this war game, crime victims and defendants, along with members of the judiciary, the prosecution team, and the defense team, are encouraged to assume that the system is so flawlessly designed that if both sides work and fight hard, and the judge/referee is neutral, truth will emerge and justice will be served.

In reality, the power is not balanced, the resources at the disposal of the prosecution and the defense are not equal, and political and economic agendas of both lawyers and the judge, who are the central figures, are decisive in determining the outcome of many cases. Opportunities for abuse of discretion (especially that of the prosecutor, who has the lion's share) and for corruption, racism, sexism, and class discrimination—personal and institutional—abound.

It is a system of jurisprudence full of abstractions that often feel—to victims, defendants, jurors, and witnesses—quite removed from the realities of what has taken place, and from the historical, relational, and psychological context within which a particular crime has occurred. This system makes a pretense of separating judgments of guilt, responsibility, and justice from personal identities and demographic characteristics of the parties involved, but in reality its process and results uncannily reflect the way in which social goods—economic wealth, political power, and cultural status—are apportioned out among various groups in the society.

The retributive, adversarial criminal justice system under which we operate, while presenting a pretense of making victims feel better by exacting revenge on their behalf, is not set up to benefit crime victims any more than it is to help offenders. Although the situation varies by location, for the most part crime victims are either marginalized and expected to be passive on the one hand, or manipulated and exploited as good witnesses and/or good public-relations tools for the parties seeking a conviction on the other. The system discourages them from feeling or expressing any openness to understanding, meeting with, or reconciling with the designated offender, and discourages them from having anything to do with the defense lawyers. The converse is true as well. Funds to compensate for their losses, both material and psychological, are usually dispensed by the prosecutor's office and dependent on "cooperation" with that office.

In contrast, some countries like Finland compensate victims from government funds. Whether a person is compensated, therefore, is not dependent upon apprehending the perpetrator, or his or her ability to pay restitution. Compensation in such a system becomes a right, supported by the state, to help the survivor be restored to wholeness.

The adversary system discourages defendants from being active and outspoken, and discourages them from expressing remorse or meeting with the victim. It is little wonder that many in both groups—victims and criminal defendants—feel that the court process is not about them, but instead is a game, or racket, played for the convenience and interests of lawyers and judges, and that they are mere pawns on the chessboard, manipulated by those who know the rules (because they wrote them) and are completely in charge.

The adversary system also discourages both survivors and offenders from resolving the conflict. Reconciliation between survivors and offenders is not considered to be a possible, much less desirable, outcome of any criminal case. The court process becomes a form of combat in which each side, represented by lawyers, tries to either "extract a pound of flesh," on the one hand, or "beat the rap," on the other.

Every day, in large and small courthouses throughout the nation, thousands of examples of this adversarial drama are played out, often with enormous consequences for the lives and the freedom of both defendants and crime survivors and their families. Yet, with the occasional exception of the showcase trial that captures the attention of the media, the vast majority of these cases are decided in relative obscurity by "plea bargain" or a perfunctory and short trial. Plea-bargaining is a process by which district attorneys, defense attorneys, and judges bargain back and forth about what to charge and what sentence to "offer" if a defendant is willing to plead guilty. It is a coercive process that has very little to do with determining what actually happened or who is actually responsible.

Often there is little input by the crime victim. Often the defendant meets his or her lawyer ten minutes or so before having to decide whether or not to plead guilty to something he or she may or may not have done. Often the disposition of the case depends on deals struck between prosecutor and public defender rather than on the merits of the case, the needs of the victim, or the moral culpability of the defendant.

In the large minority of cases (a majority in the federal court system), there are no individual, human, primary victims. The offenders are drug addicts, recreational drug users, small-time dealers in illegal drugs, prostitutes, or people charged with running small illegal gambling operations. They are their own major victims. They have not intentionally violated anyone else, though there often are, to be sure, secondary victims galore. But their "crimes" are, in one sense, either self-inflicted or consensual. In another sense, their offenses are often symptoms of profound disease or sickness. The pretense of "justice" in such court cases is, to a discerning eye, even more glaring.

Prosecutors who excel in this system (that is, who get lots of convictions and prison sentences), and judges who mete out stiff prison sentences, are seen as "tough on crime"—never mind the issue of effectiveness. Defense lawyers, at best, are able to divert a few of their clients to treatment instead of punishment, win an occasional acquittal against long odds, avoid or limit some clients' incarceration time, or get a life-without-parole sentence instead of death. At worst, they simply participate uncomplainingly as a cog in the machine of an ineffective and illegitimate system massively weighted toward the state, which does little good for most of their clients, most crime victims, or society as a whole.

The Pre-trial Process

During the period between when the primary law-enforcement activities in a given criminal case—investigation and arrest—take place, and the time the case is decided by judge, jury, or guilty plea, there are typically a series of court hearings in which important decisions are made. At a preliminary hearing, or a bail or detention hearing, the court makes a decision whether or not to keep the person detained and set bail (and, if so, how much), release the suspect on his or her "own recognizance," or release the person into the custody of a third party contingent on the satisfaction of certain conditions (for instance, drug testing). Such decisions are usually made according to the defendant's record; the nature of the current charges; his or her presumed dangerousness; his or her presumed likelihood of showing up for trial if released; and whether or not the defendant is employed, uses drugs, and has local family ties. Issues of race, class, lifestyle, and politics often play into such subjective decisions.

The consequences of these decisions may be very important for the defendant and his or her family alike. Studies have shown that defendants who have been free pending trial are more likely to be acquitted, have their charges dropped, or receive a lighter sentence if convicted than those who are locked up until the trial or plea bargain. This is largely because in jail defendants are much less likely to be able to help their own defense by gathering records, finding witnesses, and working with their lawyers.

The pre-trial detention, bail, and/or release decision can also be important because many local county jails are harsh, unhealthy, and violent places where defendants (who are constitutionally innocent until proven guilty) can experience brutality and exploitation that can mark them for life, regardless of what adjudication their case later receives. A lot of suffering and trauma can happen in seven months, which in 1998 was the mean time between arrest and sentencing across the nation (Pastore and Maguire 2002).

In the small number (fewer than 10 percent) of cases in which the prosecution does not make a plea bargain offer or the defendant does not accept it, the average time from arrest to sentencing is more than one year. It is obvious that the lengthy period between arrest and trial (despite the constitutional guarantee of a speedy trial) can be a powerful incentive for defendants to plead guilty to something, whether or not they are in fact guilty, just in order to get out of jail with a sentence of "time served." This is especially true with the massive caseloads and inadequate resources of many public defenders, which prevent them from spending the necessary time on many cases. Having a felony on one's record can later cost a person dearly under today's "two strikes" and "three strikes" laws (Durose, Levin, and Langan 2001).

County Jails

In most states, jails differ from prisons in that counties or clusters of counties, rather than the state or federal government, operate regional jails. Private prison companies operate some on contract with county governments. Currently jails also differ from prisons in that they tend to be less overcrowded. Jails were at 10 percent below rated capacity in 2001; state prisons were at 100 to 115 percent of rated capacity; and federal prisons were at 131 percent of rated capacity that same year. But this is only because construction of local jails has proceeded rapidly in the last decade or so. From 1990 until 2001, the nation's county-jail population increased from 405,000 to 631,000, representing an increase in the jail incarceration rate from 163 per 100,000 residents to 222 per 100,000 (Beck, Karberg, and Harrison 2002; Harrison and Beck 2002).

Of this 631,000, almost 8,000 were juveniles incarcerated in adult jails, and a majority of all jail prisoners were black (41 percent) or Hispanic (15 percent). The growth rate in the jail population between 1990 and 2001 was 6.3 percent annually for adult females, versus 3.8 percent for adult males, mirroring the population growth trends in state prisons during roughly this same period (Beck, Karberg, and Harrison 2002; Harrison and Beck 2002). The significance of this demographic information often goes unnoticed. Vulnerable populations held in jails—women, youth, the mentally ill—are put at great risk, especially when they are insufficiently separated from more powerful groups of prisoners. The fact that these are locked systems with little public accountability means that prisoners can suffer abuse, rape, or even death before any public attention is brought to bear. The largest mental institution in the country is located in the Los Angeles County Jail, but its primary purpose is not delivery of mental health treatment. Prisoners are in danger of being underserved medically, and at risk as a result of jail conditions, insensitive staff, and other prisoners.

The legal and jurisdictional status of persons held in county jails varies more widely than the status of those incarcerated in state and federal prisons. As summarized by the United States Department of Justice, jails hold:

- suspects awaiting arraignment and trial, or in process of being tried;
- convicted persons awaiting sentencing;
- convicted persons sentenced to relatively short terms of incarceration (usually less than one year);
- individuals held for the military, for protective custody, for contempt of court, or for being material witnesses;
- persons awaiting parole, probation, or bail revocation hearings;
- juveniles being temporarily detained pending transfer to juvenile justice facilities;
- persons awaiting transfer to federal, state, or immigration facilities if and when empty beds become available; and
- mentally disturbed persons pending being moved to appropriate health facilities.

In principle, one of most significant distinctions in jail populations is between those who, while awaiting trial, are presumed innocent and hence retain their rights, and those who have been convicted and thus have lost most of their civil rights. In practice, treatment is indistinguishable. Of all adults in county jails in 2001, 41.5 percent were convicted of a felony or a misdemeanor, and 58.5 percent had not been convicted. This represents a change from 1990, when the comparable figures were 48.5 and 51.5 percent, respectively (Beck, Karberg, and Harrison 2002, 9).

Relationships between state and county jurisdictions can become rather complex around the politics and economics of incarceration. Many states' county jails house a large number of convicted felons, most of whom are serving considerably longer time than the one-year upper limit on misdemeanor sentences. In 2001, about 11 percent of all prisoners in local jails and other local facilities were being held for federal or state jurisdictions. The states of Louisiana, Kentucky, and Tennessee led the pack, with over one-fourth of their state prisoners housed in local institutions (Beck, Karberg, and Harrison 2002, 8). To some extent, the reason for this is overcrowding in state facilities, which has led to use of the jails as a sort of temporary stopgap measure to buy time pending construction of more state facilities. In these arrangements, the state typically compensates the counties at a certain per diem for each state prisoner held locally.

Often what is temporary becomes permanent, and some counties find that they can make a profit by keeping their costs down well below the rate they get from the state. Thus, they construct larger facilities than they need for the traditional functions of the county jail (to house primarily pre-trial detainees and convicted misdemeanants) so they will have more capacity for prisoners on the lucrative state contracts. This arrangement also constitutes a great temptation for county sheriffs and/or county commissioners to hold down costs by reducing programs, health care, food, and so forth for prisoners, so the county's profit will be even greater. In many states they get away with it, since standards, regulatory mechanisms, and incentives for structures of accountability are even lower at the local level than at the state level. The result resembles what many have found in the phenomenon of private, for-profit prisons.

The downside of more and more state prisoners serving longer sentences in local facilities is that many of these institutions are not well designed for such uses. Often living conditions and both the quantity and quality of programming are even worse than in state prisons. But there is perhaps an upside: local jails are usually geographically closer to a prisoner's family, attorney, and support system than are state prisons, which may be located some distance away. But this begs the question of why it is necessary for so many people—including convicted felons—to be locked up in the first place. The overwhelming majority of such prisoners are serving time for drug offenses or other nonviolent offenses against property or public order, not against other persons.

Probation and Community Corrections

An alternative to prosecution (and therefore to incarceration) used in many jurisdictions is diversion, which usually happens at a local level. First-time offenders and others accused of less serious offenses may be diverted from prosecution contingent on their successful completion of specified programs such as drug treatment. If they do so, their charges then may be dropped, or their record may be expunged if they have been required to plead guilty prior to the diversion. They also perform their alternative service or participate in their alternative program in their hometowns. Sometimes they are monitored and supervised by state employees, but this is done locally as well.

Perhaps the most common and traditional alternative to incarceration is simple probation. Between 1982 and 1999 the number of convicted offenders on probation roughly tripled, tracking similar increases in the numbers who were in state and federal prisons and in county jails during that same period. In 1999 there were 1,300,000 prisoners, 600,000 jail inmates, and 3,800,000 probationers (Gifford 2002, 7).

If more people are on probation than are locked up at any given time, it is a function of long probation time—it is a very different story when we look at sentencing figures. In 1998, of the 930,000 adults convicted of a felony in state courts, 44 percent were sentenced to a state prison, 24 percent to a local jail, and only 32 percent (fewer than a third) to probation (Durose, Levin, and Langan 2001). When one considers that fewer than 18 percent of those sentenced that year were violent offenders, it becomes very clear that probation or similar nonincarceration sanctions would have been appropriate for a much larger percentage of the whole group.

The United States Department of Justice reports that in 1998 more than 36 percent of the 930,000 sentenced felons were ordered to do something else in addition to jail, prison, or probation. Twenty-one percent of them had fines imposed, an estimated 13 percent were ordered to pay restitution, 6 percent were sent to treatment of some kind, and 6 percent were ordered to do community-service work (Durose, Levin, and Langan 2001, 10). It is not clear how many of these additional sanctions were added on to prison sentences, and how many were coupled with probation. It seems reasonable, however, to assume that most of them were ordered to accompany probation sentences, since imprisoned persons could not reasonably comply with many of these additional expectations. In keeping with the state-dominated adversarial nature of our retributive criminal justice system, the most popular add-on sanction was fines payable to the government—rather than either restitution to the real, primary victims of crime; community service to the real, secondary crime victims; or mental health, family, or substance abuse treatment designed to get to some of the root causes of the persons' criminal behavior.

In 2001, in addition to the 631,000 persons housed in local jails, another 71,000 were supervised by jail staff in alternative programs in the community. These programs included community service (25 percent), weekend reporting programs (20 percent), electronic monitoring house arrest (14 percent), other pre-trial supervision (9 percent), drug/alcohol/mental health treatment programs (7 percent), and work release or other work programs (7 percent) (Beck, Karberg, and Harrison 2002, 8).

Due to the impossible and unconscionable caseloads common in probation departments, simple probation as an alternative sanction typically performs not much better than prison in terms of recidivism rates. Huge caseloads, the paucity of funding and resources, and the focus on revoking probation (as is also true of parole) for technical violations as well as for conviction of new crimes often make it impossible for probation officers to provide the kind of practical and personal support that many of their clients need. Better-financed and more realistic models like intensive probation and community corrections, in which professionals with much lower caseloads supervise offenders in a more comprehensive and focused program, are available in some jurisdictions, but they have not caught on, probably because of both economic and political considerations.

In some places, especially the states of Minnesota and Vermont, state policymakers have allocated resources, developed models, and instituted plans for restorative justice-oriented methodologies to be used in a number of cases on the local level, by local people. Such programs, like victim-offender mediation, family group conferencing, sentencing circles, and community-reparation boards, usually avoid major incarceration, offer significant victim and offender input, lead to successful victim restitution, and result in helpful treatment programs for offenders. They also move in the direction of transforming the adversarial, professional-dominated justice process into a more consensual, grassroots, and neighborhood-based process. But elsewhere across the country (and even in Minnesota and Vermont), most of these kinds of programs are dependent on local court personnel and prosecutorial support for case referrals, resulting in the referral of only those cases, usually minor, that they do not wish to deal with.

In most jurisdictions, we are still a long way from fulfilling the potential of alternative, community-based models of doing justice. Alternative programs are still marginalized, under-resourced, over-controlled, and used as add-ons instead of replacements for the failed punitive model that dominates our criminal justice system.

Taking Local Communities Seriously

If crime and the criminal justice system are, to a great extent, profoundly local phenomena, it only makes sense that they can be transformed at the local level. Again, this does not mean that big local government programs are what are needed to turn round the destructive forces of crime and punishment in our communities. The National Center on Institutions and Alternatives (NCIA), founded by Jerome Miller, argues that it is local people at the neighborhood level who have the primary responsibility and incentive to solve their crime and punishment problems:

> Most crime is local. Kids make too much noise, individuals suffer from drug addictions, dealers convert a vacant property into a crack house, and convenience stores lose inventory to shoplifters. The solutions to such problems are also local: parks and community gardens so kids have something positive to do with their time, drug treatment facilities, neighborhood patrols, and sentences that require shoplifters to sweep the sidewalks in the business district. These innovative, small-scale approaches to crime control are best designed and implemented by people closest to the problem. The very best crime control arises from informal neighborhood relations. Crime thrives when people are indoors and afraid. A healthy

neighborhood is one where people walk outdoors and neighbors watch each other's homes. Big government solutions like prison projects do little to foster such conditions. The best role of government is to promote problem-solving, community-oriented policing, and to free public moneys to support small-scale projects. Investing millions in a new prison does not do as much good for public safety as investing thousands in drug treatment facilities or job training programs. If the government cannot help, it should at least not interfere with neighborhoods trying to solve their own problems. Unfortunately, big government interventions like mass arrests and prison construction often do more harm than good. (NCIA 2004)

Ideally, the principle of neighborhood ownership and responsibility must go farther than this. If neighborhood people are the primary stakeholders in finding a solution to the crime problem in their community, then they should also be empowered to exercise primary decision-making authority in responding to crime within their neighborhood. This means that much of the power and burden to adjudicate situations of conflict and crime must rest with local community people, those who are most affected by the conflict and the crime themselves.

It also means, in terms of prevention, that neighborhood and community organizations need both the power and the resources to address the root causes of crime, insofar as this is possible to do on the local level. This commitment to participatory democracy and shared decision making is a basic principle of what is variously termed *community justice, restorative justice, transforming justice,* and *peacemaking justice.* We believe that a neighborhood-based solution must lean in the direction of developing an alternative to the adversarial legal system described above. Only in some such transformed, local community-based justice system can the rich potential of the neighborhood be tapped and galvanized to its fullest extent. To bring about the embodiment of such a vision on a broad scale will require a level of strategic thinking, organizing, and political struggle that we have never seen in the criminal justice arena.

In all situations involving local decision-making power, especially in criminal justice, there is a potential danger of vigilante justice, and we recognize this. That is why constitutional and statutory safeguards at the federal and state levels, coupled with active monitoring of local situations, are so important when speaking of a shift of power to the community level.

What we find, then, playing out in the criminal justice system in the United States is a broad range of social problems and social neglect. We see through this looking glass darkly—a reflection of poverty and racism. The common thread in the story is economic injustice, which gives way, very quickly, to other forms of injustice, as becomes evident as we delve more deeply into the criminal justice system.

4: SENTENCING: THE COLD HEART OF THE PENAL SYSTEM

To blacks and other minorities, criminal law may appear as an instrument of oppression; to the poor, a barrier to perpetuate an unjust status quo; to the young, a coercer of conformity to the middle-aged, middle-class, Puritan virtues; to mid-America, a frontline defense against anarchy . . . to politicians, an expedient means of relieving pressures to "do something" about politically insoluble problems.

—AFSC 1971

When AFSC published *Struggle for Justice* in 1971, it did so with the hope of taking a long look at sentencing practices—especially at the indeterminate sentence system. Prisoners were being sentenced to indefinite periods of imprisonment, often five years to life, with actual release dates determined by parole boards. The need to pay attention to sentencing trends was precipitated by Barry Goldwater's presidential campaign in 1964 and Richard Nixon's campaign in 1968, both of which exploited the theme of "law and order" for the first time in a national political context (Fellner and Mauer 1998, 47). Imbedded in their calls for order were subtle messages to whites about the need to fear black criminal behavior.

The authors of *Struggle for Justice* clearly spelled out the danger inherent in advocating any kind of change in a system already known to be utterly dysfunctional and destructive. The dangers included the enormity of the problem, the impossibility of achieving real systemic change short of radical change in the values of the dominant culture, and, finally, "the menace of good intentions," which had so often introduced new horrors (AFSC 1971, 12–13). Indeed, the book stated, "The construction of a just system of criminal justice in an unjust society is a contradiction in terms" (AFSC 1971, 16). At the same time, *Struggle for Justice* was an all-out indictment of the indeterminate sentence system that gave parole boards the broadest possible discretion to decide when people were suitable for release. It questioned the assumptions underlying rehabilitation as culturally bound and paternalistic.

The danger of addressing the ills of any part of the system is that its remedy will ultimately prop up a failing and bankrupt system. One writer has accused AFSC of hastening the day of mandatory sentences because it opposed the indeterminate sentence system, and the practice of coerced programming on which the system rested (Fellner and Mauer 1998, 44, 48). If the end of one policy leads to the inception of another, does that make the advocates of one necessarily the advocate of the other?

> *Mixing treatment with coercion in the penal system not only lengthens sentences and increases the suffering and the sense of injustice, it also vitiates the treatment programs that are its justification. . . . Is the necessary therapeutic relationship between the helper and the helped possible if the person to be helped is forced into the relationship?*
>
> —AFSC 1971

In actuality, the factors that led to the end of indeterminacy and the factors that subsequently ushered in vastly lengthened sentences are very complex, encompassing a variety of social and political realities. Specific policy changes in sentencing illustrate the complexities and the challenges they present to social change agents.

The California Example

Following the publication of *Struggle for Justice*, California became one of the first states to revamp its sentencing laws. The AFSC, along with the Friends Committee on Legislation in Sacramento and the Prisoners Rights Union, played the role of watchdog in 1975 when legislation was introduced to replace indeterminate sentences with set amounts of time chosen from a statutory range. Defendants were to be given the midrange length of time unless aggravating or mitigating circumstances dictated otherwise. But even as the bill was being debated, amendments proliferated to lengthen times and compound aggravating factors. Prisoners sentenced prior to the new law, or those still sentenced to "life," were to go before a Community Release Board whose composition did not reflect that of the community. Prisoners' rights advocates failed to secure any guidelines for board membership other than political appointment—dooming the process to a level of politicization not seen before.

In the end, prisoner advocacy groups opposed the measure, although it based midrange sentences on existing averages. They feared that the addition of aggravating factors—including carrying a weapon or having prior convictions—would result in long sentences. What no one anticipated was the impact of legislative involvement itself. Each year after 1976, when the law was enacted, brought hundreds of proposed sentencing changes—almost all of them requiring longer imprisonment. The base numbers in the original bill had no time to become operative before harsher penalties were adopted. The California prison buildup had begun.

The shift to fixed sentences amounted to a shift in discretion from the sentencing/parole boards to the political arena. Although legislators had always had the power to pass harsher sentences, they didn't exercise that power when length of incarceration could be influenced through the parole board.

In 1972, the U.S. jail and prison population was about 330,000 (Fellner and Mauer 1998, 9). Today, the jail and prison population exceeds two million. The forces that were at play in ending the indeterminate sentence included strong advocates on the political right as well as the left. James Q. Wilson, a conservative, argued for prisons to isolate and punish rather than rehabilitate. This would provide

> recognition that a society at a minimum must be able to protect itself from dangerous offenders and to impose some costs . . . on criminal acts; it is also a frank admission that society really does not know how to do much else. (Wilson 1983, 172)

Federal Sentencing Policy

The fact that legislators didn't know how to do much else became the dominant factor in subsequent decades. At the federal level, mandatory sentences were introduced in 1984 and supplemented in 1986 and 1987.[1] Up to that point, criminal law had been almost exclusively handled at the state level. There were notable exceptions, such as interstate incidents or crimes alleged to have been committed on Indian reservations. Politicians wanted to jump on the "get tough" bandwagon; even symbolic gestures would make headlines. Mandatory sentences, however, were anything but symbolic. They took discretion away from judges and made imprisonment automatic, regardless of the specifics of the crime. Once mandates were in place, they were prime targets for extension, resulting in relatively minor offenses carrying long prison terms. Some of the longest sentences were attached to drug offenses as the "war on drugs" used the punitive weapons of the criminal justice system.

A great deal of criminal justice policy mimics military policy. The AFSC sees work in this field as the domestic peace issue. In both arenas, society creates enemies, defends itself against perceived threats by engaging in armed offensives, and justifies extreme punishments, up to and including killing, all in the name of public safety. This is not to imply that buildings being bombed or people being murdered are not real threats. Yet, far too often we see highly militarized mobilizations of force directed at peace demonstrators, or the sealing off of large sections of a city to prevent an economic summit from being aware of the widespread opposition to globalization. We see guns aimed at people searching for food in the midst of a natural disaster. We see the military and law enforcement working together to profile and criminalize Muslims, suspected of "terrorism" based on nothing more than their ethnic and/or religious identities.

Nowhere is this war mentality more evident than in drug policy. So serious is this trend that Quaker Yearly Meetings across the country, beginning with the Philadelphia Yearly Meeting, are considering minutes about the drug wars:

> Friends for over 300 years have sought to live "in the virtue of that life and power that takes away the occasion of all wars." Today our country is engaged in a "War on Drugs" that bears all the hallmarks of war: displaced populations, disrupted economies, terrorism,

abandonment of hope by those the war is supposedly being fought to help, the use of military force, the curtailment of civil liberties, and the demonizing of the "enemies." While we are all affected by the "War on Drugs," we are painfully aware that particularly victimized are people of color, the poor, and other less powerful persons.

In addition, drugs continue to do terrible harm to people in our country and throughout the world. Our federal, state, and local governments need to put much greater emphasis on strategies that act to remove the causes of drug addiction and provide for education, treatment, and research into the causes of addiction. (Philadelphia Yearly Meeting, 320th Annual Session, March 2000)

Carrying Out the Drug War

The drug war is carried on at home and abroad. Globally, the United States has participated in the destabilization of whole economies, ostensibly to curb the production and export of controlled substances. It has conducted this part of the war with full-blown military intervention, with its consequent devastation of lives, infrastructure, and environments. The choices made in the execution of these policies are indistinguishable from foreign policy decisions—indeed, intervention in the name of the drug war often masks intervention for political reasons.

Within United States borders, many are beginning to question the genesis of the "crack epidemic" and the devastation it has wrought on communities of color. Serious evidence has emerged to suggest that crack cocaine was spread within inner-city neighborhoods, with government complicity. Drug profits were then used to fuel military operations in other countries.[2] This kind of operation will never be stopped until profit is removed from the drug trade.

For decades, the AFSC has called for decriminalization of a broad range of actions that are currently handled by the criminal justice system. It is imperative that drug and alcohol addiction be treated as a health problem and not as a political or moral issue calling for punishment. As long as resources are squandered on punishment, the United States will never be able to meet the demands for treatment. In addition, we will be fueling the war-like posture currently assumed by the government, and fueling the interests of those who would profit from people's addictions.

Three Strikes

Whether fighting a "war on crime," a "drug war," or any other war, stronger and stronger weapons must be found, especially if the war is failing. In the early 1990s, Washington and other states began enacting "three strikes and you're out" laws that promised to send three-time offenders to prison for life. By the end of the decade, twenty-five states had passed some version of three strikes, but the specifics and the enforcement varied considerably. Most of these laws focused on violent repeat offenders and most have been applied only in what were considered extreme cases.

The exception, once again, is California, where, as of May 31, 2001, more than 50,000 people had been sentenced under the law, compared to fewer than 1,000 in Georgia and South Carolina, the harshest of the other three-strike states. In California, the law applies to a list of twenty-six "violent and serious" offenses, including nonviolent property offenses and drug offenses. The breadth of this statute is compounded by the fact that the third strike can be charged for any felony if the defendant had two prior violent or serious offenses, and that petty theft with a prior conviction for petty theft is considered a felony in California. The results have been that as of March 31, 2001, 57.9 percent of third-strike cases were for nonviolent offenses,[3] and three quarters of those sentenced for second strikes had committed nonviolent offenses. Judges, once again, have very limited discretion in the application of these laws. Prosecutors make the key decisions. Some have charged every eligible case as a strike; others have been very sparing in their enforcement.

As with other cases of sentencing enhancement, politics play a key role. Everyone from judges to prosecutors to legislators assesses his or her moves depending on public pressure or perceived pressure. In an article on the war on drugs, Eric Sterling (former staff counsel for the House Judiciary Committee and president of the Criminal Justice Policy Foundation) emphasizes that politically driven sentencing policy is rarely rational:

> The contemporary legal culture is fundamentally indifferent to guilt or innocence, indifferent to the denial of due process, indifferent to vindicating equal protection of the laws, indifferent to perjury, indifferent to injustice. (Sterling 1999)

Sterling's conclusion is significant in that he helped write some of the harsh drug laws as a congressional staff person and later sounded the alarm about the dangers of such laws.

Both Democrats and Republicans share the blame for longer and longer sentences, and both liberal and conservative forces have had the effect of moving the issue in a similar direction. Governor Nelson Rockefeller of New York, who was considered a liberal Republican, authored the first mandatory drug sentences. President Richard Nixon seized on the crime issue to fuel his campaign, and although he was not as successful legislatively at the time, he set the ideas in motion for subsequent enactment. President Clinton presided over some of the harshest criminal law changes, and President George W. Bush pushed for even broader curtailments of civil liberties and nearly unlimited powers for domestic law enforcement. Each of these changes, when enacted, ignores the mounting evidence that longer sentences do not accomplish what their promoters promise.

The following two stories from California dramatize how the changes in sentencing policy played out in the lives of real people. Most of the decisions were made for political reasons, not sound policy reasons. Imbedded in the policies are crucial assumptions about who is dangerous, how to "send a message," and whether prisons should rehabilitate or punish.

In March of 1971, three African American young men entered a liquor store in California, intending to make a purchase. Instead, an argument broke out, and the two older youths threatened to rob the store. When the clerk reached for a buzzer behind the counter, one of the men pulled out a gun and killed him. The actual shooter was never apprehended, but the other two men were charged with "felony murder," because they had "participated" in a serious felony that resulted in a murder. One of them was under eighteen and was sentenced to the California Youth Authority. The other man, Max, was sent to state prison for "life." In those days a "lifer" was eligible for parole after seven years at the discretion of the Adult Authority. Max was released from prison in 1981, after serving ten years, and served another three years on parole. He has never reoffended.

In 1986, Byron was charged with felony murder after a "joy ride" in a stolen vehicle (grand theft auto) resulted in a fatal car accident. He and his buddies had been drinking at the time. His sentence was twenty-five years to life, and he would not be eligible for parole until he had served a minimum of sixteen years and eight months. By this time, however, the Adult Authority had been replaced by the Board of Prison Terms, which was granting very few paroles to any lifers. Byron's first parole hearing would not come until he had served the first sixteen years, and it would be unlikely that he would be given a date by the board. While he has been in prison, he has not been able to take college-level classes, as Max did, or to work a regular prison job. The only treatment program available for his alcohol problem has been the volunteer Alcoholics Anonymous group that comes when the prison is not in lockdown. Byron's overnight visits with his mother and children were discontinued in 1996, when the legislature decided lifers should not be eligible for such visits.

The Death Penalty

The centerpiece of the criminal justice system is the death penalty. It sends a message to all prisoners—and to the rest of us—that the U.S. government reserves the right to kill us under certain circumstances.

This threat exists for prisoners even in states that don't have capital punishment, because the possibility of reinstatement is ever present. Also, the federal death penalty allows for death sentences to be imposed and carried out in states that do not have the penalty. Since legislative (and even judicial) repeal of death penalty laws is always subject to change, it becomes clear that only a kind of cultural "heart and mind" change will reliably abolish judicial state killings in the long run. The AFSC opposes the use of death as a sanction for murder, treason, or any other offense. Capital punishment is the ultimate form of injustice carried out in the name of justice and is an offense to human decency.

At the same time that we stand strongly against legalized murder, we also stand with those who are outraged at the loss of life through murder. Murders occur in the home, on the streets, in office suites, in war and many other places. We decry the lives lost through neglect, through international business decisions that cut corners on product safety, through the dumping of toxic wastes in sources of public drinking water. Many of these examples are rarely considered murder and are often not even considered criminal. Indeed, one of the features of the criminal justice system is that it individualizes crime. When we are hurt personally by a violent act our outrage is understood and the wheels of justice grind relentlessly until someone "pays" for the crime. AFSC's search is for ways to honor the depth of the anger and pain without participating in more violence.

Although the U.S. Supreme Court struck down the death penalty in 1972 (*Furman v. Georgia*), different justices based their opinions on different standards of law. No majority of the court agreed on any one flaw that would render the penalty unconstitutional. When in 1976 the high court ruled in *Gregg v. Georgia* that it was possible to have a constitutional death penalty, thirty-eight states relegislated their capital punishment laws with provisions that complied with the *Gregg* standard. Over the next fifteen years, capital punishment was on the books again in those states, as well as in the federal government, which reenacted it in 1988. Actual executions resumed in 1977, with Gary Gilmore in Utah.

> *The death penalty restores no victim to life and only compounds the wrong committed in the first place. There is no justification for taking the life of any man or woman for any reason.*
>
> —AFSC Board Minutes, November 1976

The Supreme Court's expectation, clearly spelled out in their *Gregg* opinions, was that capital juries—ordinary human beings, but reasoning from comprehensible legal criteria—would now be able to decide not just about guilt, but which (relatively few) defendants' crimes sank to the level of "heinous." The decades since *Gregg* have proved otherwise. One of those justices, the late Harry Blackmun, wrote of his shattered hopes in a 1994 opinion:

> From this day forward, I no longer shall tinker with the machinery of death. For more than 20 years I have endeavored—indeed, I have struggled—along with a majority of this court, to develop procedural and substantive rules that would lend more than the mere appearance of fairness to the death penalty endeavor. Rather than continue to coddle the court's delusion that the desired level of fairness has been achieved and the need for regulation eviscerated, I feel morally and intellectually obligated simply to concede that the death penalty experiment has failed. . . . The basic question—does the system accurately and consistently determine which defendants "deserve" to die?—cannot be answered in the affirmative. . . . The death penalty must be abandoned altogether." (*Callins v. Collins* 1994)

Most of us have not had the experience with death penalty cases that Supreme Court justices have. Most of us have never even been on a capital-case jury. Most of us do not have a family member on death row. And hopefully most of us have not lost a loved one to violent crime. So we come to this issue with a theoretical notion of what the death penalty is supposed to be and to accomplish—retribution, protection of potential victims, solace for the victims' families. Opinions like Justice Blackmun's are based on the sad wisdom that public policies must be justified by their results, not their intentions.

Two structural flaws seem to underlie and enable all the other familiar flaws in death-penalty administration: the problem of a jury of one's peers, and the problem of ensuring effective legal representation for the defendant.

Jury studies, a relatively new field of legal research, show that one crucial difference between defendants sentenced to death and those punished with imprisonment is a factor termed "empathic divide." When all is said and done, can the jurors understand this defendant as a human being like themselves, despite the terrible wrong he or she did—or only as a fearful threat to all of us, if left alive? A large minority of citizens, those who oppose the death penalty on principle, are by law excluded from capital juries, and prosecutors work hard in their jury-selection process to make sure that anyone whose life experience might render her or him sympathetic to the defendant is also excused. Capital juries are thus by design not one's peers, in any psychological or social sense.[4]

Some defenders of the death penalty allow that it is an extreme punishment, but one warranted by extreme offenses. They assume that a state-sanctioned death penalty is the only way victims' families and friends, as well as the rest of us, can cope with the outrage a heinous killing generates. This understandable outrage is itself one of the chronic flaws in capital prosecutions. Media and prosecutors may use our natural repugnance to "juice up" their story with the details of the crime. And, at the trial, when a jury sits there looking at the pictures of the crime scene, when they hear from the victim's survivors in "victim impact" testimony, jury studies reveal they find it almost impossible to maintain any presumption of innocence: yes, an awful crime happened, but has the prosecutor proven this is really the one who did it?

Our vengeance-soaked culture is in desperate need of being called to higher moral and spiritual ground. Survivors of murder victims need to be free to do their grieving in natural, human ways, not skewed and distorted by sensationalist media, opportunistic politicians, and cynical prosecutors. They do not need decades of being subjected to the shifting tides of the judicial system's appellate process in the futile search for "closure" via another premeditated killing, this time by the state.

The great spiritual traditions of our peoples offer us ways of moving through and beyond our need for vengeance. To offer just one example, the Hebrew tradition's *lex talionis* ("an eye for an eye") historically represented a limit on retaliation (no more than one eye for an eye) rather than an encouragement to it. Later Jewish rabbinic authorities in the *Midrash* added so many restrictions to the use of the death penalty that a judge who sentenced one person to death in his entire judicial career was considered a "hanging judge." In the New Testament, Jesus explicitly rejects the *lex talionis,* teaching that his followers must not resist an evil person, should love their enemies, and should "judge not" (Matthew 5–7).

In Buddhism, related teachings are found in the precepts—the first of which teaches abstinence from taking life. The final chapter of the *Dhammapada* states, "Him I call a Brahmin who has put aside weapons and renounced violence toward all creatures. He neither kills nor helps others to kill" (Easwaran 1985, 187). In an article against capital punishment in the Buddhist Peace Fellowship publication, *Turning Wheel,* Damien Horigan writes: "In Buddhist terms a rehabilitated offender, even a murderer, remembers his or her Buddha-nature. For society, reforming a wrongdoer means regaining a productive member who can somehow contribute to the general welfare" (Horigan 1999, 18).

As a society, we need to find a more productive way to deal with our outrage at violent crimes. By giving in to the appetite for revenge, our death-penalty system encourages media, politicians, prosecutors, and others to appeal to what is arguably the most primitive strain in humanity.

Looking back on notorious capital cases since *Gregg,* the most common deficiency has been ill-prepared and ineffective defense attorneys. In a decision-making process designed to be adversarial, a defendant can only rely on his attorneys to tell his or her story, both of the crime and of the life before, in ways that shrink the jurors' empathic divide. Attorneys inexperienced in death-penalty cases, and attorneys overloaded with other work or personal problems of their own, have proved unequal to the tasks of determining the truth or insuring justice.

In the decades since *Gregg*, more than 120 death-row prisoners (and hundreds of other prisoners) have been exonerated, either upon proof of actual innocence, or upon exposure of their trials as legally and constitutionally inadequate. Analyzing those wrongful convictions, several problems recur again and again: eyewitness misidentification, invalid or even fraudulent lab work, false confessions, and false testimony by codefendants or jailhouse snitches. Studies indicate that death penalty prosecutions, despite all their extra cost, are more susceptible to such errors than other crimes because capital cases put more pressure on police and prosecutors to convict someone. In our system, the "players" who are supposed to detect, prevent, and expose all these problems are defense attorneys and their investigators—teams whose resources never match those of the district attorneys.

Given these structural inconsistencies, the criticisms that dogged capital cases pre-*Gregg* have continued. Some hailed the advent of DNA analysis as promising greater moral certainty for juries, but the majority of homicides produce no useful DNA evidence.

A disproportionate number of poor people and people of color continue to be sentenced to death in every jurisdiction that retains capital punishment. Discrimination by race of the victim is even more disproportionate in most death-penalty states. Nationwide, blacks make up more than 40 percent of death-row prisoners, although fewer than 20 percent of those arrested for murder are African American. African Americans killing whites are particularly liable to this extreme penalty.

In our system, prosecutors are given an inordinate amount of discretion in determining which homicides get "tracked" as death-penalty cases—and 90 percent of prosecutors are white. Although whites make up only about 45 percent of all homicide victims in the country (Rennison 2002, 5), 84 percent of the victims of death-row prisoners are white.

Since the first U.S. execution—George Kendall, a Virginia councilor who was shot in 1608 as a spy for Spain—85 percent of executions have occurred in the states comprising the old "Slave South," and one state, Texas, has inflicted more than a third of all these. Racism, however, is more contagious; Pennsylvania in recent years was the death row with the worst ethnic imbalance.[5]

Although only a small percentage—1.5 percent—of prisoners on death row are women, among these are defendants whose convictions followed trials in which they were labeled as lesbians in court. Prosecutors worked on their juries to portray the defendant not as a woman, deserving of empathy, but as a violent predator who deviates from feminine norms.

> *The more "manly" her sexuality, her dress, and her demeanor, the more easily the jury may forget that she is a woman. In essence, she is de-feminized by her sexual orientation and then de-humanized by her crime.*
>
> —Tonya McClary, AFSC, Winter 2002

Recent historic Supreme Court decisions *Atkins* and *Simmons* (*Atkins v. Virginia* 2002; *Roper v. Simmons* 2005) have ruled that executing mentally retarded prisoners, or those who committed murder while still younger than eighteen, amounts to cruel and unusual punishment as proscribed by the Eighth Amendment. Our nation's death rows also hold, however, prisoners with significant mental illness—estimates range between 10 and 20 percent. This may turn out to be the next frontier in "chipping away" at the death penalty.

The United States prides itself on high standards of due process, but evidence shows that this claim is blatantly untrue. In 1996, the federal Anti-Terrorism and Effective Death Penalty bill (AEDPA) expanded the federal death penalty to apply to an additional fifty-one crimes, and seriously limited prisoners' appeal rights. Many AEDPA provisions targeted murders related to drug dealing, and racially skewed enforcement has produced a federal death row, in Terre Haute, Indiana, with 84 percent people of color (Snell and Maruschak 2002, 6).

Other court rulings have further eroded due process in United States death-penalty cases. The U.S. Supreme Court found it constitutional to reject a death-penalty appeal based on actual innocence so long as no procedural oversights were detected (*Herrera v. Collins* 1993). Such pivotal constitutional errors as inadequate counsel, lawyers or jurors falling asleep during proceedings, and prosecutors withholding evidence from the defense have all been declared "harmless error" by appeals courts in death-penalty cases.

In the post-*Gregg* rush to reinvent capital punishment, states adopted statutes that specified "special circumstances" that would qualify a murder for the maximum sentence. In the intervening years, these circumstances have grown into long lists that encompass almost all murders, based on the description of the victim, number of victims, method of murder, and accompanying crimes. Even the requirement of premeditation, an element in death-penalty law for two hundred years, has been dropped in cases where a murder occurs "during the commission of a felony," regardless of whether the defendant actually pulled the trigger.

Whatever you think about the death penalty, a system that will take life must first give justice.

—John J. Curtin Jr, former president of the American Bar Association, testifying to House Judiciary Committee in 1991

There is no such thing as a "good" murder. Killing is wrong. To devise laws that purport to distinguish between degrees of seriousness is a dubious task. The millions of dollars spent trying these cases would be much better spent helping to heal the survivors and working with the offenders.

Some would argue for the death penalty in wistful, theoretical terms—it *ought to be* possible to administer such a punishment equitably. The whole history of executions argues to the contrary: its flaws are not incidental, not fixable, and they arise from a fundamental misconception—you cannot do a wrong thing in a right way.

One final, huge logical inconsistency confronts those who might still hope, despite discouragingly recurring evidence of inherent problems, that it might somehow be possible to administer executions justly. This mountain of evidence is the decades of empirical experience of nations—now more than 130—without a death penalty, of those U.S. states (and the District of Columbia and Puerto Rico) who have abolished their death penalties, and of the huge preponderance of U.S. homicides—more than 97 percent—punished by sentences other than death.

If death were the only logical and just punishment for homicide, how are these folks—not by nature any more virtuous than the rest of us—managing to get along without executions? If a death for a death were the only way grieving families could heal, how do all the families of these others cope? Beyond the debates back and forth about moral values, statistics, and good intentions, here is a home truth rooted in real human experience: if they can do without it, we can do without it.

Throwing Away the Key: Life without Mercy

In the past twenty years, a new criminal sanction has found its way into statutes in at least thirty states: a life sentence without the possibility of parole or release (LWOPP). Although life sentences have been common in all states, there had always been a mechanism for releasing prisoners when it was determined that they had served long enough.

Some have argued that LWOPP serves as an alternative to the death penalty, and that the LWOPP option has the effect of reducing the number of death sentences. Yet in their day-to-day work, AFSC criminal-justice program staff members have seen the populations on death row skyrocket at the same time that more and more people are sentenced to LWOPP. There has been only limited research on whether LWOPP has reduced the number of death sentences more than it has reduced the number of regular life sentences. As of July 1, 2004, there were 3,490 people on death row nationally (Fins 2004), and 31,000 serving life without release. Life without possibility of parole or release is used as a sanction not only for capital cases, but as a sanction for a wide variety of offenses. No western European country has such a penalty except Britain, which has twenty people serving life without parole (Bergner 2003).

Life without possibility of parole or release makes no allowances for changed behavior, or for reconsideration of the gravity of an offense. It throws away the key. Like the death penalty, it is a signal that our criminal justice system has given up any goal or possibility of rehabilitation. Although prisoners can continue to appeal to courts for redress, the limitations that have been placed on habeas corpus drastically limit legal appeals for wrongful imprisonment. In our many years of work with prisoners, we have seen people change, and we have seen firsthand the extent to which people's lives are wasted in prison—through enforced idleness, abuse, neglect, and societal attitudes of revenge. We have worked closely with families of prisoners, whose lives are deeply and often irrevocably affected. We have documented the many ways that the court and law-enforcement systems are highly discriminatory and disproportionately punish poor people and people of color.

Quakers believe that every person has the potential to respond to God's initiative. AFSC's goal is therefore to create conditions that foster and nurture such an understanding. Life without possibility of parole or release is incompatible with this vision. It removes hope from the lives of prisoners and their families and assumes that people's lives are irredeemable. It also precludes the possibility of the society as a whole changing in its punitive stance toward offenders.

These attitudes toward LWOPP distinguish the AFSC from a number of other anti-death penalty groups. Typically these groups do not work on criminal justice issues as a whole, and are not aware of the impact of these lifetime prison sentences overall. The death penalty often serves as a lightning rod for criminal justice reformers, who tend to see anything less than death as humane.

Parole: The Terminating Program in the Rehabilitative Model

Parole epitomizes the treatment/punishment model. If a prisoner cooperates with a treatment plan, so the theory goes, he or she is eligible for parole. Noncooperation with treatment results in parole rejection. Sometimes individuals are repeatedly rejected for parole for reasons that are presently beyond their control, such as "the nature of the offense." In such cases, no amount of cooperation with program plans results in release. If parole is achieved, the prisoner answers to a parole officer. Historically, the role of the parole officer has been to strike a balance between support and surveillance. Over the last twenty years, parole officers' primary responsibilities have become law enforcement and surveillance. Parole officers have permission to carry firearms and have broad discretion to return an individual to prison. The modern parole officer has been described as a walking judicial system.

The AFSC and many other prisoner-rights advocates opposed the model of indeterminate sentencing and parole within the treatment/punishment model for multiple reasons:

1. There is little evidence that indeterminate sentencing and parole release and supervision reduce subsequent recidivism.

2. Parole and indeterminate sentencing are unjust and inhumane, especially when imposed on unwilling participants. Not knowing their release dates keeps prisoners in a state of suspended animation and contributes one more pain of imprisonment.[6] Prisoners and ex-prisoners report that indefinite sentences are one of the most painful aspects of prison life.

3. Indeterminate sentencing permits authorities to use a great deal of uncontrolled discretion in release determination, and these decisions are often inconsistent and discriminatory, based on race and class bias.

Today, the criminal justice system has moved away from the rehabilitation model and embraced sheer retribution, disguised as deterrence and incapacitation. It seeks to isolate and punish prisoners. Increasing numbers of human beings are serving natural life sentences, or "life without mercy" as defined by some states. The implementation of truth-in-sentencing laws (sentencing laws that give an absolute minimum number of years that a prisoner must serve, thus eradicating "good time") has resulted in prisoners spending unprecedented amounts of time in prison. As a result, family contacts are minimized, as are other social supports, leading to increased social isolation upon release.

Of the fifteen states where parole authorities have discretion to release prisoners, most use formal risk-prediction instruments to predict the risk of recidivism, based on the original crime and the offender's background. As states allocate more resources for the building of prisons, fewer resources are available for parole services. Parole officers, over-burdened and under-resourced for their jobs, are increasingly likely to return parolees to prison because they are unwilling or unable to assist parolees to find work or housing.

The recent trend toward mandatory-sentencing laws gives the impression that parole boards around the country are being abolished or having their power severely restricted. But where parole is abolished, often the parole board remains, and in reality continues to wield a great deal of power over the futures of thousands of prisoners who were sentenced under the old law. Thousands of ex-prisoners must still serve a period of parole or post-release control. In addition, even since the technical abolition of the federal parole system, almost all federal prisoners sentenced under the new law are still subjected to several years of "supervised release" after finishing their sentences.

Most parole hearings and decisions are completed in a matter of minutes. Although incorrect information can be present in a prisoner's file, and humans can make mistakes when interpreting records, it is extremely difficult for prisoners to prove that a parole decision was made based on incorrect information and that, if the information had been correct, the decision would have been different. In some states, there is no right of appeal of parole-board decisions. Parole decisions are considered administrative in nature, and prisoners do not have due-process rights regarding parole-board actions. The following factors contribute to unequal treatment of prisoners by the parole board:

- Survivors of crime have increasing influence over individual decisions within the criminal justice system. While survivors should certainly have the opportunity to express their feelings about the crime, allowing victims to influence the outcome of parole hearings goes against the very foundations of sentencing structure. A sentencing system is intended to impose upon offenders equitable sentences for similar crimes in a more impartial manner than could be done by those closest to the crime. This goal is threatened by the fact that many states have created a position on the parole board specifically for a crime victim. It is the job of the parole board to be dispassionate and to evaluate the readiness of the prisoner to return to his or her community, not to retry the crime. Victims' groups frequently conduct letter-writing campaigns to keep specific prisoners in prison. Anecdotal evidence suggests that letters or testimony from survivors can result in repeated parole rejections regardless of the person's accomplishments while incarcerated or his or her remorse about the crime. Survivors of crime are entitled to play a role in the resolution of the incident that affected their lives, but not to play a deciding role, which more properly belongs to disinterested parties whose job it is to weigh conflicting interests. The growing power of retributive crime victims in pressuring parole boards to deny parole can be attributed in part to the fact that the present justice system gives survivors very limited options in terms of how to participate constructively in the process. If we move to a restorative paradigm (see chapter

8), there would be a commitment to addressing survivors' needs from the beginning.

- Parole board members often assume that prisoners whose convictions were the result of a plea bargain of guilty to one or more charges must have been guilty of all of the original charges. They may require prisoners to serve extra time for the crimes with which they were charged rather than releasing them after they have served an appropriate amount of time for the crimes of which they were actually convicted. This amounts to retrying the case without due process. When making parole decisions, the board often gives considerable weight to the specific circumstances of the crime, which may be "established" with the use of hearsay evidence. Repeatedly, the courts have ruled that practices such as these are permissible.[7]

An Ohio survey of judges in 1996, conducted by Citizens United for the Rehabilitation of Errants (CARE) in Ohio and the Correctional Institution Inspection Committee, asked judges how long they expected prisoners to serve. The survey found that most assumed that the people they sentenced would serve less than the statutory minimum sentence or the minimum sentence imposed. Thirty-six percent of Ohio's common pleas judges responded to the survey. Of those who responded, 52 percent expected an offender with an indefinite sentence to serve at least the minimum, and then, if the offender had demonstrated positive institutional adjustment, he would be released. Thirty-two percent expected the offender to serve less than the minimum (at least 70 percent), and as long as the offender had demonstrated positive institutional adjustment, he would be released. Only 5 percent indicated they expected the APA to add years to the minimum based on the severity of the crime or that they expected the offender to serve his/her entire sentence (CURE 1996). The parole board, on the other hand, works back from the maximum sentence and views a parole any time prior to the expiration of the maximum sentence as a privilege to be earned and can by no means be guaranteed. Prisoners who have difficulty understanding the parole process or advocating on their own behalf are at a disadvantage in the parole system. Mentally ill, illiterate, learning-disabled, and non-English-speaking prisoners may be overlooked for parole time after time because they cannot speak for themselves, or because they cannot correct mistakes in their files upon which parole decisions may be based.

The widening of the criminal justice net of social control is exemplified by the trend of requiring people to serve longer periods on parole. Whereas the usual period of parole was once the balance of one's sentence, people convicted of sex offenses and other violent crimes are now routinely assigned lengthy parole in some states. In many states, some people are being required to accept life-long intensive parole supervision in order to be released. Holding people beyond their actual sentence, out of fear that they might reoffend, is a form of preventive detention that should be unconstitutional.

While on parole, people must abide by restrictions of their activities and are more vulnerable to being returned to prison. In addition to the usual restrictions placed on all parolees—such as not going to bars, associating with other parolees, or leaving the immediate area without permission from a parole officer—some politically active parolees are forced to accept conditions restricting their free speech. Several Ohio parolees, including Indian rights activist Little Rock Reed, were told not to speak publicly about the prison system or the parole board while on parole. Washington state prisoners' rights activist Ed Mead was not permitted after his release to work for *Prison Legal News,* which he had coedited while incarcerated.

A person who is accused of breaking one of the conditions of parole can be returned to prison on a technical parole violation. A technical violation is not a new criminal charge. The parole board, as an administrative body, does not have to meet the same standards of evidence as do the courts. There are parallels in the use of technical violations to the application of the old Black Codes, in that they are used primarily to return black men to prison for offenses that are not crimes.

Extra Punishment for Sex Offenders

Although parole policies are governed by few, and often narrowly restrictive, rules, the rules governing certain offenses are changing midstream. Some states are requiring or allowing for the extension of sex offenders' sentences by adding civil commitments to criminal incarceration. This often means transfer to a mental health facility for indefinite confinement.

In the wake of a few very highly publicized cases, many states have enacted legislation authorizing the confinement and treatment of sex offenders following the completion of their prison sentences. These laws are similar in many respects: commitment follows a criminal sentence, the laws target repeat sex offenders, and evidence regarding the individual's likelihood of future violence is central to decision making.

Few crimes offend us as deeply as do sexual offenses, especially those perpetrated on children. Politicians gain easy points with the public by flying the "get tough" banner regardless of how strict laws may already be against such prisoners. Though the conditions that give rise to sexual abuse are serious and complex they are not untreatable, as is often asserted. Few have contributed more over the years to pioneer programs that realistically address sex offenders than the late Quaker Faye Honey Knopp.[8]

Laws that extend sentences when fear is running high have had a profound effect on the criminal justice system and the notions of punishment reflected by this system. The purported need for these statutes has been underpinned by the assumptions that sex offenders are likely to offend again, and that treatment is ineffective. However, evidence gathered over the past sixty-four years (Michigan began treating "sexual psychopaths" in 1939) through treatment of sex offenders does not support these assumptions. Untreated sex offenders in Canada, the United States, and Europe have a 17.6 percent recidivism rate for sexual offenses (Alexander 1999, 107–8). This recidivism rate drops to 7.2–13.9 percent if the sex offender goes through a sex offender treatment program coupled with a risk-reduction assessment and plan. If treatment is coupled with intensive parole and ongoing treatment after release, recidivism drops to the low single digits.[9] A 1998 Massachusetts pilot program, Intensive Parole for Sex Offenders, had a zero recidivism rate for sex offenses after three years of operation.[10] It has been proven that sex offenders not only are treatable, but also can become contributing members of their communities.

The legal expenses of committing someone civilly after the completion of their sentence range between $60,000 and $80,000. The annual cost of civil commitment is between $85,000 and $110,000 per person. In contrast, the annual cost of the Massachusetts pilot program is $5,675 per person.[11]

In 1994, a federal statute was enacted that made dispensing portions of federal crime-control money to the states contingent on the adoption of a sex offender registration program. By 1996, all states had adopted a sex offender registration law (commonly called "Megan's Law"). These laws require all people who are released after having been convicted of sex offenses to register at their local police stations, and to provide their names, addresses, places of employment, and photographs. Failure to register is a misdemeanor that could result in additional imprisonment.

There have been many problems with the implementation of these statutes. Many of the laws are retroactive, and sex offender registry boards are poorly equipped to conduct classification hearings for the thousands of people in each state who are affected by this legislation. Little distinction is made between dangerous individuals and those whose offenses were minor (public urination, exposure, or lewd and lascivious behavior). An eighteen-year-old boy having sex with his sixteen-year-old girlfriend is classified in the same category as someone who has raped a six-year-old child. People who have registered and are living well-ordered lives are exposed and harassed by neighbors and by law-enforcement personnel. Some have been forced from their homes because of this harassment, and some have killed themselves. The registries are very expensive and thus make it difficult to fund actual treatment for released sex offenders by the criminal justice system. Some jurisdictions have put the sex offender registry on the Internet, thus increasing the likelihood of abuse and harassment of ex-offenders.

Because these laws are retroactive, they have the power to destroy the lives of individuals who have been leading productive lives for many years. In some states, individuals who were released from prison fifteen years ago, and who have a spotless post-release record, have been forced to register as sexually dangerous. Their employers have been notified, and many have lost their jobs. In the cases of individuals who have married and fathered children, some have been forced from their homes in order to keep the department of social services or the department of youth services from taking custody of their children. Those individuals who pled to a sex offense as a juvenile in order to avoid lengthy incarceration are being forced to register as sexually dangerous.

These laws affect prostitutes who have pled to the lesser charge of lewd and lascivious behavior in order to avoid a mandatory drug sentence. These pleas are a common tool of prosecutors. Depending on the circumstances surrounding the incident, such a person may be classified as sexually dangerous. In some states, two such pleas could cause a person to spend the rest of his or her life in prison.

In light of the fairness problems posed by these policies, and the short- and long-term expense of their implementation, the necessity and the wisdom of this trend in public policy must be reexamined. In order to reduce sexual offenses, we must be proactive in supporting programs that prevent sex offenses involving the direct violation of one person by another from occurring in the first place. Given the success of well-structured, long-term treatment programs, we support the continuing treatment of sex offenders upon release, over civil commitment—which is cumbersome, unwieldy, costly, and in our view unconstitutional. The millions of dollars that will be spent implementing the current policies would be far more effectively spent initiating anti-violence programs, child sexuality education, and sex offender treatment programs. We would be better protected in the immediate term, and the long-term benefits are indisputable.

Criminal Records: The Permanent Punishment

Until recent decades, punishment had an endpoint, and most prisoners had a release date. Now, with longer sentences and more frequent use of lifetime sentences for crimes other than murder, those who break laws in our country often face excessive punishment. Those who document penal trends have seen punishment extend beyond the walls of prisons and into the communities from which the prisoners have come. We have seen families and communities crumble under the weight of unending punishment. Again, those who suffer the greatest burden of this punishment are invariably poor people and people of color. People with criminal records are now being excluded from low-income housing, welfare benefits, and a variety of other forms of assistance that would significantly increase their potential for success upon release.

One of the biggest barriers to post-release success is the misuse of criminal records, including arrests or convictions that are often unrelated to current jobs or job skills. Many states require criminal background checks for public employees who work in a wide variety of professions that involve day-to-day contact with clients. Many private-sector, nonprofit, and business groups that receive government funding and contracts are either jumping onto the bandwagon of background checks or being forced to do them against what they believe is in their best interest. Many employers are trying to buy a quick fix for fear of crime or to evade possible litigation. The resulting unemployment tends to decimate whole communities.

In the Criminal Offender Records Information (CORI) system, an individual accumulates a record when she or he comes in contact with the criminal justice system. Each time a person is picked up by the police, charged, arraigned, and found guilty or not guilty, the contact with the criminal justice system is recorded. The record is never expunged, even if a person is acquitted. In this way, women often acquire a record because they are in relationships with men who are breaking laws. Their contact with the criminal justice system, even if they are never charged with a crime, may be documented and reviewed by all potential employers.

Criminal records are kept by police departments, the Federal Bureau of Investigation, and a variety of jurisdictions. People of color are disproportionately represented in these records due to the racism that pervades the criminal justice system at all levels. This disproportion is found particularly in the black community, where large percentages of men and increasing numbers of women have had contact with the criminal justice system. Requiring background checks can effectively bar many in the community from access to employment, especially if employers are untrained in reading records, or the prospective employee doesn't apply for fear of discrimination.

These "rap sheets" are often inaccurate. The computer system that tracks many states to feed CORI was designed in 1970s. Customarily, this system has only two ways to search: by name and by date of birth. Information is often entered under incorrect names, and CORI files are merged. AFSC staff in Cambridge report that when this happens, it is virtually impossible to correct the information in a file. If a person has ever committed fraud while using someone else's identity, often the victim's record will be merged with that of the criminal.

Errors in over-reporting as well as under-reporting are so prevalent that when people request copies of their own records, the copies are sometimes accompanied with a form to correct inaccuracies. Definitions of crimes, which vary dramatically from state to state, are not included, so a person reading the record could reasonably assume that "lewd and lascivious behavior" or "child endangerment" are serious and violent crimes, which they may or may not be. Even if a charge against a person is dismissed, the individual is often suspected by a potential employer of getting away with something he or she did, perhaps with the help of a good attorney. This can have far-reaching effects for the family of an accused individual. Recently, after completing a course of study in early childhood education, a woman in Dorchester, Massachusetts, applied for a day-care license. She was refused a license because her husband had been charged with a misdemeanor ten years earlier. This charge had been dismissed with the payment of a $15.00 court fee.

Over the past thirty years, limitations on access to records have eroded. Records are becoming available to almost anyone who wants to investigate someone's criminal background, provided they can pay a nominal fee. State agencies have passed regulations prohibiting their contractors from even considering individuals who have criminal records for employment. In addition, most government supports to people who are returning to their communities from prison are being denied. For example, a woman returning to her community from prison with an infant child will not be permitted to apply for subsidized housing. If her family of origin lives in subsidized housing, this woman and her newborn will not be able to live with them without jeopardizing the family's housing situation.

Permanent punishment is causing severe civil disability within poor communities. More and more people have fewer and fewer avenues for exercising their rights of citizenship and investing in their communities. They are prohibited from voting, working, living in public housing, and securing educational resources. Through this policy, we are creating a sector of society that is permanently disenfranchised. This is dangerous in very concrete terms as well as in social, psychological, and spiritual terms. People who are denied basic human rights find it difficult to believe that government is concerned with the common good of their communities.

These laws not only create dysfunction and powerlessness in poor communities, they ensure that these communities will remain in poverty. They ensure that crime will be concentrated in these neighborhoods. We are actively legislating our way into a two-tiered society made up of those who have resources and those who do not, those who are punished and those who are not, those who have hope and those who do not.

Gay, lesbian, and transgender people are disproportionately arrested and charged with "sex offenses." These crimes remain on their records, yet, when scrutinized, they are far more likely to be related to their lifestyle than to constitute criminal behavior. In some states, public expression of affection between members of the same gender can precipitate police reaction and even arrest. If a case reaches trial, the possibility of conviction increases because of widespread homophobia in our society. Whether or not a person is ever formally charged with an offense, the incident can still appear on the record as if it were a "sex offense." These incidents can escalate into "violence," if the person questioned refuses to cooperate with police intervention and is considered to be resisting arrest. Since employers and landlords often seek out criminal records from fear of hiring or renting to sexual offenders, lesbian, gay, bisexual, and transgender people are more likely to experience employment and housing discrimination.

Recently, women have become deeply involved in the CORI debate from a feminist perspective. Since strong women have historically been punished into obedience, feminists have experienced firsthand the impact of the criminal justice system as a tool of social conformity. Criminal records are just another manifestation of this, which may shadow outspoken women throughout their lives.

Trusting in CORI as an indicator of a person's capacity or incapacity to do good work ignores the racism, classism, sexism, and homophobia imbedded in the records. Highly qualified people are routinely deprived of employment, and thereby of a livelihood. In addition, using CORI as an indicator grounds the hiring process in suspicion and distrust. What we have seen in recent years, then, is an intensification of punishment, resulting in longer sentences, often for lesser crimes, and in policies that extend the reach of the system beyond imprisonment. The concept of paying one's debt to society has been replaced by indefinite punishment that often follows a person permanently, long after their sentence is officially served.

We turn now to what state and federal prisons are actually like.

5: CAGES: STATE AND FEDERAL PRISONS TODAY

The Corporatization of Punishment

In recent years, many prison critics have developed the notion of the Prison Industrial Complex (PIC), which rivals the Military Industrial Complex in demonstrating how corporate interests drive public policy. Basically, the PIC notion refers to the way that the profit motive—not concerns of public safety, equal justice, rehabilitation, or restitution to victims—is increasingly determining criminal justice policy in this country. The PIC concept has given new power to the critique of the ways in which the criminal justice system is being used in our society as a force for racism, social control, patriarchy, and repression of dissent, and as a dumping ground for human beings regarded as toxic waste by the dominant sectors of our society.

It is instructive to look at the PIC in comparison to the reality that preceded it, the Military Industrial Complex, a concept first articulated by former President Dwight Eisenhower in his Farewell Address in 1961. Eisenhower was concerned that the profit motive of corporate military contractors was increasingly influencing our national foreign policy. Later commentators cited the "revolving door" through which certain persons traveled between Pentagon jobs and jobs as executives and consultants for such corporations. Such individuals and corporations influence congressional votes and executive-branch decision-making through lobbyists and contributions to political campaigns.

Today, journalists and prison critics point to the political influence and power of organizations with a vested interest in expanding the use of incarceration in the United States. A partial list includes private, for-profit prison corporations; prison food-service and health-care companies; prison construction and architecture firms; bail-bond firms; long-distance telephone companies; prisoner guards' unions; the National Rifle Association; and makers of surveillance equipment, prison-cell hardware, and weapons (including some former military contractors seeking new markets in the wake of the demise of the Cold War).

Such special interests have considerable political clout within the halls of government, especially through their trade associations (for instance, the American Correctional Association). A right-wing political organization called the American Legislative Exchange Council has committees responsible for writing and disseminating "model criminal justice legislation." Representatives of private prison companies and the bail-bond industry dominate these committees (Sentencing Project 2002, 5).

Perhaps the quintessential illustration of the PIC at work is the privatization of much of the prison system. Starting with the founding of the Nashville-based Corrections Corporation of America (CCA) in 1983, a number of private, for-profit prison management and construction corporations have been competing aggressively for contracts with local, state, and federal jurisdictions, particularly across the southern tier of states, the Sunbelt. This is no accident; these states have historically higher rates of crime, incarceration, and violence. They also tend to be "right-to-work" states with weak labor movements. Since organized labor has been the principal force of effective opposition to private, for-profit prisons, it makes sense from the point of view of prison firms (most of which are based in the South as well) to have initially targeted these states for growth. After all, private prisons are following in the footsteps of the notorious convict lease system that prevailed in the South for many decades after the Civil War (see chapter 1 for a discussion of the Southern convict lease system).

Today, the practice of contracting out the traditional government function of incarceration of adults and juveniles has spread to the majority of the states. As of mid-year 2001, the number of private prison and jail beds in the United States had increased to 143,021 from 20,687 in 1992. At the end of 2004, private prison cells held almost 99,000 state and federal prisoners, 6.6 percent of the total. Texas and Oklahoma incarcerated the largest number of inmates in private prisons (Harrison and Beck 2005, 5).

> *The convict lease system was a direct descendant of slavery, and the current wave of privatization disturbingly echoes the history of profiting off human beings who have been deprived of their liberty.*
>
> —Ohio Criminal Justice Program Committee Minutes on Prison Privatization, January 27, 2000

One wrinkle that has developed in the corporate punishment business is the building of prisons by private prison companies "on spec." Here a company, adopting the philosophy that "if you build it, they will come," decides to construct a prison anywhere it can get a good real estate and tax deal, before ever negotiating a contract. The company then hires a "bed broker" (an emerging new profession) who finds a state or other government agency with a prison overcrowding problem and a low capital problem, with which the company then contracts to house a portion of its prisoners, even if they must be moved thousands of miles away from home. The market for "spec" prisons seems to have dried up over the last few years, but many prisoners are still serving time a long way from home, and thus far from their families, friends, faith communities, and lawyers. This creates immense hardship on them and all of those who give them support.

Since the late 1990s, the private prison industry has become somewhat stymied on the state level. At this writing, it is being bailed out of potential bankruptcy by lucrative new contracts with the Federal Bureau of Prisons to house immigrants who have been convicted of crimes and who will be deported after completing their sentences. The Bush administration's privatization initiatives have produced a new period of growth for private, for-profit corrections, at least in the federal system.

Private prison companies market their services to governments by claiming to be able to have new prisons up and running more quickly, and to incarcerate prisoners more cheaply. The former claim is often true, but only because the privatizing option allows governments to avoid the need for voters to approve bond issues to finance prison construction, which usually fail. Instead, "lease purchase" or revenue bond issues are used to finance prison construction. Two kinds of bonds are commonly issued by government entities: general obligation bonds and revenue bonds. General obligation bonds require voter approval because of the debt incurred, and the belief that the public should decide how many bonds to issue and for what purposes. Lately voters have been rejecting measures that call for bonds to build new prisons. Revenue bonds do not require voter approval because they traditionally have had their own revenue streams. For example, bonds to build a power plant will be repaid as the power is sold and revenue is generated. In recent years, legislatures have approved the issuance of revenue bonds to build prisons, bypassing voter approval, even though prisons do not generate revenue. Taxpayers have to foot the total bill, and interest rates for these bonds are higher than rates for general obligation bonds.

There is much controversy over private firms' claim of lower expenses. Many studies have yielded no proof that turning prisons over to for-profit companies will save taxpayers substantial amounts of money. Modest short-run cost savings (a 2001 Bureau of Justice Assistance study says these are only 1 percent) are certain to be overwhelmed by long-term direct and indirect increases as the inherent expansionist logic of tying corrections policy and practice to the profit motive plays out over time (Sentencing Project 2002, 2).

Taxpayers still have to pay to imprison people, and they also have to pay for profits to the corporate stockholders. There are also many legal questions that need to be resolved, at great expense, when the private sector takes over a previously public sector function. For the state government to attempt to wash its hands of the responsibility of running prisons does not in any way limit its legal liability, not to mention its moral accountability.[1]

Privately run prisons operated according to the profit motive make their money by cutting prisoners' educational and treatment programs, staff numbers, staff pay and benefits, staff training, prison labor costs, and the like. There are reports of private prisons transferring prisoners with HIV/AIDS to state-run institutions in order to avoid the high cost of treatment (Whitlock 2003). These private firms rely increasingly on high-tech surveillance rather than personnel for security, preferring to invest their capital on the front end instead of paying ongoing labor costs. In some CCA prisons, cost cutting has led to rationing such necessities as toilet paper, blankets, and medical care. Firms calculate that in the current legal climate, which is so hostile to prisoners' claims, they save more money by denying prisoners' rights up front than they pay out in settlements of lawsuits.

Studies have shown that such cuts are dangerous for prisoners, prison staff, and the public at large (Coyle, Campbell, and Neufeld 2003). But since profits, not public safety, are the bottom line for corporate punishment, it is actually in the interest of private prison contractors to ensure more recidivism after prisoners are released. More repeat crime is bad for most people, but for top private-prison executives and shareholders, it means repeat business and more profits. In this way, we are witnessing human beings imprisoned within our penal institutions being turned into commodities. Prison companies are paid by the day and by the "head," so their revenue is tied directly to keeping as many beds filled as possible, for as long as possible, and as often as possible by the same people.

> *The goal of the industry is to keep prisons full. A successful company locks up as many people as possible.*
>
> —Jerome Miller, former director of youth services for the Commonwealth of Massachusetts

Often guards are offered stock investments in these corporations rather than traditional benefits, thus encouraging staff to involve themselves actively in holding down costs and increasing profits. Some guards report that they do not distribute cleaning supplies because the cost of these supplies is money out of their own pockets. Private prisons tend to experience an even higher rate of staff turnover than do government-operated prisons, due to lack of training, doubts about workplace safety, low salaries, and inadequate benefits (Coyle, Campbell, and Neufeld 2003).

Some private prison corporations effectively deny prisoners their constitutional rights of access to legal remedies by failing to maintain a law library for prisoners' use and, instead, substituting a contract lawyer, paid by the corporation, to consult with prisoners having grievances against the company. Many prisoner families complain that private prisons tend to be even less family friendly and visitor friendly than government prisons.

Studies have shown that corporate prisons have a higher rate of violence between prisoners, and between prisoners and correctional officers, than government-run prisons (Sentencing Project 2002, 2).

They also have a high rate of escape. The effects of these incidents are often exacerbated by the tendency of some private prison companies to withhold information about in-prison violence and escapes, and by the fact that often it is the local and state agencies (and taxpayers) that must bear the costs of apprehending, detaining, prosecuting, and defending private prison inmates—often from other states—who are charged with crimes committed in corporate prisons or on escape from corporate prisons. There have been a number of instances where private prison companies have made promises to communities that only minimum-security prisoners, or nonviolent prisoners, will be housed in a proposed institution. After the prison becomes operational, a very different standard of admission is applied (Coyle, Campbell, and Neufeld 2003).

The profit motive creates yet another evil in the dubious social policy configuration associated with crime and the penal system. Companies that depend on high crime and incarceration rates for their profits are unlikely to support early-intervention crime-prevention programs (for instance, victim-offender mediation and victim restitution) for children or adults, or strong reintegration programs for ex-offenders, since the effectiveness of such programs will hurt their profits.

These corporations have tremendous power to get their way in state, local, and federal government. The same campaign contributions and lobbyists they pay to try to get privatization bills through the legislature can later be used to push for even longer sentences, more prison construction, fewer mandated prison programs, and other legislative action designed to line their corporate pockets. Given the great political power of corporate donors and lobbyists, if the privatization trend continues, criminal justice policy will be increasingly driven by the profit motive and by political conflicts of interests—the very essence of the PIC. Private companies' financial incentive for more prisons, more prisoners, longer sentences, and higher profits—all at taxpayers' expense—means fewer tax dollars going to provide government services like education, affordable housing, health care, mental-health and substance-abuse treatment, and incentives to give low-income people a real chance for a decent and crime-free life. A preventive, public-health approach to crime thus loses out to a fear- and profit-based system of reaction to crime after the fact.

Private Prisons and Accountability

The privatization of prisons presents a problem of diminished account-ability. One who does not like the way that one's state is running its prison system has some real options as a citizen and taxpayer. He or she can engage in a campaign of community education, community organizing, political lobbying, and/or litigation. But if CCA or another private prison company is operating a state's prisons, the only effective way citizens can hold the company accountable to the public and to the law would be to buy a controlling interest of stock in the corporation, an option closed to most citizens and grassroots citizens' groups. Civil suits by citizens tend to be an unpromising option due to the high cost of legal counsel, recent congressional limitation on both prisoners' rights litigation and class-action litigation by legal services offices, and the growing use of "SLAP" suits (Strategic Lawsuits Against Participation) by wealthy and powerful corporations designed to intimidate citizens and small organizations from seeking to influence public policy and practice vis-à-vis corporate interests. There is also the problem of inadequate disclosure of information about private prisons, since much of it is considered proprietary information not required to be disclosed to the public.

There is little positive to say about penal institutions run directly by the government.

> *We are deeply troubled by the lesser degree to which private companies are required to submit to community involvement and scrutiny. Our experience with criminal justice work has taught us that when outside people take an interest in the operation of correctional institutions, abuses are less likely to occur. Indeed, we believe that there is a mutual obligation for citizens to be aware of what goes on inside our prisons and hold those institutions accountable to humane standards of treatment and for prison officials to make information available to citizens and to promptly and effectively address problems that may arise. It can be difficult to obtain information about state-run prisons, but it is ultimately possible to do so because these institutions are part of our government and are subject to the laws governing disclosure of public information. However, private companies are not required to allow the same degree of public scrutiny.*
>
> —AFSC Ohio Criminal Justice Program Committee, January 27, 2000

But indications so far are that the specter of a mostly privatized penal regime threatens to take the PIC to a whole new level of expansion and intensity. Our experience so far with prison privatization efforts in the United States has pointed inescapably to one inevitable conclusion: when public policy decisions in the arena of criminal justice and public safety are tied to the profit motive and thus to corporate political power, the public will be the loser. Conflicts of interest, lack of accountability to the public and to the law, and the government's abdication of its inherent responsibilities will ensure that the safety and quality of life of everyone concerned—prison staff, prisoners and their families, taxpayers, and potential victims of crime—will be at even more severe risk than in government-operated prisons.

The central truth about prisons for profit seems to be that crime and punishment may mean only suffering and pain for the rest of us, but for the corporations, it means only more profits.

> *Privatization poses the threat of profound conflicts of interest, because private prison operators would profit from keeping people in prison, not from finding ways to return them to their communities. Overcrowding and reduced services would spell high profits. And private employees would inevitably be influenced in the information they provided to parole and disciplinary authorities—assuming these functions were left in the hands of the state.*
>
> —Lichtenstein and Kroll 1990

> *Claims of significant cost savings and improved efficiency from private prisons have not proven true. Furthermore, private profit interests in sentencing policy and limited public oversight of private facilities complicate the debate over expansion of private prisons. The public and policymakers would be well served by a broad discussion of the complex set of issues raised by prison privatization.*
>
> —Sentencing Project 2002

Prison Guards

Prison guards are the police of the prison system. They experience many of the same pressures, fears, and dangers as do police. They are steeped in the culture of imprisonment, which expects them to be tough, unsympathetic, and often brutal, to the detriment of prisoners and themselves. Whistle-blowing guards who shine a light on cruelty and abuse are ostracized and retaliated against, and often lose their jobs.

Prison guards are another arm of law enforcement. Yet the "law" in prison is different from the law on the streets. In prison, prisoners who are accused of breaking prison rules have no due-process rights, except when explicitly required by courts, and prisoners are presumed guilty until proven innocent. The list of punishable offenses shows little regard for a prisoner's civil or constitutional rights and includes obvious indicators of mental illness such as suicidal behavior and self-mutilation. Prisoners with mental retardation are often punished for not following rules and orders, even when it is proven that they could not understand the directions in the manner in which they were given.

When prisoners are cited for breaking a rule, the remedy is administrative. The disciplinary board accepts the guard's report as the starting point for disciplining the prisoner. This report is invariably upheld in the final report. Guards are given unlimited power to interpret the rules of the prison environment. Their first recourse against a prisoner whom they have determined has broken a rule is the use of force. Courts have upheld increasing levels of force as justifiable. These practices make prisons very violent places.

It is important to make a distinction between individual prison guards and the prison and guard culture. Some individual guards care about individual prisoners and contribute positively to the overall environment. The atmosphere of the prison is one of violence and oppression, however, which tends to eclipse the good works of particular employees. We have found abuses of power in the guard culture to be the rule rather than the exception, but we acknowledge the valiant attempts of some of its members to be fair and humane.

In some states, and typically in private, for-profit prisons, prison guards have little training to prepare them for their jobs. Some states require a six-week training course, but it is not uncommon for guards to start their jobs with no training at all. The little training that guards receive is geared to prepare them to use force or chemicals to maintain order within the prison. It is not uncommon for a guard to provoke an incident with a prisoner, and for the prisoner to be beaten up or even shot if he or she responds to the provocation. After the prisoner is subdued, the prisoner will be charged with assault. The guard will not be reprimanded. Prisoners report being treated as less than human by guards. This perception was made very real in California during the late 1990s when the prison administration placed prisoners from rival gangs on the same yard, and then opened fire when fights broke out. The fights were videotaped. Fifty prisoners were wounded in this process and five died.[2]

As the prison system becomes a larger and larger economic force, guard unions have become a larger political force. The California Correctional Peace Officers Association is the second largest contributor to California political campaigns and a major lobbyist for prison expansion. The California Correctional Peace Officers Association and guards' organizations in some other states fund a number of retributive crime-victims' groups that join the guards in lobbying for longer sentences, harsher prison conditions, and expansion of the death penalty.

The Super-max and Other Forms of Torture

Mass incarceration has brought profoundly disturbing changes in the very nature of imprisonment. Most prominent among these is the escalating use of isolation through "control units" and "super-max" prisons. Historically, isolation and lockdown (confining prisoners to their cells for twenty-three or twenty-four hours a day) have been used as temporary measures to punish individual prisoners or to control the prison environment. In these new forms of incarceration, these conditions have been made permanent for more and more prisoners. Increasing numbers of prisoners spend up to ten to fifteen years in solitary confinement. A few prisoners have been sentenced to life in solitary confinement.

This is the case with New York prisoner Willie Bosket.

For the purposes of this Convention, the term "torture" means any act by which severe pain or suffering, whether physical or mental, is intentionally inflicted on a person for such purposes as obtaining from him or a third person . . . a confession, punishing him for an act he or a third person has committed or is suspected of having committed, or intimidating or coercing him or a third person, or for any reason based on discrimination of any kind, when such pain or suffering is indicated by or at the instigation of or with the consent or acquiescence of a public official or other person acting in an official capacity.

—United Nations Convention Against Torture and Other Cruel, Inhuman or Degrading Treatment or Punishment, 1984

As Fox Butterfield reports in his book *All God's Children*, Bosket is a black man sentenced to life in solitary confinement in a special control unit designed only to imprison him. Three generations of men in the Bosket family have ended their lives in the criminal justice system. Bosket has spent the entirety of his life in state custody, much of it imprisoned. He considers himself "a monster created by the system" and believed that he was at war with the system when he stabbed a guard. This stabbing resulted in the creation of a special control unit designed to hold him in perpetual solitary confinement (Butterfield 1995). An estimated twenty-five thousand prisoners, or nearly 1.7 percent of the state and federal prison population, are now held in permanent solitary confinement.

> 1. Each State Party shall take effective legislative, administrative, judicial or other measures to prevent acts of torture in any territory under its jurisdiction.
> 2. No exceptional circumstances whatsoever, whether a state of war or a threat of war, internal political instability or any other public emergency, may be invoked as a justification of torture.
>
> —Convention Against Torture and Other Cruel, Inhuman or Degrading Treatment or Punishment; Article 2c

Another area of concern is the widespread control of prisoners through the use of devices such as stun belts, stun guns, and restraint chairs. Under international standards for human rights, all of these developments are banned as forms of torture. In May 2000, the United Nations Committee Against Torture roundly condemned the United States for its treatment of prisoners, citing super-max prisons and the use of torture devices, as well as the practice of jailing youth with adults. Such practices have nonetheless become common throughout the U.S. prison system, from federal penitentiaries to county jails.

The AFSC became involved in the issue of isolation in the mid-1980s, when a prisoner in the Trenton State Prison who had been placed in a "Management Control Unit" contacted the Prison Watch program, based in Newark, New Jersey, asking AFSC to monitor his situation. Later, the 2001 AFSC publication *Torture in U.S. Prisons* quoted the World Organization Against Torture report *Torture in the United States*, stating:

The term "control unit" was first coined at the federal penitentiary at Marion, Illinois, in 1972 and has come to designate a prison or part of a prison that operates under a "super maximum security" regime. Control unit prisons may differ from each other in some details but all share certain defining features:

1. Prisoners in a control unit are kept in solitary confinement in tiny cells (six by eight feet is usual) for between twenty two and twenty three hours a day. There is no congregate dining, no congregate exercise, no work opportunities and no congregate religious services. Access to any facilities or social services is severely limited.

2. These conditions exist permanently (as opposed to the temporary lockdowns that occur at almost every prison) and as official policy.

3. The conditions in control units are officially justified not as punishment for prisoners but as administrative measures that are within the discretion of prison officials to impose without a [court] hearing taking place. . . . Prisoners are denied any due process and prison officials can incarcerate any prisoner in a control unit for as long as they choose, without having to justify their action. (AFSC 2001, 20–21)

The AFSC pulled together the National Campaign to Stop Control Unit Prisons as it discovered that, in some places, super-max prisons were filled with both prisoners being administratively punished and those placed there without due process. The 1996 report "History of Control Units" stated, "While the specific conditions in control unit prisons may vary, the goal of these units is to disable prisoners through spiritual, psychological, and/or physical breakdown" and went on to describe some of these methods by which this goal is accomplished:

- Arbitrary placement sometimes not based on pre-established standards and procedures. In other cases people were charged with real or imagined infractions;

- Years of isolation from both prison and outside communities while being housed in solitary or small group isolation;

- Extremely limited access to services such as education, worship, or vocational training;

- Physical torture such as forced cell extractions, strap-downs, hog-tying, beating after restraint, and provocation of violence between prisoners;

- Mental torture such as sensory deprivation, forced idleness, verbal harassment, mail tampering, disclosure of confidential information, confessions forced under torture, and threats against family members;

- Sexual intimidation and violence, usually against women prisoners by male guards, using strip searches, verbal sexual harassment, sexual touching, and rape as a means of control (Kerness 1996, 1).

Manufacturing Madness

It is well established that isolation and sensory deprivation will inevitably drive many people insane. As noted in a briefing paper by Human Rights Watch (HRW), "Prisoners subjected to prolonged isolation may experience depression, despair, anxiety, rage, claustrophobia, hallucinations, problems with impulse control, and an impaired ability to think, concentrate, or remember" (HRW 2000).

Dr. Stuart Grassian, a psychiatrist at Harvard University Medical School, has been an expert witness on the impact of control units. He found, and courts have recognized, that solitary confinement itself can cause a specific kind of psychiatric syndrome, which in its worst stages can lead to agitation, hallucinations, and a confused psychotic state. Symptoms can include random violence, self-mutilation, and suicidal behavior (Kerness 1996, 3).

The cells in control-unit prisons are often soundproof, and there is little interaction with anyone other than staff. Visits, telephone calls, and mail from family and friends are severely restricted. Reading material is censored. When a prisoner leaves his or her bathroom-sized cage, a strip search is conducted, including pointedly humiliating cavity searches. This takes place even though the prisoner may not have had contact with another human being for months.

In 1994, the AFSC and a group of activists from around the country gathered in Philadelphia to form the National Campaign to Stop Control Unit Prisons. AFSC offices in Denver, Cambridge, Newark, and Dayton participated in hearings and heard testimony of serious abuses related to high-security housing units. They heard that:

- Prisoners at the federal facility in Florence, Colorado, were awakened every hour throughout the night by flashlights shining in their faces.

- Prisoners in New Jersey were awakened at 1:00 A.M., strip searched, and told to pack belongings to be moved to another cell. This happened as often as twice a week.

- Women prisoners in California were subjected to twenty-four-hour screaming by other prisoners, and lights were kept on around the clock, resulting in severe disorientation.

- The effects of extended isolation included a progressive inability to tolerate even ordinary stimulation. Some prisoners cut themselves "just so they could feel something."

Despite such reports, control units continue to proliferate. Guard unions throughout the country are in the forefront of encouraging the building and use of isolation prisons, claiming that they provide a safer work environment. Making guards "safer," however, may be making the public considerably less safe, since it is not uncommon for prisoners to be released directly to the street from the control unit when their sentence is completed.

Isolation prisons provide a place for prison administrators and line staff to commit human-rights violations with impunity. Evidence gathered by all human-rights groups monitoring super-max prisons suggests that control units are also used as a form of retribution. At this writing, AFSC is monitoring one New Jersey prisoner who blew the whistle on open recruiting by the Ku Klux Klan among prison guards. Prison guards retaliated by holding him in isolation, withholding his AIDS medication, and threatening him with transfer to another state prison that is generally known to be run by Klan members.

The AFSC has been asked to serve on the board of the World Organization Against Torture to document compliance (or lack of compliance) with the International Covenant on Civil and Political Discrimination and the U.N. Convention Against Torture and All Forms of Racial Discrimination. The United States is out of compliance with these conventions in a number of respects:

- the practice of forced cell extractions (the forced removal of a prisoner from his or her cell by six to nine armored guards in SWAT team uniforms, wielding shields and stun guns);

- the treatment of mentally ill prisoners, which not only violates their civil and political rights, but often constitutes torture when it involves leaving prisoners in restraints or naked in isolation cells;

- the use of chemical sprays and dangerous methods of restraint; and

- the classification of prisoners to ongoing isolation, which violates the convention on racial discrimination (the overwhelming majority of prisoners in isolation units are black and Latino) and due-process requirements.

Prison Gang Policies: A Threat to Our Security

In prisons, racism takes many forms. It may take the form of unequal job assignments. Black Nationalist and Muslim literature could get a prisoner identified and punished as a gang member or a member of a "security threat group" (STG). Individual guards who are racist have ample opportunity to abuse prisoners. Racism is often encouraged by prison administrators who have their own biases and prejudices and hope to keep black, brown, and white prisoners occupied fighting one another and hence more easily managed.

A common practice in prisons today is to classify prisoners to control-unit centers based on STGs or gang membership. The use of the "gang" label by prison authorities is fraught with racial stereotyping and political repression. What is sometimes labeled a gang could be a group of activist prisoners who are organizing on their own behalf. Once isolated in one of these units, prisoners report that the only way to secure release is to "renounce, parole, or die."

During the mid-1990s, state departments of corrections around the United States began creating STG policies. These policies were modeled after the Federal Bureau of Prisons protocol. They involved the separation of suspected gang members from the general population and the creation of special gang units within maximum-security prisons. These units are lockdown units, and many are control units. These policies were implemented on a hunch that street-gang members sentenced to the same prison would organize themselves into dangerous prison gangs. There was no evidence that this was about to happen. There is still no evidence that this has ever happened. In fact, there are no criteria to distinguish incidents attributed to STGs from routine prison occurrences. Yet every state has hundreds of men and women living out their imprisonment in these high-security units.

Those who are imprisoned in the gang units throughout the country are primarily young people and people of color. This is true even though every state lists the Aryan Nation and White Supremacists as traditional prison gangs. Individuals are "validated" as gang members by prison staff and administration. This is problematic, because 51 percent of the states surveyed in 1997, in an unpublished document of the U.S. Department of Justice entitled, "National Survey Results on Security Threat Groups," did not have a uniform definition of a gang or STG. Eighty percent did not have a formal validation process. Yet all but one had developed an STG policy (National Survey Results 1997).[3] With no criteria or formal validation process, departments of corrections throughout the country have spent millions of dollars identifying gang members, constructing "gang blocks" or units, and creating programs to "deprogram" gang members who have renounced their affiliation.

Gang members are identified through racial or cultural stereotyping, for their beliefs, for their language, or for their associations. There is heavy emphasis placed on identifying Latino gang members. In many states, more than 90 percent of the Latino prisoners are identified as potential gang members. In Massachusetts, 96 percent of the Puerto Rican prisoners are in the gang units (National Institute of Corrections 1991, 14).

Given the punitive nature of the response to admitting that one is a gang member, self-admission is rare. Anyone who has a tattoo is immediately placed under suspicion (National Survey Results 1997). One young man who had a tattoo of a bumblebee on his arm (the symbol of his favorite reggae group) was identified as a gang member. The gang was identified as the "Killer Bee Gang." According to Department of Corrections records, the Killer Bees were a gang of one. The Black Cat Collective, a group of young men who conduct educational programs in libraries in New Jersey, is listed as an STG (National Survey Results 1997, 26).

The symbols that are used to identify gang membership are often related only to the prisoners' culture or beliefs. Beads, a symbol of Puerto Rican and African culture, are considered gang paraphernalia.

An elderly black prisoner was seen teaching a young Puerto Rican prisoner to read; he had a poster of the Black Panther Ten Point Plan in his cell. He had had this poster in his cell for close to thirty years. In 1997, he was identified as a gang member. The gang was identified as the Black Panthers. The poster and the fact that he taught a Puerto Rican young man to read were enough to get him labeled. Speaking with others who are suspected of being gang members, especially in Spanish, will get a prisoner "tagged." Associations are made so loosely that a photograph of a young Puerto Rican man at a family gathering attended by a distant cousin who was a member of the Latin Kings in another state was enough to get this young man identified as a gang member. Internal and external documentation used to support gang identification is defined so broadly that almost any prisoner who was ever involved in a prison incident could be identified as a gang member (National Survey Results 1997, 4). Police contribute external documentation to prison authorities by passing on information gathered through racial profiling. Such identification practices become a direct assault on cultural pride as well as the criminalization of cultural consciousness.

Gang-related documentation can also include an individual's name being on a hit list. Thus, what used to be a protective-custody issue, where the institution was required to protect a prisoner, becomes a security issue, and the individual is placed in a punishment unit. If an individual is targeted by a gang and is not a gang member, placing that individual among gang members can be very dangerous. A prisoner can be placed in a gang-member category simply by being identified as a gang member by a "reliable informant" (National Survey Results 1997, 4). The nature of the information that is gathered from the informant is not shared with the prisoner, nor is the identity of the informant. In practice, the identification of gang members is slanted so that prison officials can justify placing anyone they wish into a gang unit. In Massachusetts, the street names in Roxbury, the historic black community in Boston, are translated into gang names by prison officials (National Survey Results 1997, 20). Political organizations and religions are identified as gangs. The Black Panthers, the Nation of Islam, the Five Percenters (a sub-group of the Nation of Islam), and Wicca are considered gangs in New Jersey (National Survey Results 1997, 26). On the outside, both the American Civil Liberties Union and the AFSC have also been identified as potential security-threat groups and investigated.

Placement in a gang unit has not been subject to due process. However, in the *Haverty et al. v. Commissioner of Corrections* (2002) decision, the Massachusetts Supreme Court found that prisoners were entitled to due process before being placed in controlled units. In many states gang identification is purely an administrative process, with very narrow routes for legal appeal to the courts. Once identified as a gang member, a prisoner's only way out of the unit is through renunciation of his or her membership. Many prisoners refuse to renounce because they maintain that they were never members of a gang. Renouncing membership in something one never embraced seems to imply that perhaps the prisoner was really, at one time, a gang member. Because gang profiling is done on the streets by police and information is shared between prison and law enforcement officials, prisoners do not want to affirm that they were members of gangs and give the police another reason to harass them after release. When an individual is identified on the basis of religion or culture, renunciation means renouncing those beliefs. For many, their religion and culture provide the structure for them to reconstruct their lives. Renouncing these beliefs is not an option.

When prisoners who are only marginal members of a gang are limited to associating only with one another because they have been segregated into the gang unit, they begin to rely upon one another. Their identification with this group becomes stronger. Prisoners who were not members of a gang or were only marginal members previously become committed members under the harsh conditions in these prison-gang blocks. It can be argued that prison STG policy actually manufactures stronger street gangs. Prisoners who are held in gang units report the same psychological breakdown that other prisoners in isolation experience. "Prisoners often complain about insomnia, depression, nightmares, violent mood swings, anxiety attacks, claustrophobia, paranoia, hallucinations and generalized feelings of nervousness, irritability, and anger" (NIC 1991, 14). These unintended consequences of prisons' STG policies actually decrease the safety of these prisoners' communities after they are released to the street.

The state of New York does track known gang members within a prison, but "does not deal with inmates as gang leaders or members; no attempt is made to glorify gangs" (Kassel 1998). We believe that the interests of the prison system and of communities of origin of "identified" gang members would be better served by treating all prisoners fairly based solely on their behavior in prison. Prison rebellions have many causes: prisoners are bored because there is a dearth of productive programming; the food or medical care is bad; the prisons are overcrowded, unsafe, or unsanitary; or the prison is poorly managed, with ill-defined lines of accountability. It would make more sense to solve these problems rather than create a policy that deliberately creates these conditions.

Political Prisoners

We are mindful that the U.S. judicial system is promoted by many here and throughout the world as one of the most progressive and protective of individual rights. The claim that the U.S. does not have political prisoners has gone generally unchallenged. We believe that the evidence presented at the Tribunal overwhelmingly established the opposite case. The U.S. government uses its judicial system to repress legitimate political movements opposing the government.

—Verdict of the Special International Tribunal
on the Violation of Human Rights of Political Prisoners
of War in United States Prisons and Jails, 1990

In 1990, U.S. political activists and legal experts called for an International Tribunal in accordance with the precedents of the Nuremberg and Tokyo Tribunals and following the procedures approved by the Economic and Social Council of the United Nations (Resolution 1503 [XL VIII]). The tribunal used the following definitions:

- *Prisoner of War:* Those combatants struggling against colonial and alien domination and racist regimes, captured as prisoners, are to be accorded the status of prisoners of war. Their treatment should be in accordance with the provisions of the Geneva Conventions Relative to the Treatment of Prisoners of War, of 12 August 1949 (U.N. General Assembly Resolution 3103).

- *Political Prisoner:* A person incarcerated for actions carried out in support of legitimate struggles for self-determination or for opposing the illegal policies of the United States government and/or its political subdivisions.

Based on the evidence submitted, the tribunal found that "within the prisons and jails of the United States exist substantial numbers of

Political Prisoners and Prisoners of War." Yet the United States government continues to say there are no political prisoners in this country. The tribunal also found that "political people have been subjected to disproportionately lengthy prison sentences and to torture, cruel, inhumane, and degrading treatment within the United States' prison system" (Verdict of the Special International Tribunal on the Violation of Human Rights of Political Prisoners of War in United States Prisons and Jails, 1990).

During the invasion of what is now North America by Europeans, Native people resisted to the brink of extermination. Ever since African people were captured and brought here as slaves, there has been resistance. Slave records document 150 shipboard revolts in the three hundred-year history of the Middle Passage. The struggle for peace, equality, and self-determination on the part of oppressed groups has been constant. The existence of political prisoners, prisoners of war, and prisoners of conscience who engaged in organized resistance to government policies reflects the historical criminalization of the very act of resistance.

International tribunals have recognized many of the actions of political prisoners and United States prisoners of war as acts of conscience. What a person is charged with and convicted of may be incidental to the actual aims of a particular struggle, especially when the legal apparatus is being used to suppress rebellion. People are not charged with political crimes: they are charged with such things as robbery, possession

Those who labor under structures of injustice and violence will set their own course for breaking free from oppression. We will not support the choice of violence, but where basic human rights and social equity are at issue, Quakers and the AFSC need to be engaged in common cause to the limit of our beliefs, resources and program capacity. In crises and protracted struggles we should share widely our experience and insights about nonviolent strategies for change. . . . When AFSC staff form personal and programmatic associations with groups struggling toward social justice, these relationships should not be terminated solely because acts of violence have been carried out in the name of such organizations, any more than AFSC should break off from dealing in love with the forces in power who turn to violence in the same setting. . . . But respect for the oppressor cannot still the insistence upon movement toward social justice.

—AFSC, "Perspectives on Nonviolence in Relation to Groups Struggling for Social Justice," 1981

> *There can be no healing without truth, and the greatest love is that which is based on justice.*
>
> —Leonard Peltier, political prisoner, American Indian Movement

of weapons, or conspiracy. Often the political motivation for prosecution comes out in the sentencing phase, where defendants are given very long sentences for seemingly "ordinary" offenses.

The AFSC is well aware that some of these individuals and the organizations they represent did resort to violence in the course of their struggle to break free from oppression. It is "the insistence upon movement toward social justice" that inspired the actions of the men and women recognized as political prisoners and United States prisoners of war. Along with these individuals, we continue to struggle to bring about a just world without violence. Their liberty and vision are necessary to bring about this world.

Immigrants in the Criminal Justice System

In 1797, 70 percent of the prisoners in the Walnut Street Jail in Philadelphia were immigrants. The first line of action against the waves of immigrants who have come to the United States has always been the criminal justice system. Prison was used to make "gentlemen" out of offenders who were largely immigrants. In other words, our prison system was used to acculturate and assimilate those people whose behavior was not accepted by the dominant culture. Immigrants who were active in the labor movement were specifically targeted for criminal charges. After World War II, the United States Immigration and Naturalization Service (INS) developed a network of detention centers, and the focus of immigration policy shifted from imprisonment and acculturation to detention and expulsion. In reaction to the events of 9/11, the Homeland Security Act of 2002 led to a reorganization in which the former INS was

> *Our struggle for justice and against injustice is based on the right not to be oppressed, not to be subjected to abuse, but to be able to stand up and live free, and proud, and equal, and in peace. These rights are our birthrights, we cannot be stripped of them, and these rights are higher than all laws.*
>
> —Kazi Ajugun Toure, former political prisoner, New African Liberation Movement, and AFSC staff member

incorporated into the new Department of Homeland Security. The detention function of the INS has now been taken over by the Bureau of Citizenship and Immigration Services (BCIS).

The U.S. border with Mexico has been thoroughly militarized. Barriers have been constructed under the Gatekeeper Program begun in 1996 and are patrolled by the armed forces. Between 1994 and Fall 2005, approximately 3,600 people died crossing the border in California, Arizona and Texas. Fiscal year 2005, which ended on September 30, was the deadliest year on record: 460 people lost their lives crossing the border, according to the AFSC San Diego office.[4] The agricultural industry relies on migrant Mexican labor. These workers are sometimes undocumented or use incomplete or false paperwork. This fact puts these men, women, and children at the mercy of two exploitative industries, one that relies on cheap, manual labor—the agricultural industry—and the other that turns prisoners' bodies into commodities—the prison industry.

> We know from painful experience that freedom is never voluntarily given by the oppressor; it must be demanded by the oppressed. . . . You express a great deal of anxiety over our willingness to break laws. This is certainly a legitimate concern. . . . One may well ask, "How can you advocate breaking some laws and obeying others?" The answer is found in the fact that there are two types of laws: There are just and there are unjust laws. I would agree with Saint Augustine that "An unjust law is no law at all."
>
> —Martin Luther King, Jr., "Letter from Birmingham City Jail"

If an immigrant, documented or not, is accused of committing a crime, he or she is charged and set to go to trial. If charged with a felony or facing the death penalty, the immigrant's home country is to be notified, according to international law. This rarely happens. Conviction rates are high among immigrants charged with crime. If they do not speak English, they often go through their trials or the plea-bargaining process and on to prison without understanding what has happened to them or whether they have had an adequate defense. All decisions in these cases have to be made by United States citizens—whether acting as prosecutors, hearing officers, or juries—and xenophobia often plays a role.

These individuals are sent to United States' prisons where they must complete the minimum portion of their prison sentence. After completion of their sentence, they are paroled to BCIS. Then they are deported, even if the felony was minor, even if they were permanent residents before conviction, and even if the rest of their family members are law-abiding permanent residents. This deportation process can take months or years. Some immigrants who have finished their prison sentences face indefinite detention because their home countries are not accepting deportations from the United States. This is the case despite recent court decisions in immigration law that require timely release of immigrants who are not deportable.

Youth who are not naturalized are particularly at risk. Many young people from immigrant families never become United States citizens even though they may have come to this country with their families as infants. Some have never seen their countries of origin, and some do not even speak their parents' language. When these young people are convicted of crime, they go through the same deportation process. Eventually, they are deported to a country they do not know at all.

Families often use considerable resources to immigrate to the United States. When one member of the family is convicted of crime, the entire family's economic safety in this country is shattered and their ability to return to their home country is compromised. Families, most often women and children, become trapped in poverty. In this manner, families are destroyed by BCIS policy. If a partner's prison sentence is long, the remaining spouse must choose between staying and supporting the individual who is sentenced to prison or returning to the home country, leaving the loved one to survive prison and deportation without an advocate. The isolation of convicted immigrants within prisons and the separation from their families and friends are an additional pain of imprisonment.

The word *detention* belies the reality of immigrants captured by BCIS. Some deportations are swift, but in the case of those who come from countries that are not accepting deportees from the United States—most notably, Cuba, Vietnam, and China—detentions can continue for years. Some Cuban immigrants have been held in United States prisons for more than fifteen years without a criminal conviction. The conditions that these immigrants face are harsh. Often, they do not have extensive family networks here and contact with the family at home is very difficult, if not impossible. Access to attorneys is not guaranteed by law. Immigration attorneys are often very expensive, and pro bono immigration clinics few and small. The legal arguments to protect a person seeking residence or asylum in the United States have narrowed dramatically in the past decade.

Immigrants report increased tension and fear of the criminal justice system. This fear exists for those who have visas and green cards as well as for those who have insufficient documentation. They report that little things that would be very inconsequential for citizens take on monumental significance for them. Driving slightly above the speed limit, having a taillight out on one's car, or leaving one's driver's license at home can result in permanent separation from one's family and home. Immigrants walk a very fine line as they struggle with the increasingly pervasive and hostile presence of law enforcement in their lives.

This rise in imprisonment of immigrants and asylum seekers has been coupled with the aging and dismantling of regional BCIS detention centers. In order to accommodate the increasing numbers of immigrants in detention and the decreasing number of facilities, the old INS entered into contracts with state prisons, county jails, and private, for-profit prisons.

When a prison would enter into a contract with the INS, it would agree only to house the detainee in the prison—security level and conditions of confinement were not specified. These contracts specify a per diem cost for housing the individual. The prison's goal is to make the actual cost of housing the individual equal to, or less than, this charge. This results in severe deprivation for immigrants. Detainees are usually not permitted to participate in programs that are available to other prisoners. Immigrants are placed wherever there is an empty bed in the prison. This has led to BCIS detainees being held at very high security levels, often in control units. Given language and cultural barriers, immigrants are often in conflict with guards and with prisoners. Conflict results in more punishment and increases the punitive environment for the detainee.

The increasing use of private prisons for immigrant detention is of concern to those who advocate for the rights of immigrants and those who advocate for prisoners' rights. Private prisons win their contracts through lobbying and campaign contributions to politicians, and they exist to make profit on the imprisonment of people. Since private prisons are so well connected, there is increasing interest in privatizing all immigration detention centers. Corporations such as Corrections Corporation of America and GEO (formerly Wackenhut Corrections) are actively and successfully lobbying for the contracts to design, build, and operate prisons that would allegedly cater to the needs of BCIS detainees. On some levels, this is appealing to some advocates for immigrants. It would relieve the unnecessary deprivation that they think immigrants experience when housed with criminal convicts.

Yet the privatization of immigration detention facilities is no solution. Private prisons are not subject to the same level of government supervision and monitoring as state- and county-run prisons. Once an immigrant is sent into a private prison, it is very difficult for anyone to follow up on that individual and make sure that he or she is being treated properly. Since the goal of private prisons is to make profit on the people detained, the privatization of such facilities could create an infinitely expanding capacity to detain immigrants.

Immigrants in detention report being given food to which they are unaccustomed and which, in some cases, causes them to be sick. Immigrants report being terrorized by both prisoners and guards. Women in detention report being given stained underwear and being subjected to racist and sexist jokes. If housed in a prison, the detainee is often limited to one phone call a week and must choose between maintaining contact with family members or consulting with an attorney. Since telephone rates in prisons are three times the cost of a collect call outside, when these collect calls are international, the cost can be prohibitive. Prisoners housed in a federal prison are not allowed to make collect calls.

Immigrants are being detained hundreds or thousands of miles from their families and lawyers (if they are lucky enough to have one). Immigrants are often held in rural prisons with prisoners and guards who are unprepared to deal with issues of diversity. This increases the likelihood of overt hostility. Immigrants are brutalized regularly in prison. Some have been left permanently disabled as a result of prison assaults. Some have died.

In Arizona, the state legislature has passed laws permitting ranchers to capture and detain migrants who look suspicious. In essence, these laws allow individual citizens to create jails on their own property. There are no regulations describing where and under what conditions these individuals will be held until they are turned over to law enforcement. Ranchers are permitted to shoot migrants who are trespassing on their property. These laws have led to increasing reports that migrants have "disappeared." Families fear these individuals have been murdered.

In California, the six hundred-plus bodies that have been found in the mountains, deserts, and canals since the Gatekeeper program began are known as the *"no indentificados,"* or the unidentified. These six hundred bodies, in unmarked graves, lie in silent witness to a failed law-enforcement solution to a human problem, and to the low value the United States places on lives of vulnerable, poor people who are considered the "other."

Sexism

Sexism causes unfair application of laws against women and is reflected in the treatment of women in prison. Central to an understanding of this problem is the recognition that laws that directly affect women are generally formulated and applied by men and reflect the expectations and limitations of traditional gender roles.

Our society has defined a woman's role as primarily that of mothering children, serving a man's physical needs, and maintaining households for others. Women who assert themselves strongly or otherwise rebel against traditional roles are often punished from an early age in an effort to enforce conformity. The criminal justice system is too frequently a part of this enforcement effort.

Most of the young women held by the juvenile justice system have entered it for "status" offenses (for instance, truancy or being a runaway). As teenagers, girls are more likely than boys to be institutionalized for assertive behavior that does not involve crime. In the past, many women were sent to mental hospitals for such behavior, while others, often low-income or women of color, were sent to the criminal justice system. As mental institutions have been phased out, women who defy gender "norms" can find themselves incarcerated.

Women of color suffer the dual oppressions of racism and sexism. The legacy of unique oppression of black women is long and painful. As early as 1662, the child servitude statute assigned all children of African women to slavery, and all children of white women to freedom, regardless of paternity. This reversal of patriarchal tradition ensured that black women would be reduced to "breeding stock." The degradation of black women as the carriers of a tainted motherhood continues today with the persistence in blaming black women for the problems within their communities.

In the 1960s, the Moynihan report singled out "domineering Black matriarchs" for disempowering black men and destabilizing the family structure. In the 1990s, female crack addicts were singled out for special prosecution. These economically poor women were portrayed as incapable of responsible motherhood. Civil courts have terminated the parental rights of thousands of women whose infants test positive for drug addiction. Pregnant women have faced criminal prosecution for prenatal drug use under child abuse statutes involving charges of neglect, manslaughter, and delivering substances to a minor. Empirical evidence shows that maternal drug use is consistent across race and class lines at about 15 percent (Logan 1999, 123). "Protective" incarceration, the practice of imprisoning a pregnant woman convicted of charges unrelated to her drug use, who would not ordinarily have gone to prison until her baby is born, has become common and is almost exclusive to poor black women. Nearly all criminal convictions sustained in these prosecutions have been overturned on appeal. But litigation is expensive, and women and children have lost years in the process.

Because of the focus on the War on Drugs in communities of color, women of color are entering prisons at an unprecedented rate. In some parts of the country, their rate of imprisonment has tripled in the past five years. The removal of women of color from their communities, and the judgment that they are unfit mothers, has thrown already fragile families into crisis.

With reflection on the real imperatives driving the criminal prosecution of crack-addicted mothers, policy makers might begin to devise programs that empower pregnant addicts and allow them to be good mothers to their children. The policies pursued thus far have done little good for crack-exposed babies and have only helped undermine the fragile world into which they were born.

—Logan 1999, 136

Sexism also has a major impact on men in prison. The sexist roles prescribed for men in our society support patterns of dominance that lead to an exaggerated macho image. It is not surprising that these patterns are heightened in prison settings. Prison culture is a culture controlled by violence, the threat of violence, and the concentration of all real power in the hands of guards and prison administrators. The strongest prisoners prevail among their peers. Being able to protect oneself is necessary to survival. Strength may be defined physically or intellectually (as in the case of jailhouse lawyers and long-termers who "know the system").

Internalized sexism, self-loathing, and sexual deprivation foster violence against and abuse of those men who do not fulfill the accepted male image. Because prisons are controlled by threat of violence, guards are encouraged to behave in a sadistic manner and to ignore and exacerbate the abuses of prisoners against one another. This, in turn, becomes additional cruel and unusual punishment for those prisoners who do not conform to traditional gender models. Because life inside prisons mirrors life outside, these patterns support the perversion of family and community life into struggles for dominance when prisoners return to their communities.

Women

Nowhere is the futility of imprisonment clearer than it is with incarcerated women. The question must be asked: What possible benefit could the policy of mass incarceration of women serve? In the vast majority of cases the "crimes" that involve women represent failed social policies and lend themselves to social solutions. While we argue along the same lines for all prisoners, tending to economic disparities, domestic violence, drug addiction, and gender inequality would virtually empty the courts of women defendants. It would also save the children who are now orphaned by the system.

As incarceration rates have increased nationwide, the number of women incarcerated has increased at even more dramatic rates. According to United States Bureau of Justice Statistics, there was a 60 percent increase in imprisonment of males between 1990 and 1999, and an 84 percent increase among females sentenced to prison (Beck 2000). (As the number of women increased, however, the percentage of women doing time for violent crimes decreased, from 49 percent of the imprisoned population in 1979 to 32 percent in 2001 [Beck, Karberg, and Harrison 2002].) One-third of these women are serving sentences for murder. Approximately one-third of the women serving homicide sentences have killed someone with whom they were intimately involved. Sexual and physical abuse are factors in a majority of these cases. Seventy-one percent of female prisoners in California have experienced ongoing physical and/or sexual abuse before the age of eighteen. Sixty-two percent have experienced ongoing abuse as adults (Owen and Bloom 1995). The constantly demeaning treatment of prisoners, often with sexual overtones, reopens old wounds.

Such issues cannot be addressed, however, in the prison setting, where psychological devastation is considered part of the punishment.

Drug laws with mandatory sentences have resulted in long sentences, often for less culpable offenders, while drug dealers— usually men—who can afford to pay for good legal counsel do less time. In this way, women are being swept up into the criminal justice system while their children are left behind.

As a result of the War on Drugs, fewer women are being charged with property crimes, and more women are being charged with drug-related crimes. This change in the charges does not reflect a change in the nature of the crimes committed by women, but a shift in social policy, with devastating effects. Like all aspects of this war, drug enforcement is targeted toward those who are poor and from communities of color. Black women—nationally the fastest-growing class of prisoners—now comprise almost half the population of women in prison. In this respect, the use of drug laws becomes another form of racial profiling for women.

Many women in prison are doing time because of the men in their lives. This phenomenon is partly attributable to the structure of drug laws, the injustice of conspiracy statutes, and the number of women incarcerated for killing their batterers or their pimps. Conspiracy laws convict people for having knowledge of a crime, regardless of whether they actively participated. It is common for wives, mothers, and girl-friends to receive long prison sentences because they failed to cooperate with the police when their loved ones became involved in crimes.

Incarcerated women bear a double burden of punishment: their children "do time" along with them, because most imprisoned women are single parents. Eighty percent of women in prison are mothers, and two-thirds have children under 18 (Owen and Bloom 1995). The children are cared for by relatives or foster parents and may or may not be able to maintain contact with their mothers. The fear of losing custody, or all contact with their children, is a threat women are under at all times that they are under the control of the criminal justice system.

Many people are unaware of the special problems that women face in prisons. They are thrown into an environment created by and for men, forced to wear men's clothes, and subjected to the military-style regimentation that governs prison life. Community and interpersonal relationships, on which women depend, are stifled if not directly forbidden. The primary punishment represented by prisons is isolation and separation from community. The impact of such isolation is often considerably more devastating to women than it is to men. The Federal Bureau of Prisons in the early 2000s decided to limit federal prisoner's phone calls to three hundred minutes per month. The target of the new regulation was alleged abuse by certain men. The impact on women trying to maintain family ties was far more punishing than on most male prisoners.

Since the primary purposes of incarceration are separation and isolation, and since criminal sanctions are a one-size-fits-all proposition, it stands to reason that the injustices of the system would be compounded for those people whose "size" can't be made to fit. Women are among the worst victimized by criminal justice policies and practices.

Sexual Relations and Prison Rape

Certain male prisoners are targeted for sexual assault the moment they enter a penal facility: their age, looks, sexual orientation, and other characteristics mark them as candidates for abuse. Specifically, prisoners fitting any part of the following description are more likely to be targeted: young; small; physically weak; gay; a first offender; possessing "feminine" characteristics such as long hair or a high voice; being unassertive, shy, intellectual, not street-smart, or "passive"; or having been convicted of a sexual offense against a minor. Prisoners with any one of these characteristics are much more likely than other prisoners to be targeted for abuse.

To some extent, the talk of predatory homosexual prisoners is groundless, if not homophobic. Since prisoner-on-prisoner rape is by definition homosexual, in that it involves persons of the same sex, its perpetrators are unthinkingly labeled predatory homosexuals. This terminology ignores the fact that the vast majority of male prison rapists do not view themselves as gay. Rather, most such rapists view themselves as heterosexuals and see the survivor as substituting for a woman. From this perspective, the crucial point is not that they are having sex with a man; instead, it is that they are the aggressor, as opposed to the victim, the person doing the penetration as opposed to the one being penetrated. Indeed, if they see anyone as gay, it is the victim (even where the victim's sexual orientation is clearly heterosexual).

It is not surprising that mentally ill or retarded prisoners, whose numbers behind bars have increased dramatically in recent years, are at particular risk of sexual abuse. An Indiana prisoner suffering from schizophrenia told Human Rights Watch that he was constantly being coerced into unwanted sex (HRW 2001). Clearly there is no commitment on the part of prison administrators to prevent rape or to protect vulnerable prisoners. Indeed, rape is discussed with amusement, with derision for victims, and with underlying homophobic assumptions. To many, it is considered part of the "punishment." It remains to be seen what will be the effect of the federal Prison Rape Elimination Act of 2003, which mandates state-by-state studies of the extent of the problem of rapes in prison.

Equal and voluntary gay relationships do not fit comfortably within this dichotomy. Although outsiders may perceive male prisons as a bastion of gay sexuality, the reality is quite different. Gay relationships typical of regular society are rare in prison, and usually kept secret. Indeed, many gay inmates—even those who are openly gay outside of prison—carefully hide their sexual identities while incarcerated. They do so because inmates who are perceived as gay by other inmates face a very high risk of sexual abuse.

For women, voluntary sexual relationships are both easier and harder. Lesbian relationships among women prisoners are not greeted with outright taboos. Women are generally more physically affectionate with each other, and lesbian relationships are not seen as precluding heterosexual relations on the outside. Sexual exploitation certainly occurs, at the hands of both prisoners and guards, but by far the more dangerous are male guards who prey on incarcerated women. Correctional institutions are beginning to clamp down on staff caught raping prisoners, but in an environment that generally condones abuse and requires that certain people have power over others, prohibitions against sexual exploitation sound hollow.

Women prisoners don't always welcome harsh responses to sexual activity. Although there is clearly a power imbalance between guards and prisoners, women do not want to be patronized or made to feel that they can never freely consent. Some want to be able to "exploit" the relationship for their own gains. Few want society's strict sexual mores, which may have put them in prison in the first place, to define what sexual behavior is appropriate for them. At the very least, it is safe to say that it is difficult, if not impossible, to have healthy sexual relationships inside prisons, and a system that depends on violence and power can hardly be expected to find mature, nonviolent responses to sexual occurrences.

Transgender Prisoners

Prisons present a challenge for virtually anybody incarcerated in them, but transgender and gender-variant prisoners face special hardships. It is important to remember that transgender and gender-variant people may be in different stages of gender transition. For some, the transition may be primarily behavioral and emphasize clothing choices. For others, the transition is also physical, so issues of privacy and physical violence are especially volatile.

> **Clandestine Kisses**
> **for Linda and her love**
>
> *Kisses*
> *bloom on lips*
> *which have already spoken*
> *stolen clandestine kisses*
>
> *A prisoner kisses*
> *she is defiant*
> *she breaks the rules*
> *she traffics in contraband*
> *   women's kisses*
>
> *A crime wave of kisses*
> *bitter sweet sensuality*
> *flouting women-hating satraps*
> *in their prison fiefdoms*
> *   furious*
> *   that love*
> *   can not be arrested*
>
> *   —By Marilyn Buck*
> *   (Used by permission.)*

The standards of care for people who identify as transgender or gender-variant are well documented in the outside medical world. These include access to hormone therapy; appropriate psychological counseling; and bras and other supportive underclothing that enable the individual to live as their self-identified gender. State courts have held that hormone therapy is a necessary medical treatment for transgender prisoners.

One prison in California offers targeted medical and mental health-care services to transgender and gender-variant prisoners. California Medical Facility, Vacaville, provides access to counseling, hormone therapy, and supportive clothing for male-to-female transgender prisoners. There have been no negative repercussions as a result. In fact, it would be logical to assume that expanding medical and mental health care in this way would only improve conditions inside for everyone by setting a more realistic bar for what proper services could look like.

However, the California example is the exception, not the rule. It would be difficult to overstate the complexities of gender variation in an environment that is so backward on most gender issues and on matters of sexual identity. Prisoners experiencing conflicts about their gender identity may find a receptive counselor in a particular institution, but they are more likely to keep their concerns a secret for safety reasons.

Prison and Disability

Prisoners with disabilities constitute a rapidly growing, yet still largely invisible, segment of the United States' prison population. The deplorable conditions in which many prisoners live are further exacerbated for those with physical and mental disabilities. Like their counterparts in the outside world, disabled prisoners face discrimination and often life-threatening abuse and neglect on a daily basis—except that, in a prison environment, they are even more vulnerable.

Although conclusive data are not available, several surveys of adult and juvenile prison populations in different geographic areas have found that the prison population has a large percentage of disabilities. One study notes that hearing loss, for example, is estimated to occur in 30 percent of the prison population (Russell and Stewart 2001, 61). People with all types of disabilities, such as quadriplegia, deafness, blindness, cerebral palsy, head injuries, and diabetes, are found in the prison system. The deinstitutionalization of mental institutions, which occurred without provision of adequate community-based support, has resulted in a marked increase in the numbers of mentally ill prisoners—perhaps up to 55 percent of incarcerated juveniles nationwide (Russell and Stewart 2001, 61). Research suggests an extremely high prevalence of learning disabilities among prisoners, most of whom were never diagnosed or accommodated by the educational systems in their communities. Longer sentences and the aging of the prison population are almost certain to lead to a further increase in the number of disabled prisoners.

A variety of factors contribute to the high rate of disability among prisoners. Our prisons are filled with poor people who are survivors of substandard living conditions, inadequate nutrition, and minimal or absent health care, all of which lead to disabling conditions. The 70 percent unemployment rate among people with disabilities is evidence of the increased difficulty they face in their efforts to get out of poverty.

The prison environment itself causes or contributes to disabling conditions. Overcrowding and other tensions often lead to violence, which may result in permanent disability such as spinal cord injuries or head injuries. The high noise level in most prisons can contribute to hearing loss. Unsafe and unregulated working conditions for prisoners, such as the unprotected handling of asbestos, may result in permanent injury or chronic disability. Lack of preventive medical care in prisons and inadequate care for medical conditions, including HIV and AIDS, results in disability, shortened life expectancy, and death. General prison conditions, as well as the increasing use of isolation, are responsible for the extremely high incidence of clinical depression and other mental illness among prisoners who were not mentally ill when they entered prison. Finally, as one study notes, as a result of locking up people for longer and longer periods due to mandatory sentencing, the prison population is aging—and along with age comes increasing disability (Russell and Stewart 2001, 73).

Like disabled people in general, disabled prisoners vary greatly in their degree of comfort with their disability and in the compensatory coping skills they have acquired. Given that prison programming is minimal or nonexistent in the vast majority of institutions, few disabled prisoners receive the specialized rehabilitation and training they may need. Compounding the problem is the fact that prison staff sooner or later brand virtually all disabled prisoners as malingerers, no matter how severe and obvious their disabilities. This accusation is then used to justify denying the assistance or accommodation they require. Prisoners who have developed alternative ways of accomplishing things that nondisabled staff think a disabled person can't do are sometimes accused of faking their disability and denied assistance when they do require it.

The standard for "reasonable accommodations" is very low in prison, and the conditions that many disabled prisoners endure on a daily basis are truly horrific. Wheelchair users whose chairs break down may wait for months or years before repairs are made. Confiscation of a prisoner's wheelchair, sometimes for months on end, is a popular form of discipline, rendering a mobility-impaired prisoner unable to move from his or her bed. Prisoners with back injuries are sometimes given top-bunk assignments. Prisoners who spend most or all of their time in bed develop pressure sores, because the "egg-crate" mattresses they require to help prevent skin breakdown are denied. Pressure sores—the leading cause of death among people with spinal cord injuries in Third World countries—easily become infected in a prison setting. Prison medical staff tends to be willfully ignorant of the proper care and treatment of this condition. Women prisoners with mobility impairments may lie for hours or days in pools of menstrual blood.

Deaf prisoners endure their own hardships. They go through disciplinary hearings not knowing what is being said and are unable to tell their side of the story because no sign-language interpreter is provided. Nor are interpreters provided for counseling, educational programs, on-the-job instruction, religious services, medical appointments, and so forth.

While the United States Supreme Court has ruled that state prisoners are covered by the Americans with Disabilities Act (ADA), and disabled prisoners are winning some important victories in the courts, the ADA cannot be relied on to solve all disabled prisoners' problems. Many people still resent the ADA in general, and are even more adamantly opposed to extending rights to disabled people who are imprisoned. Disability rights activists often share the prevalent public prejudice against prisoners and fear that aligning themselves with disabled prisoners may negatively affect the disability rights movement, which is already embattled. Prisoners' rights and human rights organizations have been slow to bring the specific abuses of disabled prisoners to the forefront in their campaigns.

Advocacy for the rights of disabled prisoners has often been carried out without a foundation in basic disability rights perspectives, and sometimes without more than a cursory knowledge of the specific characteristics and appropriate accommodations for particular disabilities. With the growing number of disabled prisoners, it is vital that we challenge ourselves and other prisoners' rights activists to increase our understanding of and attention to disabled prisoners. Action by prisoners' rights and disability rights activists, based on the recognition of this mistreatment as a form of human rights abuse, is urgently needed.

The Mentally Ill

There is a direct relationship between the lack of treatment of the mentally ill in the community and the number of persons incarcerated in jails and prisons across the nation. This tension between addressing mental illness as a community problem and hiding it, or institutionalizing it, has existed since the late 1700s when asylums were first created. Quakers were at the forefront of mental health treatment since the opening of The Retreat in 1796 in York, England. Friends Psychiatric Hospital in Philadelphia and Bloomingdale Asylum in New York were early examples of Friends' involvement in mental health treatment in the United States. The belief in those days was that a cure was possible in the right setting, and so the stage was set for removing the mentally ill from family and community in favor of institutions and experts. In his classic history, *The Discovery of the Asylum*, David Rothman demonstrates that the institutional solution to many problems—for instance, from almshouses and orphanages to asylums and penitentiaries—all had their roots in post-revolutionary North America (Rothman 1971).

The mentally ill moved back and forth between psychiatric hospitals, jails, and prisons, depending on the extent to which they were charged with crimes. The introduction of the McNaughton Rule in 1843 further complicated the issue. This legal development allowed defendants to plead "not guilty by reason of insanity" or "incompetent to stand trial." Although these options opened the door for treatment rather than strict imprisonment, they have never been widely used. The insanity defense is estimated to be used less than one-half of one percent of the time. One of the main reasons for this is that offenders often face more time in psychiatric settings than they do under a fixed prison sentence. There is also widespread public skepticism about the insanity defense, which renders it unpopular with defense attorneys.

During the 1930s and 1940s, the population in psychiatric hospitals increased considerably. Gradually, public awareness of mental illness improved, as did public concern for conditions in hospitals and the lack of civil rights for patients. Families of the mentally ill began to organize, and conscientious objectors from World War II who did their alternative service in psychiatric hospitals amplified the voice. A nationwide push toward deinstitutionalization resulted. But others, less concerned about patients' rights, eyed the emptying of hospitals as a way of saving government money. Promises to shift care of the mentally ill to the community were never translated into dollars, leaving patients on the streets, fending for themselves.

Many mentally ill persons on the streets are arrested for everything from vagrancy to assault. Jails and prisons have become the new psychiatric institutions. Of course, these institutions are ill equipped to deal with this new population:

The Bureau of Justice Statistics has reported that 238,000 individuals with mental illnesses were confined in U.S. jails and prisons in 1998. Overall, 16% of all inmates self-reported current mental illness or an overnight stay in a mental hospital and an additional 14% had received other mental health services in the past. Almost one-quarter of incarcerated women were identified as mentally ill. . . . Significant as these numbers are, many mental health experts believe they understate the problem. (Sentencing Project 2002)

It is common for a person suffering from mental illness to deteriorate once imprisoned. The nature of prisons is that they are anti-therapeutic. At best, imprisonment entails discomfort and isolation; at worst, high levels of stress and abuse. Overcrowding, segregation, victimization, and sensory deprivation all compound their illnesses. Mentally disabled prisoners end up in disciplinary segregation and are labeled "bad" in addition to "mad."

Correctional policy is based on the misguided assumption that seriously disturbed prisoners are malingering, hoping to receive some kind of special attention. Mental illness is viewed as another "con" played by prisoners, and prison authorities focus their energy and resources on not being "manipulated." Most prisoners who claim physical or mental problems are suspect in the eyes of many prison staff, making it difficult for them to receive timely medical assistance.

In this discussion, we are focusing on the severely mentally ill—those suffering from schizophrenia, bipolar disease (manic depression), or major depression as diagnosed in the *Diagnostic and Statistical Manual of Mental Disorders IV* (Frist 1984). The practice of making treatment available only to people diagnosed in those three categories means that all persons suffering from any other mental illness are not being treated. Such restrictions apply not only to the mentally ill in jails and prisons, but also to indigent sufferers in the community. In a recent study done in California to determine the number of mentally ill persons who were not receiving treatment, 460,000 persons received public mental health services, while approximately 600,000 did not. This was out of a population of 33 million (Richardson 2001, 5).

Common conditions that go unrecognized and untreated are posttraumatic stress disorder (common in veterans), anxiety (particularly common to sufferers of child sexual abuse), severe personality disorders, and head injuries. In addition to untreated illness, misdiagnosis is widespread. For example, self-mutilators and suicidal prisoners, perhaps those most at risk, are treated as management problems rather than patients. In general, their behaviors are seen as antisocial and manipulative, not as manifestations of mental illness and therefore a matter of safety and treatment.

Further complicating the diagnosis and treatment of the mentally ill has been the tendency to "self-medicate." Patients treat their own symptoms with alcohol, nonprescription drugs, marijuana, cocaine, crack, or whatever is available. This trend became catastrophic with the advent of much harsher drug laws, resulting in a vast increase in mentally ill persons sentenced to jails and prisons.

Another complicating factor is the new anti-psychotic drugs that have come onto the market, turning mental health treatment into a pharmacy visit rather than a counseling session. Patients sometimes have been helped by these medications, and sometimes have resisted them, often depending on the side effects. In either case, they have made it possible to "treat" the mentally ill without actually relating to them very closely.

The positive side of these new medications has been the recognition that mental illness is a disease of the brain chemistry—not simply the result of poor parenting, harsh living conditions, or lack of employment or housing. This new understanding has been empowering to families of the mentally ill, and to the clients themselves, who have become more organized. Class-action suits were introduced across the nation to demand treatment in jails and prisons, and corrections departments have been under court order to spend millions improving care. Still, the priority of custody over care in prisons continues to hamper most viable treatment programs.

The dance between treatment provided by mental health departments and punishment overseen by corrections departments goes on. In Massachusetts, New York, and, to a large extent, California, state hospitals have been taken over by the department of corrections, shifting the primary mission from health care to imprisonment.

Some states have even contracted imprisonment of the mentally ill to private corporations, just as they have contracted for other forms of managed health care, and other forms of incarceration. The old hospitals for civilly committed patients are now virtually empty and have been auctioned off to private developers along with large parcels of land. The privatization of prisoner health care—like the privatization of imprisonment—creates new dilemmas. Quality mental health treatment costs money; the purpose of managed care is to reduce costs. It is difficult to recruit, train, and retain qualified staff in the prison health-care field. Prisons are usually built in rural areas, far away from urban centers and from institutions of higher learning. In addition, the prison environment is not viewed as an ideal workplace. Health-care professionals are far more apt to accept these jobs when delivery of care is handled by mental health departments and not by custody-driven departments. In both cases, however, oversight of the care provided is thin or nonexistent. Even institutions under court order to improve care rarely comply.

The most recent development in the plight of the mentally ill prisoner is that many states are passing laws allowing civil commitment of prisoners who have completed their criminal sentence, on the grounds that the person is too dangerous to be released. It is almost as if the McNaughton Rule has come full circle: instead of being sentenced initially to the psychiatric hospital as forensic patients, and being treated for their mental illnesses, prisoners languish for years in prisons without treatment and then have their sentences extended because they are not "cured." Sex offenders are in particular danger of being resentenced as civil commitments—and even having their parole revoked, often after years of success in the community—because of the fear that they might do something in the future. Extended sentences often come on top of the longest possible prison time because mentally disabled prisoners frequently lose their "good time." Good time is awarded based on behavior. With poor coping skills, or an inability to conform to institutional norms, these prisoners often have long "disciplinary" records.

We believe that we should stop treating mental illness as "criminal" behavior, and use health-care responses rather than police responses to behavior that results from mental illness. If there is a return to greater use of mental hospitals, these should be available to patients and their families on a voluntary basis. Instead of continuing investment in more prisons to house mentally ill persons in facilities not equipped to treat them, we should invest more in secure but treatment-oriented hospitals for the violent mentally ill, and in community mental health services to treat nonviolent mentally ill persons as outpatients.

Health Care

If universal health care were available in the outside world, the right to adequate medical care in prisons might be more easily understood. Instead, health care is only available to those who can afford it, or to the very poor, and assuring qualified, humane care for prisoners is not always recognized as a right, but rather considered a privilege. If the state chooses to deprive certain people of their freedom, it is absolutely the state's obligation to provide basic services they cannot secure for themselves. Medical care in prisons, however, is a scandal and a disgrace to civilized society. With the increase in HIV/AIDS, hepatitis C, and tuberculosis, failure to provide adequate health care to the incarcerated also endangers the general public.

Researchers Rita E. Watson and Jessica Riceberg say that although the medical professions have denounced the gap in care between those with HIV/AIDS in the community and those in prison, the combination of budget cuts for AIDS and the national trend toward longer prison sentences threatens to seriously compromise our public health (HIV PLUS 1999–2000). Prison care is compromised not just by lack of resources, but by attitudes. Prison rape is a fact of life, and is even "condoned by guards as a form of disciplinary action, despite what we know today about AIDS transmission" (HIV PLUS 1999–2000). Interruptions in medication, lack of access to medication, and poor monitoring are all too rampant in the prison setting. Prisoners returning to their families untreated are walking carriers. However, individual programs in Massachusetts and Rhode Island have demonstrated that by implementing a continuum of care program, former prisoners have often had the courage to reach out to their home communities to help others understand the health risks.

Recent Bureau of Justice statistical reports reveal that the HIV rate in prisons and jails is eight to ten times greater than in the outside population. AIDS accounts for almost one-third of all prison deaths. A greater percentage of women prisoners, 2.8 percent, were HIV positive, compared to 1.9 percent of men (Maruschak 2005, 1).

Nearly one-third of all people infected with hepatitis C in the United States have passed through the correctional system. National estimates of hepatitis C in prison are 17 to 19 percent, but surveys of individual systems show up to 40 percent infection rates. It has been estimated that prisoners are nine to ten times more likely to be infected with hepatitis C than people in the general population (Wagner 2003, 30).

Rather than providing prisoners with prevention tools—notably, condoms for safe sex and liquid bleach for sterilizing needles and syringes—prison administrators frequently bar the entry of these items. Even HIV/AIDS education, as well as information on hepatitis C and tuberculosis, is sparse and inconsistently available.

Spanning Generations: Impact of Prisons on Families

A child reaches to say goodbye to his father. He presses his small hand against the glass. On the other side, his father does the same thing. They mouth goodbye.

A middle-aged woman who works as a janitor arrives at Norfolk prison in Massachusetts, the prison where Malcolm X was held. She stands in line to go through a metal detector. She is asked for her shoes and her glasses, then her wig and finally her dentures before she is allowed to walk into the trap. She complies because she wants to see her son.

A woman who is talking to her new cellmate confesses that she was born in this very same prison. Her family always predicted that she would end up there.

A little boy is turned away from visiting his father because his shorts are too long. He cries as he is led away by his mother. He is three years old.

A grandfather piles his two granddaughters into his car for their Sunday visit to their mother. He does this every Sunday for the eight years that his daughter is in prison.

A young man's father is executed. His mother's husband adopts him. He is always told that he is "just like" his father. He is arrested, charged, and convicted of armed robbery. At sentencing, the judge pronounces a very harsh sentence stating, "This city views you as part of a certain family."

One grandmother has a t-shirt with pictures of all of her grandchildren on it. She wears this shirt to the prison on visiting day. Her son has been in segregation for five years. He is allowed one visit per week, so he never sees his nieces and nephews. He has never touched any of these children and they have never touched him. His mother has not touched him since he was arrested. His mother taught him sign language so that the guards would not be able to hear them saying, "I love you" at the end of their visit. Her visits were stopped because they were accused of throwing "gang signs." This woman has watched two of her older brothers die in prison and is trying to get the third, who is very ill, released, so he can die at home. She also holds a full-time job and takes care of her grandchildren one day a week.

Many of the costs of prison are not measurable in charts or in dollars. Yet they whittle away at the fabric of families and communities, slowly crushing hope and self-esteem. This cost is infinite.

Many prisoners have other members of their families in prison or grew up with a parent in prison. Children who grow up with a parent in prison are six times more likely to spend some part of their life in prison, too (LIS 2002, 1). It sounds as if the determining factor in going to prison is having a parent in prison. This statistic does not take into consideration the social and economic impact of having a parent in prison.

It is devastating for a child, especially a young one, to have his or her mother in prison. Children of incarcerated men also face serious disruptions in their relationships to their fathers. The still-prevalent attitude that men are not as important in the lives of their children is reinforced. We have worked with many male prisoners, as well as women, for whom contact with their children has provided the lifeline they needed to make permanent lifestyle changes. Separating these parents from their communities by imprisonment impoverishes the prisoners, their families, and their communities.

The criminal justice system is structured to humiliate those who come into contact with it. Many poor defendants are treated as though they are convicted from the moment of their arrest. They await trial in jail where they do not have the freedom to schedule appointments with their attorneys, choose the clothes they will wear in court, or begin to address the issues that affect their behavior. Thus, they are not able to mitigate their sentence by demonstrating to the court that they can use their time well. The judge, the jury, and their family never see them without leg irons on. When they come to court, they are brought in and out by police and are cuffed as well as shackled. All of these images create the perception that the individual is guilty. All of these images humiliate the family.

When a family member goes to prison, the economic well-being of the entire family is affected. The family must face the loss of a wage earner compounded with the additional costs of having a loved one in prison. Telephone calls alone can run close to two hundred dollars a month. When the government decides to charge a prisoner for doctor's visits, or haircuts, they are charging the family. It is the family that sends money to cover the prisoner's costs. With prison wages as low as seventeen cents an hour (and not every prisoner has a job), a jar of peanut butter can cost two days' wages. Money spent on vending machines by visiting families can be twenty dollars or more a visit. Add to that the costs of transportation, possible overnight stay, loss of wages, and child care, and visiting becomes a huge burden. Prisons typically are not located near city centers, and many prisoner families do not have cars. Going to visit their loved one usually means taking a bus, train, and/or taxi.

At many prisons, when families arrive at the gate, they are still not assured that they will be able to visit their loved one. Their clothes might be wrong. An elderly grandmother in a wheelchair was turned away from prison because she had a sleeveless shirt on. The implication was that she was going to allow her grandson to touch her breasts. A guard might decide not to tell the prisoner that he or she has a visitor, and the visitors may be told that the prisoner does not want to see them. While visiting, women may be required to keep both feet flat on the floor. Menstruating women may not change their tampons or sanitary napkins. They may not go to the bathroom without effectively ending their visit.

Everything takes time. Families wait for hours before they are called for their visit. While they wait, passing guards look at them, and if they do not comply with every request, their visit may be canceled. If they are seen speaking to others while waiting to visit, they may be accused of organizing, and their visit will be canceled. Their cars can be searched. Some prisons have "sniffer machines" that check their hands and feet for drug residue.

Families of prisoners will often say that they too are punished. They are punished by the cost of having a loved one in prison. They are punished and humiliated by the treatment that they receive when they go to prison. They say that they feel like they are being treated as if they too are criminals. They feel this regardless of the position that they hold in society. One leading black legislator was refused entrance into a prison twice, once because she did not have her legislator's card (this despite the fact that all the guards greeted her by name when she arrived at the prison), and once because she was wearing an underwire brassiere. After families visit, they feel that they have lost their right to be human and to be treated with respect, solely because a loved one has committed a crime and because they have chosen not to forget that person.

Over time, this breaks a family down. Parents worry that their children will go to prison. Children perceive prison as a possibility—or probability—in their future. Because poor communities and communities of color are targeted for heavy law enforcement, and because these same communities do not have the social supports and resources that more affluent communities have, some families see members of each generation convicted of crime and going to prison. In this manner, the criminal justice system has disenfranchised whole families. In this manner, whole neighborhoods have lost their power to participate in government. In some neighborhoods, 70 percent of the adult men cannot vote due to felony convictions. These men also cannot easily find work or housing.

This process is exhausting to families who have loved ones in prison. Every visit to the prison means unpacking the family history. Workdays are spent at work, days off at the prison. Everything that happens to their family member in prison affects them intimately. Since the prison environment is closed, families live in anxiety about what may be happening in the intervening time between visits and phone calls. They cannot call the prison just to check up on their loved one. If a loved one does not call for a few days, the family becomes anxious. If they go to the prison to visit and they are refused, they expect the worst. If they finally see their loved one and the prisoner shows evidence of being beaten, it is as if that beating happened to the whole family. And they can do little about it. All of these factors make it very difficult for family members to stay in the lives of their incarcerated loved ones. It can have an impact on their experiences at work, school, or church, or their participation as members of their communities.

A majority of family members live in fear of their friends or coworkers discovering they have a family member in prison. They are forced to lead secret lives. This has an even more destructive effect on children. Well-meaning teachers regularly assign homework about

family histories. Children of prisoners, along with children in nontra-
ditional families and children who may not know who their fathers or
mothers are, face shame and bullying. Some children choose to make
heroes of their imprisoned ancestors, parents, or grandparents out of
self-defense or pride.

Lesbian, gay, bisexual, and transgender youth who are incarcerated experience an added isolation. Due to their sexuality these youth
often face rejection from their home communities. Support from their
home community, as with all prisoners, is critical for their success both
while they are locked up and when they get out.

Few people are aware of the impact that having people in prison
has on their home communities. With two million people in prison,
this impact is growing. Whole families and their communities are having their vision narrowed by the reality of imprisonment. It is hard for
individuals to remain healthy, let alone invest themselves in improving
their communities and neighborhoods.

And yet they do visit. But they do so at tremendous cost to themselves and to future generations. They pay with their liberty and with
their hope.

Prison Ministry

> *A prison chaplain has two options: he* [sic] *can compromise his integrity
> and become an accomplice to the crime of prison control or he can . . .
> witness to his . . . beliefs and be fired.*
>
> —Thomas O. Murton, "The Prison Chaplain:
> Prophet or Pretender?" *The Reformed Journal*

For people of faith, a major criminal justice issue crying out for honest,
creative attention is the place of ministry within the confines of punitive institutional settings. The institution of government-employed
prison chaplaincy—the dominant model used both for providing
some religious services and for recruiting/gatekeeping/coordinating
other religious services provided by groups from the community—has
undergone recent challenges. Some challenges have come from states
unwilling to pay for government chaplain positions. Others question
the integrity of a state-paid system, as the quotation above from an
Arkansas prison warden who was himself fired for shaking up the
prison system there illustrates.

The modern system of prison chaplaincy in the United States is rooted both in the historical American Puritan equation of crime and sin, and in the origin of the concept of "chaplain" itself: "literally a clergyman responsible for the prince's prayers" (Yoder 1984, 210). In keeping with this generic origin, chaplaincy within the prison setting, like that in other institutions (military, academic, medical, and industrial), "retains the administrative (and usually financial) dependence upon the ruler to the exclusion of any more popular ecclesiastical base within the people 'served'" (Yoder 1984, 210). Thus, neither prisoners themselves, nor outside religious institutions, but rather the state that incarcerates and controls prisoners assumes the authority to appoint, oversee, and, in roughly 90 percent of cases, pay their ministers.

A third root source for the current prison chaplaincy system—what one former prisoner has called a "symbiotic relationship between church and state" (Seiber 1984, 9)—is the First and Fourteenth Amendments to the Constitution. An analysis by legal scholar Barbara Knight of state and federal case law surrounding religion in prison has assessed the results in terms of courts' responsiveness to a "balanced triangle" of constitutional rights: "free exercise of religion, protection against establishment of religion, and equal protection of the laws" (Knight 1984, 437).

In addition to the constitutional considerations, it is clear that a broad range of other considerations have been brought to bear in other court decisions, including:

1. the distinction between freedom of religious belief, which is protected absolutely, and religious practice, which may be restricted;

2. the ambiguity of the meaning of "establishment" of religion;

3. the distinction between what must be *permitted* and what must be *provided* by prison officials;

4. considerations of administrative convenience and limitations of available funding;

5. the prison environment's particular requirements for order, safety, security, and rehabilitation; and

6. religion's potential for use as an instrument to promote discipline, order, and rehabilitation among inmates and to enhance institutional security.

From this matrix of constitutional and more pragmatic considerations, the courts have tended to rule that state and federal governments' provision of prison chaplains in "a representative but partial selection" of particular faiths and denominations at a given institution is both "necessary to secure to prisoners their guaranteed free exercise" and sufficient, "since . . . prison chaplains . . . are not intended to be emissaries of their particular churches" (Knight 1984, 445–46). Hence, many states' correctional policies seek to cover their flanks against any potential allegations of moving too far to either side of this delicate balance by providing for government chaplains. These chaplains are expected to avoid active proselytizing, yet to provide nonsectarian worship services and to facilitate access by and to outside faith communities who wish to provide religious services within their own faith traditions.

Most U.S. religious groups have accommodated rather happily to this uneasy legal compromise, despite the problems it raises with respect to the separation of church and state. One reason for their compliance may be because it relieves them of primary responsibility for ministry with a constituency often regarded as marginal, unattractive, and controversial.

Quite aside from constitutional and other legal considerations, some critics argue that this conventional system of state-paid prison chaplaincy is structurally inadequate in several respects:

1. By giving individual religious groups an excuse to do nothing themselves, it fosters an irresponsible hands-off posture on the part of churches relative to prison ministry.

2. It inherently compromises chaplains' ability to gain the trust, confidence, and respect of many prisoners, due to their employer.

3. It renders chaplains virtually powerless to speak out forthrightly in the face of perceived prison abuses and injustices without running a high risk of losing their jobs.

To the extent that they exist, these structural flaws—which clearly can limit both the pastoral and the prophetic dimensions of ministry in a prison context—have their effect no matter how much faith, commitment, skill, and integrity an individual chaplain may have.

On the other hand, many state chaplains counter that they can uphold prisoners' rights and humane treatment more effectively by quiet persuasion of the authorities from inside the system than they could from a posture of more independence. They also note that in those few states (for instance, Virginia and Colorado) where state employees have been replaced by private-sector prison ministers on contract with the state, the ministers have tended to be fundamentalist and overly evangelistically oriented in their vision and practice of ministry in such settings.

Neither the established government chaplaincy nor the individualistic evangelical model of prison ministry includes a strong and effective advocacy component geared toward changing criminal justice policy and practice in this nation. While the predominantly Christian faith communities that sponsor these ministries claim to believe in such values as fairness, peace, equality, justice, reconciliation, and forgiveness, too often their leaders and members tacitly or aggressively support a criminal justice system that routinely violates all these basic spiritual and ethical principles in massive and immensely damaging ways. This is largely true of both the middle-class, "mainline" denominations, which often have liberal official positions on criminal justice issues (usually not preached and not practiced), and the more working-class groups and sects, whose members at least go to prisons to "save," or just to be with, their people there.

From a perspective that takes seriously the whole church's responsibility for ministry in prisons and jails, there should be more than these two alternatives of a professional chaplaincy structurally beholden to Caesar and theologically and politically controlled by his agenda, on the one hand; and a narrow, fundamentalist ministry that focuses on saving the souls of a captive audience and usually looks the other way when confronted by evidence of abuse to their bodies, their minds, and their spirits, on the other.

This situation cries out for a new model of ministry in the arena of criminal justice that transcends both of these inadequate models. As long as prisons are with us, faith groups must understand ministry comprehensively as faith-based intervention with persons, organizations, and systems. It must be more holistic, more ecumenical and interfaith, more critical, more prophetic, and more transformative in its approach to the criminal justice system and to those caught up in it as survivors, offenders, family members, and workers.

The ministry must also move far beyond the jails and prisons themselves and begin to raise the consciousness of people of faith about the theological and moral dimensions of the many ways in which citizens interface with the penal system—paying taxes, voting, serving on juries, testifying as witnesses, responding to crime victimization, and so on.

Over a quarter of a century ago, the National Interreligious Task Force on Criminal Justice (NITFCJ) issued a consensus paper that addressed "the dilemma of today's prison chaplain, of individuals, and of churches engaged in prison ministry: can one be in the prison world and not of it?" (NITFCJ 1980, 1).

Declaring that "changing the prison system . . . needs to be the highest priority of the religious community," the task force argued:

> A critical question relates to who should pay for prison chaplaincy and for programs. . . . The source of funding for chaplaincy may relate directly to numerous other issues such as advocacy and church volunteers. There is considerable reason to support the concept of church-paid chaplains. (NITFCJ 1980, 13–14)

People of faith who share the AFSC's critique of our nation's penal system are in a unique position to initiate a dialogue with leaders of their faith communities and institutions in order to enlist their partnership in developing and implementing an alternative model for what faithful, responsible, and progressive ministry would look like in the context of crime and the criminal justice system. A related aim would be to collaborate with them to develop resources designed to facilitate their ability to lead their people into new avenues of engagement and relationship with those caught up in the criminal justice system, with the destructive policies and practices of that system, and with those, like the AFSC, who are working to transform it.

6: YOUTH, POVERTY, AND DELINQUENCY

Just as the criminal justice system is in crisis, so is the juvenile justice system. Our youth are in grave danger. The United States spends less than any other industrialized nation on nurturing its children. Increasing numbers of young people are ravaged by poverty, insufficient health care, under-funded and mismanaged schools, fear of adult violence, and the internalization of adult stereotypes about them. Parents are working more jobs for less money and with less outside help than has been the case since World War II.

A 1997 study from the Children's Defense Fund, *Poverty Matters*, showed that children born into a family during a period of poverty have a much harder time succeeding later in life than their siblings who are born during a period of relative prosperity (Sherman 1997). This contradicts theories that would blame "poor parenting" or a "culture of poverty" for troubled youth. Instead, it brings to light the direct harm caused to young children by economic distress in the family and in the communities where they live.

The U.S. child poverty rate continues to be unusually high from an international perspective. The United States has the highest poverty rate of sixteen industrialized countries, and invests the lowest amount in social expenditures. Countries with the lowest child poverty rates allocate the highest proportion of gross national product to social expenditures (Allegretto 2004).

In spite of these dismal poverty rates, violent juvenile crime in the United States has been declining for ten years. The United States Justice Department statistics show that, for 1992 and 1994, only 6 percent of all juvenile arrests were for violent offenses. Juvenile homicides, most of which are firearm-related, account for only one-tenth of 1 percent of all juvenile offenses, and the rate of juvenile homicides went down 14 percent in 1995. The juvenile arrest rate for violent crime fell 41 percent between 1994 and 2000, and the juvenile arrest rate for murder fell 74 percent from its peak in 1993 to 2000 (Mennonite Central Committee 2003). It fell again in 2003 to a level 77 percent below the peak year of 1993 and half of what it was in 1980.[1]

Yet at least forty-three states have passed laws since 1993 making it much easier for children to be tried as adults. The option of trying certain children as adults has almost always been possible in the United States juvenile justice system, but until recently it was used only in the rarest of cases, and a juvenile court judge always made the decision. In 1998, Congress made money available to states contingent upon their enacting policies that allow children over fourteen to be transferred to adult court. In 1996, one-half of the cases waived to adult court were nonviolent drug or property offenses. Forty-three percent were offenses against a person, 37 percent property offenses, 14 percent drug offenses, and 6 percent public order offenses (Stahl 1999). In 1999, juveniles charged with crimes against a person, property crimes, and drug crimes about equally likely to be transferred to adult court (1 percent or less often). Black children were 1.6 times more likely to be transferred than white defendants (Pastore and Maguire 2002, 456).

Just as the rules for prosecuting juvenile cases have changed, new definitions of crimes have brought more youth into the system. Minor acts that at one time would have been dealt with at school, family, or community levels are now brought into the justice system and often punished with imprisonment. Much youth detention takes place without due process, especially if the youth has no adult advocate within the family or community.

History of the Juvenile Justice System

The American juvenile justice system traces its origins to 1899, when the first juvenile court was established in Chicago. Nineteenth-century champions of a separate legal system for youth offenders were responding to the atrocious conditions in adult jails and the long-term harm this could cause children who served time in them. The idea behind the new juvenile court was that children are not adults; they understand their actions and the world differently, and this requires different responses from the adult community. The courts were created to provide individual treatment and services geared toward the specific needs of the child in question with the ultimate goal of that child's rehabilitation. Juvenile detention facilities and state juvenile corrections institutions were created to take the place of adult jails and prisons precisely because young offenders were recognized to show great potential. Reformers realized that nobody's interests were served by traumatizing children, sometimes irreparably, in adult courts and prisons.

The joint concepts of reform and provision of services became the principles of the juvenile justice system in the twentieth century. In 1974, Congress passed the federal Juvenile Justice and Delinquency Prevention Act, which built upon previous protective legislation and prohibited states from confining "status offenders" (those convicted of offenses that would not be considered crimes if committed by adults) in locked facilities, and from housing convicted youth offenders with adults. The purpose behind this legislation was to decrease the abuses children suffered while incarcerated. Violent youths were to be separated from nonviolent youths, and all youths were to be separated from adults by at least "sight and sound." It is important to note that compliance with this law did not happen everywhere. Children as young as eleven years old have always been housed with adult prisoners at Parchman Farm in Mississippi. These children are brutalized and often die before they are released. By 2001, the reforms of the last one hundred years were being abandoned wholesale in many states. How could this have happened and what consequences can we anticipate?

The Language of Demonization

The rhetoric of juvenile justice "reform," as proponents of punitive legislation nationwide call it, has made our children into an internal enemy. Judy Briscoe of the Texas Youth Commission uses the "super-predator theory" to explain Texas's remarkably punitive juvenile justice system. Changes were made in state law (trying youths as adults and making sentences very harsh), she says, precisely because of the threat posed by criminals who grow up surrounded by "deviant, delinquent, and criminal adults in chaotic, dysfunctional, fatherless, Godless, and jobless settings where drug abuse and child abuse are twins, and self-respecting young men literally aspire to get away with murder" (Bazelon 2000, 200–201).

On a national level, in their book *Body Count*, John DiIulio, William Bennett, and John P. Walters predicted a coming wave of violent crime in the United States on the part of juvenile "super-predators" by the turn of the century. Their ideas and terminology showed up directly in Congressman Bill McCollum's (R-Florida) initiative, the "Violent Youth Predator Act" of 1996. This kind of rhetoric lends itself to a form of demonization that we have seen develop when the nation wants to go to war against an "enemy," when we are considering punitive immigration policies, or when any category of people has become unpopular. It is a rhetoric that has been rampant in the post-9/11 environment.

The DiIulio-Bennett-Walters prediction never materialized. In fact, as we have seen, the rate of juvenile violent crime dropped precipitously in the late 1990s. DiIulio, while defending his data and his study, now apologizes for any "unintended consequences," at the same time insisting, "I am not responsible for teenagers going to prison" (Becker 2001). But the damage had already been done: creating a spate of state legislation moving juvenile offenders into the adult criminal justice system.

Statistics from Louisiana belie the "super-predator" theory by showing that both the kinds of crimes committed by the majority of youths in the system and their own personal circumstances do not fit the label. Fewer than 25 percent of the youths there are incarcerated for violent offenses. Approximately 70 percent have mental health problems (20 percent of which are serious), more than 70 percent are below the eighth-grade level in school, African American boys are much more likely to be put in secure custody than whites, and the recidivism rate is double for children who were in secure (as opposed to nonsecure) care (Juvenile Justice Project of Louisiana 2004).

Rather than being super-predators, youth in America could instead be characterized as super-prey. United States youth are twelve times more likely to die by gunfire than those in other industrialized countries. Guns are the primary cause of homicides among children. Twenty-three percent of all crime survivors in the United States are children. Nearly 5,000 children die each year from child abuse; 18,000 are permanently disabled, and 150,000 sustain serious injuries (Currie 1998, 82).

Campaigns to criminalize youth have done away with the term *child* altogether, preferring the law-enforcement term *juvenile.* Proponents of harsher penalties pit "juveniles" against "the public," making new legislation a matter of "public safety." Prosecutors can refer to their job of protecting society when questioned about transfers to adult court or stiff punishments for relatively minor crimes— and because campaigns against children have been so effective, this false separation between children and society has proven to be persuasive.

One group that is overlooked and underserved within the juvenile justice system is sexual minority youth. Youth who are grappling with sexual identity issues can be irreparably damaged when subjected to the pressures of a locked facility. Guards, as well as other prisoners, have harassed, abused, and

While concrete data estimating the precise number of lesbian, gay, bisexual, and transgender (LGBT) youth in the juvenile justice system do not exist, social science research documents the paths through which LGBT youth commonly enter the system and suggests their overrepresentation in the juvenile justice population. Social stigma and rejection—stemming from problems with family members and peers, and frequently leading to substance abuse, mental health problems and rebellion—often results in LGBT youth leaving home. Whether removed by the child protection agency due to parental abuse or neglect, kicked out of their homes, or feeling they have no choice but to leave, LGBT youth often end up homeless. In fact, up to 40 percent of homeless youth are believed to be LGBT.

—Feinstein et al. 2001

ostracized lesbian, gay, bisexual, and transgendered youth at a time when they are particularly vulnerable. It should be said that all teenagers are discovering sexuality, and no prison is a safe place in this regard. While sexual acts are officially prohibited, prisons and youth facilities create an environment that weaves sex and power together. Many youth form unhealthy sexual relationships that often lead to fights and new charges. All developmental needs of imprisoned youth go ignored or are exacerbated, adding new dimensions to the punishment. Indeed, the recognition that youth, by definition, are developing is being intentionally ignored.

Lesbian and gay youth are often the targets of physical, sexual, and verbal abuse from both other youth and staff. Often, gay boys are targets for sexual abuse by other boys, resulting in many allegations of rape or sexual molestation. Taunting is also common for those boys who are open about their sexuality. These youth face discrimination on a regular basis, including incidents of a teacher threatening a boy with disciplinary action for crossing his legs, and girls not being allowed to attend church because they are lesbians (Whitlock 2003).

Criminalization of Youth

One hundred years after laws were created to protect children, new legislation across the country is threatening an entire generation of children by making them responsible for the ways in which the system has failed them. Children, families, and communities of color are bearing the brunt of this legislation. However, the system is rapidly expanding to encompass an ever-widening net of youth from poor white communities.

Increasingly, harsh penalties for children, trying children as adults, incarcerating them with adults, empowering prosecutors to decide if a child should be tried as an adult, allowing the privatization of the entire juvenile justice service-provision network from detention centers to secure facilities to boot camps—all add up to a massive increase in the number of children experiencing the traumatic and destructive effects of the "justice" system. The vast majority of these children are not serious offenders. They are troubled teens, foster children with nowhere else to go, or young people accused of crimes so minor that the involvement of the justice system is shocking. These recent trends in policy and practice do not "rehabilitate" children or rebuild communities. They do harm public safety. They may get politicians re-elected. They do line people's pockets.

Youth of color are seriously overrepresented at all levels of the juvenile justice system—from arrests to incarceration with adults. In 1999 in California and Texas, 100 percent of youths held in adult jails awaiting trial were of color (Schiraldi 1999).

Adult facilities are extremely dangerous. Their imprisonment may be the first time these children have ever been away from home. Studies show that children commit suicide 7.7 times more often in adult jails than in juvenile detention facilities (Flaherty 1980). Children are also much more likely than adults to be sexually abused and assaulted by adult prisoners and guards. Horror stories emerge across the nation as children are jailed with adults. A fifteen-year-old girl in Ohio ran away from home and was put in the county jail to "teach her a lesson." There she was raped by a deputy jailer. A fifteen-year-old boy in Idaho who had not paid a $73 traffic fine was held in an adult jail where he was brutally tortured and eventually murdered by other prisoners in his cell. In Milwaukee, a twelve-year-old girl was one of six in the facility to try to hang herself since its opening in 1996. She succeeded.[2]

Creating Gangs

Two legal developments in the prosecution of juvenile cases have made the likelihood of conviction much stronger: anti-gang legislation and conspiracy laws. Anti-gang legislation and policies have resulted in some of the worst abuses of children's civil and human rights. The Office of Juvenile Justice and Delinquency Prevention has identified 25,136 gangs nationwide. Criteria for gang membership can be types of jeans, relation to a gang suspect, tattoos, specific brands of sneakers, use of pagers, certain hairstyles, or wearing jewelry. These criteria offer no specific or verifiable proof of gang activity and therefore serve to put the vast majority of teenagers under suspicion.

Despite the vague criteria for establishing gang membership, local police districts around the country are creating gang databases. Inclusion in the database is often based solely on police suspicions, and the databases have been proven to be thoroughly discriminatory. In Denver, for example, eight of ten youth of color in 1992 were listed

on the database. In Orange County, California, an appalling 92 percent of its list in 1997 were youth of color (though fewer than 50
percent of the total youth population were of color).

Laws passed since 1988 have enhanced penalties for gang-related
activity and created new crimes specific to gangs. This raises considerably the stakes of wearing a certain article of clothing. If a youth is
arrested and convicted of a property offense, for example, and in addition is charged with committing the offense as part of his or her "gang-
related activity," the child can be tried in adult instead of in juvenile
court and receive a much harsher sentence. Gang policies penalize
youth for the crime of "association" and subject them to sentencing
enhancements based on knowing what their friends were thinking of
doing. Often, youth are tried under gang provisions or as co-conspira-
tors. Children can be prosecuted for activities of their friends merely
because there is evidence that their friends talked to them about their
plans. Although "talking big" has always been a recognized part of ado-
lescence, whether in the locker room, in the sorority/fraternity house,
or on the telephone, such behavior is now being treated as criminal.

Some criminologists have argued that gang policies are actually
creating gangs. Groupings of youth are identifying themselves as gangs
in reaction to the attention and stress they are placed under by law
enforcement or the adults in their lives. This process is known as cohesion. There is evidence that anti-gang policies on the street and in
prison increase cohesion among youth and set up a "them vs. us" construction that may not have existed before.

Zero Tolerance

The trend in recent years to undo humanitarian policies toward youthful offenders is also mimicked in many school disciplinary policies.
Spurred on by a handful of shocking crimes committed on school
campuses, "zero tolerance" policies cropping up across the country
require drastic disciplinary action, usually on a mandatory basis, in
response to broader and broader types of behavior. Where schools
were once safe havens for youth with troubles at home, now the philosophy governing relationships between students and their teachers is
punitive rather than educational. A recent Harvard University study
unearthed a wealth of evidence that "zero tolerance" is interfering with
children's education and achieving little in return (AP/CRP 2000).

The study documents case after case in which disciplinary policies stretched any definition of common sense. For example, two ten-year-old Latino boys in Virginia were charged with felonies after putting soap in their teacher's water. Not so long ago, such an act would have been considered an ill-conceived prank, and would have been dealt with among teacher, school, and parents.

Other manifestations of an intolerant approach are suspension and expulsion practices. Racial disparities in the application of disciplinary policies have been documented by various agencies, including the Department of Education. The most recent data from the department show that African American children, who account for 17 percent of public school enrollment nationally, constitute 32 percent of out-of-school suspensions. Students of color are disproportionately disciplined for the most serious offenses, such as "assault"; for the most subjective categories of offense, such as "defiance of authority"; and for minor infractions such as "disturbing schools." In South Carolina, where black children were overwhelmingly charged with "disturbing schools," 70 percent of the cases were referred to a law enforcement agency. Of these, 72 percent were referred for suspension, and 21 percent were referred for expulsion (AP/CRP 2000).

The Mississippi Legislature recently passed a "three strikes, you're out" policy for its schools, which will affect youth as young as thirteen. Mississippi public schools are 51 percent black (from Mississippi Public Schools: An Overview, www.mde.k12.ms.us/public.htm), but the school boards are overwhelmingly white (though children of board members very often attend private, all-white academies).

School disciplinary policies can be traced directly to changes in school integration policies. As federal law began to implement equal protection provisions guaranteeing all children the right to an equal education, new ways were found to segregate children within the schools. In addition to suspension and expulsion, special education classes have been widely used to separate children of color and immigrants from others. Parents who advocate on behalf of their children are often caught between the role of "enforcer," to satisfy school authorities that they are supervising their children, and the role of nurturing parent.

Parents in all walks of life are often lacking in the most basic information about their and their children's rights once a child comes in contact with the juvenile justice system. The absence of a parent or guardian at a court hearing can spell the difference between incarceration and release, as work with foster children shows. Without active parental insistence on, and hiring of, legal representation, many children will be assigned counsel or will waive their constitutional right to representation. Many parents mistakenly trust that their children will be well provided for or at least protected while in secure care. Some parents contact the juvenile justice authorities when they are having a hard time controlling their children. They do so without the knowledge of the stiff penalties for noncriminal offenses. Such calls can result in the prosecution of their children.

In South Dakota, a mother called the police because her son had stayed out all night. She was hoping the police would help her regain a degree of control over him. Instead, he was arrested and, after a juvenile court hearing, sentenced to a boot camp. There he was placed in solitary confinement in a freezing-cold, air-conditioned cell, where he was allowed to wear only his underpants. He was subjected to cold showers (if he complained), and thrown back into his frigid cell without being allowed to dry off. Although he received a sentence of only four months, it took his mother a full two years to finally get him out of the juvenile justice system.

In Massachusetts, a sixteen-year-old girl and her mother were having an argument. In the course of the argument the girl hit her mother. The mother dialed 911 and stated that she was having trouble controlling her daughter, hoping to receive support in mediating the argument. The police were dispatched and, after listening to the mother's side of the story, arrested the sixteen-year-old. Against her mother's wishes, she was ultimately charged and convicted of assault and battery. She was sentenced to five to seven years in prison as an adult.

Judge Eugene Moore of the Oakland, Michigan, Family Court said, "If we put more kids into a failed system, although we may house them where they cannot do any damage for a period of time, we should not be surprised when they emerge as more dangerous and hardened criminals. . . . Instead of spending money building prisons, we should be spending money preventing crime and rehabilitating youthful criminals" (Shepherd 2000).

There is no room for zero tolerance in the raising of our children. If we allow no room for mistakes, misjudgments, and testing of limits, we have effectively taken away childhood. Schools must return to their mission of educating children, and parents must be given the support they need to love, nurture, and guide. The participation and support of all adults is critical. As allies, we can reverse the demonization of children; the responsibility of the broader society to its children can be reexamined. The struggle to disentangle our children from the criminal justice system is also part of the struggle to allocate this nation's resources in an equitable and ethical way. The criminalization of children allows society to wash its hands of its own culpability. Youth have always baffled their elders and presented challenges that were difficult to meet. However, current policies institutionalize our fear of youth in ways that are damaging and permanent for all of us.

7: AN ALTERNATIVE VISION OF JUSTICE

Survivors

Beloved, do not die. Do not dare die! I, the survivor, I wrap you in words so that the future inherits you. I snatch you from the death of forgetfulness. I tell your story, complete your ending—you who once whispered beside me in the dark.

—Krog 1999

The first step in taking the need for community seriously, in the redefinition of justice, is to take the needs of survivors of crime seriously.[1] Survivors know, from painful personal experience, the cost of the current social policy. They are most often portrayed as middle-class people who have been tragically harmed by violent offenders who are the "other"—and in a small percentage of cases, they are. Yet most survivors of street crime (as distinguished from corporate and white-collar crime) come from the same communities as their victimizers, most often, in their own families or immediate neighborhoods. Frequently, people are victimized for years in silence. More and more, survivors remind us that solutions that destroy their families and neighborhoods are not solutions at all. These solutions maintain silence in the face of great harm. Survivors need to be able to come forward, without fear of punishment of themselves or of their family members, and ask for help and support.

Policymakers, prosecutors, and judges often use survivors' voices to leverage the harshest of penalties and the most vengeful of crime policies. Survivors, like offenders, are harmed by the criminal justice system. They are often victimized repeatedly and never permitted to move beyond the tragedy they have experienced. Their voices are used when they are the most vulnerable, often immediately after a murder has taken place and before they have received any kind of support. A "good" victim in the eyes of some prosecutors is one who never heals. Murder victims' surviving family members who ask for mercy toward the victimizer and advocate healing are occasionally told that they really did not "love" the person who was murdered.

Often, an entire trial will take place with no recognition that the survivor or the survivor's family is in court. The only time they are required to come to court is when they are required to give evidence against the defendant. Survivors often describe being "left in the dark," without information, during a trial. Survivors are ill prepared for the realities of a trial, the adversarial nature of criminal proceedings, the requirements of due process, procedural fairness, or the focus on establishing the guilt or innocence of the accused. Survivors often walk away from the trial frustrated.

Those who have experienced violence know that crime is much more complex than the legal procedure reflects. They know that their perception of "the truth" shifts as their understanding of the crime deepens. They also know that they need to be able to tell this truth over and over again as their understanding changes, in order to weave what was lost in the act of violence back into their lives and into the history of their communities.

In recent years some survivors have been advocating a new kind of justice, a justice that would heal them, the people who have harmed them, and their communities. Unsupported by the criminal justice system, they often act on their impulses alone, making up their process as they go along. Some meet with the offender in the crime so that they can resolve unanswered questions, and then go on to do work in nonviolence or violence prevention. Many do this work in memory of their loved one, as a way to make sure the story of their loved one is told. Through their positive actions, survivors make sure that what was lost is not forgotten. Their stories teach us something about justice, and they remind us that no two crimes are the same, no two offenders are the same, and no two victims are the same.

At a recent death-penalty hearing, Tom Lowenstein, the son of Congressman Al Lowenstein, who was murdered in his office in 1980, petitioned the Massachusetts legislature not to reinstate the death penalty.

> I know the need for revenge and I am not sure that forgiveness is possible, but if you want to do something in my father's name, put money into education, create prevention programs for troubled youth, pass universal health care, make drug treatment available to all, but do not pass this bill—not in my name.[2]

Punishment

Punishment is central to criminal justice practice in the United States. Punishment is the act of making someone suffer for a fault or crime. According to the 1994 *Merriam-Webster Dictionary*, "Punishment stresses the giving of some kind of pain or suffering to the wrongdoer rather than trying to reform the person." Punishment, as a response to violation, grows out of the revenge concept of justice—returning pain for pain. In terms of the criminal justice system, punishment is the legitimized use of force and violence against individuals who have violated laws.

According to Kobutsu Malone, a Rinzai Zen Buddhist priest:

> The physical or emotional pain or injury of punishment done to a child or an adult creates only fear and trauma, it not only damages the person being punished but it damages and enslaves those who inflict the punishment. . . . The net result of any kind of punishment is internalized oppression, humiliation and degradation for both the giver and the receiver of the punishment. It is difficult indeed to really see the profound depth of this truth because we as individuals and collectively as a society live within an oppressive and coercive environment. . . . Arrogance and aggression permeate our society, our history, our religious traditions, our so-called judicial system to the point that we can not dare to even question the premise of punishment without drawing shocked response from our fellow citizens. We live in a nation surrounded by violence. We worship violence and the infliction of pain in our entertainment, in our day-to-day interrelationships with each other. (Malone 2000)

Increasingly, American policy-makers have come to believe that we can punish our way to a healthy society. Through law and policy, we have created an elaborate system of punishments and rewards. Even the basic human needs of housing and the means to earn a living have become part of the punishment system. Rings of punishment extend out from that center through the criminal justice system and into the child welfare system, health system, educational system, and beyond—into our family system at home, where child abuse and domestic violence are practiced at alarming rates with terrifying fatality, often in the name of punishment. The actions that are punished by these systems are grounded in realities over which the offender has little control: poverty, mental illness, addiction, poor education, race, sexual orientation, or gender.

Society punishes ostensibly to teach offenders a lesson, with the belief that if people are made uncomfortable enough, they will understand that their actions were not in their best interests. This is usually referred to as the "deterrence" argument. We are told that if sentences are harsh, people will think twice before committing a crime. This argument is most often made in debates over the death penalty. This concept is

Five years after Arnold went to prison for the murder of John Labanara, my brother decided that he must spend the rest of his life in atonement for the life that he took. Arnold was 18 when he went to Walpole prison. He faced a natural life sentence. He has always taken responsibility for this murder. He decided the best way to atone for this life that was taken was to help young men, particularly young black men like himself, not to go down the same path. Arnold embarked on a course of preparation that would allow him to do this work. At 18, . . . he completed his GED, he committed himself to a life of sobriety, he went on to get his bachelors degree and his masters; he is working on his Ph.D. He runs a sobriety support group for young men who have elected to be sober in prison. He began a mentoring program for youth who are in trouble with the criminal justice system. He has had 30 successful furloughs where he worked in the community with youth. Youth are referred to him for counseling, and their parents drive them to the prison where he helps them look at and change their lives. I can honestly say that my brother, after 30 years in prison, at the age of 48, has long since repented.

—Marva King, speaking
on her brother's sentence
commutation request

largely invalid; it is further evidence of our cultural ignorance of the true causes or motivations for criminal behavior. Few perpetrators stop to think about the consequences before they commit a crime. Street crime is typically an act of desperation, insanity, drug-induced behavior, or sometimes all three. Making punishments harsher does nothing to prevent crime; it serves primarily to satisfy the desire for revenge and retribution. Society believes in this false logic of punishment for deterrence and does little or nothing to alleviate the problems that led to the offense. Anyone who has raised children knows that children do not stop misbehaving merely because they are punished. If we punish a child without nurturing, mentoring, and loving, we create at least a dysfunctional adult—and sometimes a dangerous adult.

Another rationale for punishment is incapacitation. Whether or not fear of the consequences will prevent wrongdoing, keeping people locked up and isolated (or killing them, in the case of the death penalty) will prevent them from reoffending. To some extent this rationale makes sense, but it is hard to argue that our preferred ways of carrying it out constitute a sustainable social policy. Should all of the two million people currently incarcerated in the United States be kept in prisons on the chance they could commit another crime? Would killing all murderers eliminate future murders?

There are other methods of incapacitation besides execution and incarceration, although these two have been dominant practices in the Western world (Zimring and Hawkins 1995, 158). The other two most frequently used methods of incapacitation are house arrest and electronic surveillance. Confiscating automobiles from chronic drunk drivers would also constitute incapacitation.

For millennia, societies have punished to set an example, and yet people in all societies continue to offend. Scientific studies have consistently failed to find convincing evidence that the death penalty deters crime more effectively than other punishments. The most recent survey of research findings on the relationship between the death penalty and homicide rates, conducted for the United Nations in 1988 and updated in 2002, concluded that "it is not prudent to accept the hypothesis that capital punishment deters murder to a marginally greater extent than does the threat and application of the supposedly lesser punishment of life imprisonment" (Hood 2002, 230). The United States, the only Western democracy that still uses the death penalty, also can boast the highest murder rate in the industrialized world.[3]

Perhaps the most loathsome of reasons to punish is to exact revenge. We legalize our desire for revenge in our criminal code. Justice Oliver Wendell Holmes wrote:

> The first requirement of a sound body of law is that it should correspond with the actual feelings and demands of the community, whether right or wrong. If people would gratify the passion of revenge outside of the law, if the law did not help them, the law has no choice but to satisfy the craving itself, and thus avoid the greater evil of private retribution. At the same time, this passion is not one that we encourage, either as private individuals or as law makers. (Williams 1957, 120–21)

If this quotation makes us uncomfortable, it should. How far should the state go to satisfy some people's craving for revenge? Is legal murder through the death penalty the endpoint? Do we still really believe that revenge brings balance to our communities? .

What is the answer? The AFSC criminal justice programs are opposed to the use of punishment. Inherent in punishment is retribution, which runs contrary to the basic beliefs of Friends. We recognize that the recipient may view the imposing of any sanction for law violations as punishment, regardless of society's motives. People of good conscience are deeply divided on what constitutes just and humane societal responses to behavior that has a destructive impact on human lives and rights. Nonetheless, it is painfully evident that the Western—and especially American—penal experiment has been a dismal failure.

The peace-building justice paradigm that we articulate in our final chapter does not include punishment in response to the breaking of laws. It includes repentance, reparation, and reintegration. Repentance involves three components: acknowledgment—a truthful, public accounting for what was done; an apology; and the will to atone for the action. Acknowledgment and apology confirm the victim's experience as real and begin the accountability process. Atonement, as used here, means actual change of behavior.

The importance of a public repentance or accounting for crime was the centerpiece of the Truth and Reconciliation Commission (TRC) in South Africa.

Other countries emerging from civil war or despotism are also deciding that a public truth telling is a crucial step to democracy. It is critical for citizens to know what was done, for offenders to admit their wrongs and apologize, and for survivors to tell their stories and tell the government what they need to be whole. In South Africa, the truth and an outline for reconciliation were the foundation for the new nation. Repentance preceded reconciliation. Reparation was to be determined by the survivors, by the people—from the bottom up. Choices about what kinds of reparations would be appropriate could still be a matter of public policy—enabling jurisdictions, for example, to limit reparations to fines, work exchange, community service, or a host of creative responses. This is radical justice. The fact that the reparation stage of the process has still not been acted on is a testimony to how difficult it is to enact true justice. Until the process is complete, reconciliation will continue to be elusive.

Reintegration can occur at different levels. In most instances a perpetrator does not have to be removed from the community for acknowledgment and healing to take place. But if separation does occur, the ultimate goal must be to find a way to reincorporate the person into family, neighborhood, and economic structures. Without this, wholeness is not possible.

> *The Scripture of Islam exhorts its adherents to faith and to obedience, to exemplary life, to brothers and sisters, and to the building of community. The tenets of the Qur'an could be characterized as the foundation of a theology of restoration. . . . If an offense is committed, restitution should be made. If an offender repents, the Imam can pardon and an act of expiation can be performed. If an offender does not repent, or if a victim does not forgive, penalties may be exacted. Forgiveness among human beings is considered a virtue.*
>
> —Mackey 1981, 31–32

We acknowledge the difficulty in moving beyond punishment, as Kobutsu Malone suggests. We currently live in a violence- and revenge-ridden culture. But just as the first step toward healing comes with truth telling, the first step advocates of social change must take is to articulate a different reality.

Forgiveness

In order for a true discussion of forgiveness to take place, all of us—not just survivors of crime—must learn to see those who commit crime as human beings. It is easy not to forgive when applying the assumption that the person who has caused harm is less than human, incapable of doing otherwise or of changing for the better. Only by rehumanizing those who commit crime is forgiveness possible.

If truth telling and reparations are crucial to a new justice equation, so is a third step: the element of forgiveness. Almost gone from our current vocabulary and culture, forgiveness is the actual act that enables healing. When discussing forgiveness, it is important to distinguish between the role of individuals, particularly survivors of crime, and the role of social policy. Individual survivors will come—or not come—to forgiveness in their own time. It cannot be coerced, cajoled, or provoked by guilt. Survivors must be in charge of their own healing.

Here we focus on forgiveness as essential in social policy. At the dawn of the new millennium, there is little evidence of any form of forgiveness—even for children who commit crimes. The practice of clemency, one way of practicing forgiveness, was once commonplace, even in American colonial jurisprudence. Now it is practically extinct. Yet without it there is no hope—and certainly no hope for a new justice paradigm.

> *It isn't easy, as we all know, to ask for forgiveness, and it's also not easy to forgive, but we are people who know that when someone cannot be forgiven there is no future.*
>
> —Archbishop Desmond Tutu, *No Future Without Forgiveness*

Breaking the Cycle

Our tradition, our culture, speaks clearly about the concepts of judgment and punishment. They belong to Creator. They are not ours. They are, therefore, not to be used in the way that we relate to each other. People who offend against another (victimizers) are to be viewed and related to as people who are out of balance—with themselves, their family, their community, and their Creator. A return to balance can best be accomplished through a process of accountability that includes support from the community through teaching and healing. The use of judgment and punishment actually works against the healing process. An already unbalanced person is moved further out of balance.

The legal system's use of incarceration under the guise of specific and general deterrence also seems, to us, to be ineffective in breaking the cycle of violence. Victimization has become so much a part of who we are, as a people and a community, that the threat of jail simply does not deter offending behavior. What the threat of incarceration does do is keep people from coming forward and taking responsibility for the hurt they are causing. It reinforces the silence and therefore promotes, rather than breaks, the cycle of violence that exists. In reality, rather than making the community a safer place, the threat of jail places the community more at risk.

—Community Holistic Circle Healing Program
Hollow Water First Nation Position on Incarceration, Canada

The Navajo nation has its own system of courts and prisons. On the reservation, there are 28,000 criminal cases adjudicated each year; however, there are only 220 beds in the Navajo prison (Yazzie 2000, 37). Rather than resort to prison building, in January of 2000 "the Navajo Nation quit jailing people for dozens of offenses that used to land people behind bars. Now tribal courts are turning to be peacemakers" (Yazzie 2000, 36). The Navajo practice of *nalyeeh*, "confronting someone who hurts others with a demand that they talk out the action and the hurt it caused so that something positive will come of it" (Yazzie 2000, 36), underpins this peace-building system. Western criminal justice defines the problem as the actor. Imprisonment is designed to work on convicts. Navajo justice deals with the action itself. The questions are not, What happened? Who did it? How will they be punished? The questions are, Who got hurt? How do they feel? What can be done about it?

The U.S. penal system is built on suspicion and distrust, and it assumes the worst about the people in custody. This attitude permeates the system so strongly that individual staff members who relate positively to prisoners are marginalized by their peers. People rarely make positive changes in a setting that expects the worst of them. Institutional violence against those who commit crime is never justified, nor is the deprivation of their human or constitutional rights.

When punishment involves imprisonment, the risk of violence in society increases because of the culture of violence that exists within prisons. This culture of violence is caused by the extreme concentration of power in the prison administration, and the absence of any independent, public checks on that power. Closed systems, which prisons invariably are, invite abuse of authority and often sanction cruelty, both officially and unofficially. In prison, control—whether the overarching control exercised by prison officials or the more limited control exercised by some prisoners over others—is maintained through the threat of violence. Examples of this violence on the part of prison officials can be found throughout the prison system: in beatings, body-cavity searches before and after visits, restraint chairs, and isolation units.

Many of the prisoners (some against their will) also participate in this violence—occasionally against guards, but most often against each other or vulnerable prisoners. It is a tragic reality that sometimes the only way to survive in prison is to become violent. As the numbers of prisoners increase, so do the numbers of individuals who have experienced the brutality of prison. The violent culture of prison spills over into our communities each time a brutalized prisoner is released, and often when a stressed-out, brutal, or brutalized prison guard comes home from work.

There are people who are so dangerous that they need to be separated from society, but they do not number in the millions. They may not even number in the thousands. Secure, humane institutions should be established where these relatively few individuals can live their lives safely separated from society, but always with the potential for repentance and possible reintegration. They should have every opportunity to develop themselves and contribute to society. They should be separated, but not punished.

Is there an alternative to penal systems? There always has been. We must be willing to wrestle *seriously* with the root causes. It requires fundamental change in how people within the community see one another—particularly the way they view those who are struggling or outcast, or who sometimes harm themselves and others. Respecting the fundamental humanity of those who violate the social order, as well as recognizing systemic imbalances, are prerequisites to developing a new paradigm. The only way to end crime is to address the real causes, among which are poverty, mental illness,

> *The purpose and justification of a sentence of imprisonment or a similar measure deprivative of liberty is ultimately to protect society against crime. This end can only be achieved if the period of imprisonment is used to ensure, so far as possible, that upon his return to society the offender is not only willing but able to lead a law-abiding and self-supporting life.*
>
> —United Nations Standard Minimum Rules for the Treatment of Prisoners, Article 58

despair, and broken relationships. The concrete alternatives are head-start programs, family support systems, nutrition programs, improved education, employment opportunities, housing programs, and adequate family incomes. Together these alternatives would constitute a radical justice.

8: SEARCHING FOR A NEW JUSTICE PARADIGM

Can Prisons Rehabilitate?

From the outset, one of the fundamental purposes of the penitentiary system has been rehabilitation within the prison system. At its core, this belief is laudable—even noble—because it recognizes people's ability to change. However, within the context of a punishment model heavily reliant on coercion, is rehabilitation possible?

Outside of the prison system, the guiding principle for professionals in the various rehabilitation fields is that an individual's needs can only be addressed successfully in the full context of his or her family, neighbors, and community, not in isolation. Within the prison system, however, rehabilitation

- is based predominantly on an individual treatment model, focusing on the individual prisoner and not on the crime or the survivor. This narrows the focus of the process to one person, marginalizing the survivor and absolving the broader community of any responsibility. It says, "If we can fix the person, we have fixed the problem." This is a fundamental fallacy, because it isolates the individual from family, social, and economic contexts, thus ignoring the importance of relationships and systems in both forming individuals and enabling them to change. There have always been some courageous professionals within the system who have tried to reach beyond the individual model and work contextually, but they rarely receive the support they need to sustain the effort and are often beaten down by a custodial prison culture.

- is reliant upon indeterminacy; the individual is released when he or she is deemed to be "cured" of criminality.

- involves great discretionary power in which a small group of gatekeepers decides the fate of prisoners who are vastly different from themselves. Discretion in decisions about release compounds and reinforces the class and race discrimination that has infected the process from the beginning.

It is difficult to imagine a penal rehabilitation scheme that does not translate into a form of behavior modification to coerce the prisoner into conforming to expectations of the dominant culture. It is inevitable, since the focus of rehabilitation within the prison system is on the person, not the crime. Society has a legitimate interest in stopping people from committing robbery, murder, and other harms, but that interest is distinguishable from reinventing the person. A better role for prisons, if they are going to be in the rehabilitation mode, is to make available the widest possible educational, vocational, religious, and psychological opportunities. They must also keep every avenue open for prisoners to maintain and improve family contacts. Self-improvement is the best hope for success upon release.

In searching for a peace-building paradigm, one must ask, What is a person being "habilitated" to? To a culture already fraught with violence, greed, and racism? To a culture that measures achievement in dollars, material possessions, and power over others? Do we ultimately ask prisoners to become saints before they are released—people who never resort to violent responses even when violence continues to be heaped onto them? People who never resort to theft even when the job market is closed to them because of their past? This double standard of expectations of former prisoners and people in the general public perpetuates the present system and creates a revolving door. There is ample evidence that many special interests depend on people failing upon release. Guards' unions, heavy contributors to political campaigns in some states, are a prime example. Their failure keeps the system going. Their failure lines the pockets of many, albeit legally. Their failure also fans the fears of the public, which wants to be safe.

From Prison Abolition to a New Paradigm

The International Conference on Penal Abolition, with AFSC participation from its beginning, has shifted from prison abolition to penal abolition, signaling a recognition that the entire apparatus must be abandoned.

The AFSC recognizes that the existence and continued expansion of the penal system represent a profound spiritual crisis, and its job as a Quaker organization is to address it as such. It is a crisis that allows fellow human beings to be demonized. It is a crisis that legitimizes torture, total isolation of individuals (sometimes for a lifetime), sensory deprivation, and abuse of power. It is a crisis that extends beyond prisons themselves into judicial, parole and probation, law enforcement, mental health, and public education systems. It further damages not only crime survivors and offenders, but also the families of both survivors and offenders. As the system becomes more and more dependent on profit-making companies, the "public mission" of the system is lost behind the self-interests of every group wanting to make a buck—from the unions representing the guards on the tier to the corporate food-services companies, from the construction firms to the for-profit detention corporations.

> *Lawlessness and the prison are both manifestations not of a political issue but of a spiritual crisis that affects us all. It is a crisis wherein we persist in choosing death even though God has chosen life on our behalf. When we focus on this spiritual crisis, we see that violence and disrespect for life are the same no matter what manifestation. And so we cannot talk about robbery on the streets of our cities without also talking about the robbery that takes place when we eat from full tables while one-third of the world remains malnourished. We cannot talk about violence on the streets of our cities without seeing its direct link to the fact that, as a nation, we are armed to the teeth with enough nuclear weapons to obliterate our planet.*
>
> —Griffith 1993

All participants in this system are damaged by it: defendants, prisoners, guards, police, lawyers, judges, and survivors. We are all confined by a set of assumptions about "the other" that will make justice unattainable.

This spiritual crisis is no simple matter. People called to abandon a deeply ingrained system are in danger of being left frightened and exposed. Are they aligning themselves with such figures as Francis of Assisi or Gautama Buddha, who gave up all trappings of human comfort for a hard-to-articulate ideal?

The answer is both resounding and terrifying. As people of faith, our choice is clear. The alternative is to remain enslaved by fear and beholden to false idols. This crisis of allegiance is precisely the same one AFSC faces when it addresses the need to abandon the military apparatus. We cannot simultaneously build peace and prepare for war.

The other part of the spiritual crisis that the penal system represents is the long-term harm we do ourselves by legitimizing extreme abuse, and even murder, of fellow human beings. From the very beginning prisons carried the "attraction" of locking away people society found offensive. As the prison industry has expanded, so has the legitimizing of such isolation and the brutality that accompanies it. We accommodate what appears to be the "necessary evil" of enforcing harsh conditions. We accommodate the "collateral damage" represented by the children left behind. We accommodate the beatings and "justifiable" homicides that go with police work. After awhile, our own humanity is compromised. Unless the system can be overturned, the damage to us is permanent.

The entire criminal justice apparatus has spun out of control. The United States must reexamine the fundamental purposes on which the system rests.

Reform vs. Abolition

There is an ongoing debate between the reform approach to the criminal justice system and a stand for penal abolition. Abolition assumes that the system itself cannot be "rehabilitated." The AFSC's 1990 publication, *America's First Penitentiary,* pointed out that the penitentiary experiment has failed.

> It has failed to rehabilitate, failed to bring crime rates down, failed to protect the public. The failure will not be rectified by further tinkering with prisons or penitentiaries. (Magnani 1990, 74; see also Sentencing Project 2005)

Reformers, like those who advocated for the first penitentiary, believe in prisoners' ability to change, as well as the system's ability to be adjusted in ways that overcome its deficits. However, too many factors militate against the possibility of the system adjusting. Powerful economic interests are at play. The legacy of slavery and continued racism is mixed into the cement of every prison and jail in the country. The system depends on the role of guards, police, prosecutors, and judges as legitimized oppressors. The needs of survivors and the need to make communities whole again are lost. Enforcement cannot be achieved without violence.

> We submit that the basic evils of imprisonment are that it denies autonomy, degrades dignity, impairs or destroys self-reliance, inculcates authoritarian values, minimizes the likelihood of beneficial interaction with one's peers, fractures family ties, destroys the family's economic stability, and prejudices the prisoner's future prospects for any improvement in his economic and social status. It does all these things whether or not the buildings are antiseptic or dirty, the aroma that of fresh bread or stale urine, the sleeping accommodation a plank or an inner-spring mattress. (AFSC 1971, 33)

Finding ways out of the spiral of violence represented by the penal system is not simple. In fact, the first step must be to insist that there are no simple solutions. Solutions to problems of crime and violence must be rooted in the community and determined by the community, yet we cannot be naïve about the existence of cohesive communities in most neighborhoods throughout the country. Still, there must be systemic efforts that address economic and social problems. Solutions must be complex and revolutionary in a society as dependent as ours on solving problems through police powers and repression. They must begin with a serious effort to decriminalize behavior that involves homelessness, mental illness, drug addiction, or consensual sex between adults. These behaviors are better addressed through housing subsidies, universal health care, substance-abuse programming, job training, and education.

Alternatives

Over the past thirty years, many alternatives to imprisonment have been offered. These alternatives have included bail release programs, drug courts and treatment, job referrals and training, community service, survivor/offender reconciliation, and restitution options that take into account economic disparities. Largely, these "alternatives" have been implemented as "programs" and have become add-ons to the criminal justice system, serving a new class of individuals who would not have previously been prosecuted or incarcerated. As a result, these programs rarely divert people from prosecution or incarceration. Alternative programs have widened the net of people caught up in the criminal justice system and weakened the web of community concern by professionalizing those who administer these programs.

It is also fair to say that virtually all alternatives work—that is, that they are better than incarceration. They do less harm and often provide a lifeline to someone in need. They have been so severely underutilized, or aborted midstream, that good research on alternatives is hard to find. The best programs are the product of creative and innovative individuals working in a particular area with a particular expertise. In evaluating an alternative, an important question to ask is whether it replaces prisons or expands the reach of the criminal justice system.

Restorative/Peace-building Justice

In recent years, indigenous communities, followed by faith communities, have pioneered new concepts in "restorative" or "transformative justice,"[1] which shift the definition of crime from a breaking of legal codes to an act of harming another person or a community of people. The question becomes, "How do we heal the harm?" not "How do we punish the criminal?" Implementation of restorative justice practices would shift the goal of the justice system away from punishment and retribution (or revenge) and replace it with a healing approach that addresses the needs of survivors, offenders, and the community. This restorative or healing justice is truly a new paradigm—an entirely new framework for handling violations that tear the social fabric. Such alternatives cannot be instituted on top of existing punitive systems, but must replace sanctions with mutually agreed-upon solutions to specific cases. Neither can they be successful unless systemic issues, which may have contributed to the offense, are addressed. This requires the community to accept responsibility by committing itself to implement the changes in social structures that will genuinely prevent crime at its roots. Peace-building justice presupposes a functioning community capable of promoting institutional, and thus social, change.

Unlike other forms of alternative dispute resolution, peace-building justice recognizes participants as survivor and offender, not as codisputants. The process emphasizes truth, often described as "speaking from the heart." Emotional expression is encouraged and valued.

In peace-building justice, survivors are clearly not considered responsible for the harm they suffered and are involved in developing active strategies for changing their situation. Survivors are given space to control their own healing, even when it involves the desire to reconcile with the offender. The importance of human relationships is central, and the building of com-

> *All the efforts at restoration and healing will be piecemeal and, I think, ultimately futile if we can't bring ourselves to do the true peace work: the truth-telling. As long as the lies continue, nothing can be resolved.*
>
> —Jensen 2001

munity is the outcome. Communities are expected to provide both the support and enforcement necessary to stop violence and repair harm. It has long been held that community organization and support decrease violence. Conversely, when community is dysfunctional or absent, criminal behavior and victimization increase. The community supports the survivor by acknowledging his or her harm and by offering concrete help or resources. The community can also make an impact on the offender's behavior through social disapproval. This concept should not be confused with "shaming." Most offenders have already been subjected to a lifetime of shame, which has questionable healing value. When strong communities are in place, their involvement can be more appropriate from a cultural, racial, or class perspective. Social disapproval is contextualized within a specific community (for example a tribe) and conveys a community standard.

The practice of peace-building justice is not outcome-driven.[2] It focuses instead on the healing process. Healing for the survivor occurs as a result of storytelling in an environment that both encourages the telling of the story and validates the truth of the survivor's experience. Offenders are supported in their efforts to change. Even though his or her actions may be condemned, the offender is shown that he or she can be welcomed back into the community as someone who is capable of change, someone capable of reestablishing covenant with the community. Perhaps most importantly, practices that function as community builders, bringing disparate sides together, make community healing possible as well. Lastly, healing justice has the likelihood of increasing reports of previously hidden abuse because it offers a flexible spectrum of responses.

In advocating a new justice paradigm, it is easy to become discouraged, because punishment seems so entrenched and revenge is characterized as a natural human response. Philosopher Kathleen Dean Moore says that we respond to wrongdoing by meeting evil with evil—thinking that our job is to create a counterforce to the wrong we have been done. As long as we are committed to such a response, we will be among the creators of evil.

> Another possible response is forgiveness. One of the greatest human capacities is the power to forgive—not to forget, but to renounce resentment and begin the process of healing. It's the only way to triumph over evil. (Jensen 2001)

The most convincing examples of this approach can be found in nature, Moore suggests. Observe the way a formerly polluted river restores itself or the way a landscape that has been decimated by fire comes back to life. Rather than an idealistic dream, this concept, based on forgiveness, is a natural one toward which life forces flow.

Healing justice is a purely extralegal practice when it is at its best. It does not deal with the question of legally defined wrongs, but rather with the impact of harmful behavior on people and communities. It focuses on questions of truth, rather than fact, personal experience rather than legal evidence, and reparation rather than punishment. It is only when healing justice is seen as its own system, not as an add-on to the existing criminal justice system, that it actually works. When it is combined with the existing system, many problems surface.

Problems with Restorative Justice

Restorative justice is about healing the community, restoring harmony, and building peace. The process means that relationships among people must change, resources must change hands, and societal norms must be redefined. Problems occur when those who benefit from the current system recognize that they must give away some of their resources. They attempt to salvage parts of the existing system by implementing the new approach in pieces, jeopardizing the capacity to really heal the community. Advocates of restorative justice must be vigilant to ensure that it is not co-opted by the criminal justice system.

Peace-building justice practices assume that the survivor and offender are emotionally, psychologically, spiritually, and intellectually ready to enter into a healing process with each other. They carry a clear risk of emotional trauma for survivors. Both survivor and offender need to be carefully screened and prepared to enter into the process.

Over the past few years, the restorative justice movement has moved from the periphery of criminal justice practice. This is happening at a time when criminal justice policy is almost uniformly mean spirited. The rapid acceptance of restorative justice parlance belies the failure to implement serious changes in criminal justice practice. Language is being used without any intention of putting into practice the principles it represents. Programs are instituted without the development of the necessary value base. Usually these programs do not work or have disastrous consequences. Examples of this are Victim Impact Panels. Under the name of "reintegrative shaming," these panels often have been used to punish offenders further rather than to provide opportunities for understanding and healing. Restitution is being added on to long prison sentences, resulting in prisoners being released with crippling financial debt. We continue to see alternatives to incarceration appropriated for small-time offenders who would ordinarily not be handled by the criminal justice system, while the number of people in prisons keeps increasing. In Canada, where a form of "restorative justice" is being adopted by the criminal justice system, and lip service to restorative justice ideology is being implemented inside prisons, there is sizable growth in the rate of imprisonment and an intensification of imprisonment. There is great danger that the movement for restorative justice will be discredited by such truncated and often dishonest "reform."

Many poor communities and communities of color see restorative justice as one more thing imposed upon them by middle-class white communities. They are disturbed by white practitioners who go to indigenous communities (Native American or African), become trained in restorative justice practices, and then return to communities of color in the United States and proceed to teach them about themselves. These leaders in communities of color see the restorative justice movement as another wave of cultural imperialism. If restorative justice practices are to be meaningful, the communities that practice them must develop them.

Creating a climate for a sustaining, nourishing, restorative justice practice is extremely labor intensive. It demands unceasing dedication from those involved. Solutions are not reached quickly. Sometimes survivor and offender are engaged in the process for years. The Hollow Water First Nation reports that it often takes up to four years to bring restoration involving sexual abuse and incest to fruition (Hollow Water Report 1995). Restorative justice solutions cannot be supplementary to a bankrupt criminal justice system. They must replace the system from its foundations. They will require a commitment from the whole community to the whole community. Any system that leaves out immigrants, or the "undeserving poor," or people whose lifestyle is disapproved of by some, will not lead to wholeness. In short, there are no easy answers and no quick fixes. Politicians will not be able to provide remedies without a strong commitment and impetus from constituents on the ground.

Examples of Peace-building Justice

Reparations to Japanese Americans

One of the best models for peace-building justice in the twentieth century can be found in the movement for reparations to Japanese Americans interned during World War II. Following the bombing of Pearl Harbor, 125,000 Japanese American citizens were sent by Executive Order #9066 to internment camps, where most remained for more than two years. Many lost money and property in the frantic efforts to pack belongings and comply with the "legal" order. One person who refused to comply, Fred Korematsu, challenged the legality of the order in court. He lost his case when it came before the U.S. Supreme Court in 1944, and he was incarcerated for his defiance. In 1983, the case was reopened on the grounds that the withholding of evidence had resulted in an unjust decision. Although the government offered to pardon Mr. Korematsu rather than reopening the case, he refused to accept the offer on the grounds, "We should be the ones pardoning the government" (Alonso 1998, 87).

The reconsideration of the Korematsu case may have set the stage for reparations legislation. The judge, in upholding the claim, said that the true value of the case was as a warning for times of war: "During such periods, we must always to be especially careful to protect our constitutional rights" (Alonso 1998, 95).

In 1948, Congress passed the Japanese-American Evacuation Claims Act. Those who had been interned could file claims for money or property lost. Claims for property loss were hard to prove, however, and much documentation was lost. Out of 26,000 claims filed, only 232 were settled. Other steps toward redressing the wrongs committed against Japanese Americans followed slowly.

In 1971, President Nixon signed a law requiring that in the future such an action could not be taken by executive order, but would require congressional action. In 1976, President Ford signed a law repealing the provisions of Executive Order #9066, even though it had long since gone out of use. At the same time, Ford admitted that the government had made a mistake, an essential step toward true reconciliation.

Finally, in 1988, a reparations bill was signed, granting $20,000 in tax-free money to each prisoner of the camps who was still alive at the time the bill was signed. It would be two more years before actual payments were made. A total of 60,000 people qualified.

There is a difference between reparations for wrongs done to a people and compensation for financial losses. Clearly, financial losses should be redressed. But it is rare that the government accepts responsibility for mistakes that it has made, apologizes, and makes amends. The passage and implementation of the Japanese-American reparations bill sets the stage for other types of peace-building actions, where the community owns up to its responsibilities for wrongdoing and takes steps to repay survivors. African Americans are stepping up and demanding that similar steps be taken to redress the horrors of slavery. Although there are complex issues to sort out, there are real opportunities for healing deep wounds of racism and injustice.

To some people the concept of reparations may appear remote to the wounds of traditional street crime. But it is important to continually remind ourselves that "crime" is too often confined to individual occurrences when the greatest harms are frequently collective. It is also essential to be students of successful attempts at systemic reparations in order to fully understand systemic causes of crime.

The Sentencing Circle—Community Healing Process

The Hollow Water First Nations in Canada began developing the Community Holistic Circle Healing (CHCH) when they realized that sexual victimization was at the core of many of the community's problems. They began to develop a healing process based on traditional principles used to deal with conflict: bring it out into the open, protect the survivor and minimally disrupt the functioning of the family and community, hold the offender accountable for his or her behavior, and offer the opportunity for balance to be restored to all parties.

Prior to the development of this process, community leaders had attempted to cooperate with the court system to reach equitable solutions to problems. The legal system was a partisan system, however, and each side had its own agenda, which prevented a healing process from taking place. The end of the process was the punishment of the offender. The CHCH developed sentencing circles, which had two primary purposes: (1) to promote community healing by providing a forum for the community to address the parties of the victimization, and (2) to allow the court to hear directly from the people most affected by the pain of the victimization.

Sentencing circles occur inside court buildings and include the survivor, offender, support people and family members of each, other community members, and court officials. The support people usually include a psychologist for each of the primary parties. Court officials often include a judge, prosecutor, defense lawyer, and police officer.

A number of practices traditional to First Nations people are incorporated into the preparation and carrying out of the circles, including offering tobacco, a pipe ceremony, smudging of the court building (ritualistic burning of herbs or incense), placement of the community drum and eagle staff in the courtroom, serving food to participants from outside the community, opportunity for a sweat lodge ceremony, personal smudges, and opening and closing prayers. A specific seating arrangement around the circle is maintained. The inner circle is made up of people who wish to speak as part of the process, and the outer circle includes observers and listeners. A series of questions are asked, beginning with, "Why did you come today?" Everyone around the circle has an opportunity to answer in order. In the second round, participants speak to the survivor. In the third round they speak to the offender and tell how the incident affected individuals, families, and the community. In the fourth round, participants make suggestions about how to restore balance to the community. In the end, the judge gives a decision concerning sentencing, and closing prayers are offered. Participants are invited to stay and use the circle for sharing and debriefing if they wish.

The sentencing circles are supplemented by circles that continue to work with both the survivor and the offender over a period of months, and often years. It is understood that sentencing is only one step in the healing process. But by combining people most directly affected by the incident with community members and representatives of the court system, the needs of all parties are addressed. The offender is both held accountable and supported to make any necessary changes. The Attorney General's Department and the Federal Justice Department support the process, after working with it over time (Hollow Water Report 1995).

AFSC-Sponsored Dialogue

Over the years, many AFSC programs have participated in or initiated efforts that constitute peace-building justice. One example in the Pacific Mountain Region was the "community conversations" AFSC facilitated among survivors, family members, and former prisoners. The backdrop of these conversations was an interactive art installation by artist Richard Kamler, who constructed the "Table of Voices." The table mimicked a prison visiting-room table, with glass down the center and telephones on either side. In an actual visiting room, prisoners would be "visiting" with family or friends on either side of this table, through the telephones. In the art piece, visitors to the exhibit picked up telephones on one side of the table and heard a victim's family member tell the story of the crime that affected their family and the loss they were experiencing. When visitors picked up the phones on the other side of the table, they heard a perpetrator's story. Kamler, partly inspired by reading Sister Helen Prejean's book, *Dead Man Walking*, collected these stories over many months.

One of the most controversial aspects of the exhibit was the prisoner and victim "paraphernalia" displayed on the walls around the table. A five-year old child's handprint, submitted by the victim's family, looked very similar to a handprint submitted by the perpetrator's family. Baseball uniforms, rock collections, graduation photos, and letters from summer camp were also similar. Some victims' families did not want their mementos displayed next to those of perpetrators, even though the perpetrators were not involved in the same crime.

The AFSC hosted community conversations alongside the art installation. These consisted of panel discussions among victims' family members, perpetrators, and prisoner family members. One conversation was held on December 14, 1996, which would have been Frankie Mills's birthday. His mother, the Reverend Clara Mills, spent the day instead telling the audience at the exhibit about the drive-by shooting that killed Frankie in 1991. Frankie had come home safely from the Gulf War just a few weeks earlier. Reverend Clara reminded the audience that "the other kind of violence is a system that oppresses some people while clearing the way for others to succeed. There's the violence of neglect that emanates from people in positions of social and political power who do not understand that to whom much has been given, much will be required. It's essentially a spiritual problem. It's not about putting prayer back in schools, but of finding a spiritual center, spiritual renewal, and commitment" (Trowbridge 1997).

Community Problem Solving

Since 1998, AFSC has been working with the Newark-based "Boycott Crime Coalition." The coalition is spearheaded by Women in Support of the Million Man March (WISOMMM), in an effort to address the multi-facets of crime. The coalition primarily consists of WISOMMM; AFSC; Black Cops Against Police Brutality; Muslim, Inc.; and Allegheny East Prison Ministry Federation of Seventh-Day Adventists. This is a unique mosaic of groups committed to taking back definitions of crime and what the community response to crime needs to be. In their public forums, the coalition has openly called for the acknowledgment and cessation of the crimes of the New Jersey Department of Corrections—racism, harassment, and brutality inside the prisons. In these quarterly forums that include members of the Department of Corrections, legislators, human-rights activists, ex-prisoners, and family members, testimony is taken about prison conditions.

In May 2002, a forum on gangs focused on the Department of Corrections' definition of what constituted a gang, which varied markedly from the definition offered by participants. Family members expressed grave concern about their children being drawn into gang life and discussed how to meet the needs of their young people to "belong." The law enforcement definition of gangs as "security-threat groups" was threatening to children, family members, and prisoners in New Jersey. The Boycott Crime Coalition sought to develop ways to assist street organizations to use their considerable organization skills for the betterment of the community at large. A number of "gang members"—including members of the New Black Panther Party, which was labeled as a "security-threat group" and targeted by local law enforcement—participated in the forum.

Testimony by AFSC at the forum addressed the implications of gang policies.

> It is time to take the issue of gangs and so-called "security-threat groups" out of the hands of the authorities. We need to own the community dialogue and we need to own what is happening and find ways to stop it. We have to be watchful that "gangs" or "security threat groups" don't become another code word for domestic terrorism. Most of all we need to redirect the dollars going into prisons that belong in our communities. We need to remember that the Department of Corrections isn't only a set of institutions, it is also a state of mind.

Although these examples are inspiring, they are not a "quick fix" to the broken criminal justice system that is in place. They are not yet a new paradigm, because they are the exception and not the rule. If anything, they highlight the labor-intensive nature of such a paradigm shift. But they each contain essential elements that healing justice requires, and they begin to take steps in the direction we need to go.

AFSC's Twelve-point Plan

If prison abolition is the goal, what interim steps can be taken to responsibly move the culture in that direction? Frequently, incremental or partial solutions are co-opted by the forces that would perpetuate the existing system or have a stake in the existing system. When groups such as AFSC began calling for an end to the indeterminate sentence, conservative interests twisted the call into a strategy for lengthening, rather than shortening, sentences. This didn't change the reality that indeterminacy was and is grossly unjust to those who are subjected to it. Restoring indeterminacy would not roll back sentences now. But groups concerned with social justice must be highly critical of advocating change that falls short of the ultimate goal.

Advocates must establish principles against which incremental solutions can be tested. The first such principle would be to "do no harm." Interim steps must not, for example, create longer sentences for the purpose of rehabilitating people. They must not address a population that would not otherwise have come into the prison system. They must not expand abusive authority with the hope of producing some illusory good.

The second principle would be to examine the proposed incremental step to see if it genuinely moves in the direction of dismantling the system, rather than bolstering it. In recent years, restorative justice has become a popular add-on to the system in many jurisdictions, rather than a replacement for it. People may end up paying restitution to survivors in addition to serving a prison sentence, resulting in a new kind of debtor's prison.

The positive principles we see would be for greater fairness, more democratic processes, more individual autonomy, and greater overall social and economic justice. This would necessarily mean that the community as a whole takes responsibility for the health and well-being of all of its people, including responsibility for the brokenness of the economic system and the extent to which that contributes to injustice. It is all too easy to delegate responsibility for complex social problems to the police or to some other designated authority rather than to undertake the hard work ourselves.

We recommend the following steps be taken. Some are large and some are small. None should exacerbate the deficits of the existing system.

1. Penal Abolition

> The spirit of the LORD God is upon me,
>> because the LORD has anointed me;
> he has sent me to bring good news to the oppressed,
>> to bind up the brokenhearted,
> to proclaim liberty to the captives,
>> and release to the prisoners. (Isaiah 61:1)

Visions of a new social order can come from many sources, as old as Hebrew Scripture or as recent as the restorative justice movement. Building on the 1978 minute of the AFSC national board, which called for prison abolition, the Criminal Justice Task Force now joins with an increasing number of other national and international organizations (for example, International Conference on Penal Abolition, and Critical Resistance) calling for penal abolition. The critique offered in this document clearly demonstrates that the entire apparatus has punishment, revenge, and violence at its core. A new justice paradigm must replace this.

At the same time, good arguments can be made for sticking with prison abolition as the more radical stance, because it would preclude any use of separation or isolation as a sanction. Penal abolition, while challenging the violence of the entire legal apparatus, could permit selective, short-term incarceration in a narrow number of cases for the purpose of treatment or incapacitation. At the same time, it would clearly address the root of the problem: the coercive and violent reality of punishment, which is the linchpin of the retributive justice system, as well as the racial and economic incentives that drive it. By advocating a new justice paradigm, we necessarily address the whole existing framework. Perhaps the most important contribution, from an organization that has addressed these issues throughout its eighty-plus year history, is to raise questions, draw distinctions, and define terms in a way that deepens the discussion. Ultimately, however, fundamental change is required.

The AFSC Criminal Justice Task Force will continue to push for a moratorium on all prison construction, abolition of the death penalty, and the abolition of the mandatory sentence of life without the possibility of parole. It is tempting to separate abolition of the death penalty from penal abolition, but because the death penalty is the centerpiece of our punishment system, work to abolish it must be understood within the context of the penal system as a whole. Often groups that work exclusively on the death penalty advocate life sentences without the possibility of parole, without recognizing the long-term consequences of such a position. Seeing the issues as integrated parts of a whole is crucial. The system as we know it is evil.

2. DECRIMINALIZATION

The first step toward penal abolition is to decrease our dependency on incarceration as the panacea for all social problems. The AFSC criminal justice programs have called for decriminalization of a broad range of conditions currently handled by the criminal justice system (AFSC 1978, 8). These include mental illness, homelessness, drug use, sodomy, and same-sex sexual relations. The United States could move a long way toward decriminalization if it had universal health care and could rely on the health-care system to address problems.

Drug and alcohol dependency are too often handled as a criminal matter, and this is largely responsible for the burgeoning prison population. Although not all communities that AFSC works with would support legalization of controlled substances, decriminalization of possession and use of these substances is a first step toward individual and community health.

Funds must be redirected to nonprofit, community-based, voluntary drug treatment programs. The profit motive must be removed from drug trafficking in order to prevent commercial opportunists from preying on vulnerable populations. (We need only look at the tobacco industry to trace the ways an addiction can be encouraged for the sake of the bottom line.) As a first step, first- and second-time drug users must be redirected to community programs. Treatment, for those who seek it, must be available through all health insurance and prepaid health programs.

With regard to mentally ill offenders, significant decriminalization can occur if treatment for mental illness, in both residential and outpatient settings, is available to all who seek it. Assertive community outreach is a necessary component to making services available to those who need it. We have not found involuntary "treatment" to be nearly as effective, and we oppose measures that create involuntary methods of delivering services when voluntary services continue to be underfunded. The recent trend toward establishing mental health courts, which in practice tend to decriminalize mental illness, offers a positive move in the right direction.

For all those who find themselves in prison, we call for a full range of educational, employment, and health-care services. This is especially important for physically disabled prisoners, who may have special needs, and who are entitled to the same opportunities provided other prisoners. Similarly, mentally ill prisoners are entitled to treatment and must be protected from dangerous and abusive settings, such as security housing units. The AFSC is actively involved in monitoring prisons' compliance with the Americans for Disabilities Act and other legislation that guarantees rights to the disabled. However, our position remains clear: prison is no place for people who are disabled.

3. Elimination of Solitary Confinement

The AFSC Criminal Justice Task Force calls for the immediate end to the use of solitary confinement for extended periods, and to the building of control units. From the time of the first penitentiary, the torture connected with such confinement has been well established.

> I hold this slow and daily tampering with the mysteries of the brain to be immeasurably worse than any torture of the body; and because its ghastly signs and tokens are not so palpable to the eye and sense of touch as scars upon the flesh, because its wounds are not on the surface, and it extorts few cries that human ears can hear; therefore I denounce it as a secret punishment which slumbering humanity is not roused to stay. (Dickens 1996, 59)

The AFSC criminal justice programs across the country will lead efforts to call attention to the proliferation of solitary confinement, actual conditions associated with it, and the need for wholesale rejection of this dangerous trend. Included in these efforts will be public education, mobilization, and focus on incremental steps such as due process for prisoners sent to security housing units, monitoring of the treatment of mentally ill prisoners held in high security, and enforcement of consent decrees impacting conditions in these units.

4. Work Inside as Long as Necessary

I was in prison and you came to me.

—Matthew 25:37

As long as prisons exist, AFSC must continue to work in solidarity with the imprisoned, the survivors, and the family members. We also cannot turn our backs on guards, judges, police officers, or anyone struggling within the system—though we must always be truthful about the injustices we witness. In order to be able to speak authentically in our advocacy work, and to guard against becoming overly theoretical or abstract, we must be in relationship with the communities most affected by the criminal justice system.

Theologian Walter Wink, speaking at Friends General Conference in July 2002, said, "People of faith ought to be living the kingdom right now 'inside the shell of the old regime.'" Throughout the history of the U.S. prison system, many Quakers have pioneered programs inside and outside to alleviate the suffering created by them and to practice positive forms of rehabilitation. Racial, cultural, and class discrimination are not inherent in the concept of rehabilitation. However, the distortions of the use of rehabilitation have been more the norm than the exception. The AFSC Criminal Justice Task Force will continue to support positive, empowering programs which give prisoners options, skills, and relationships that will enable success upon release, while in all cases preferring programs to be made available in the community. Staff members who put their clients' needs ahead of the drive to punish or exploit should be supported.

> *All living things are sacred. Punishment is no solution, putting people in cages is no solution. These things happen because of fear. We believe in taking care of each other in a human way, with compassion.*
>
> —Jun Yasuda, Buddhist nun, initiator of Prison Dharma Walk

5. CITIZEN REVIEW

The AFSC continues to support vigorous monitoring of criminal justice systems, as well as of community-based programs. Independent citizen review processes need to be in place to oversee police work, all locked facilities, and community-based programs using public funds. Independent review boards must reflect the communities they serve, including ex-prisoners and family members. They must be free from conflicts of interest with the agencies they are reviewing, be adequately funded and staffed, and have power to subpoena information as well as enforcement power. Prisoners must have access to oversight boards without risk of reprisal. Reports of citizen review boards must be made public.

The AFSC has seen review boards and "special masters" (who oversee implementation of court decisions) compromised time and time again by institutional manipulation. Ultimate authority to act on recommendations is often given, for example, to the police chief, who sees the welfare of his/her department as more important than accountability for a particular officer. Often a board is given investigatory power but no staff. In Oakland, California, the effectiveness of the police commission is compromised by a clause in the union contract that requires police to appear at commission hearings only 60 percent of the time—enabling police to abstain from participation when they are particularly culpable.

Special masters, appointed by a court, may face a wall of noncooperation unless they come from within the ranks of law enforcement. Such "credentials" usually compromise independence and prejudice fair outcomes.

6. PRISONERS' BILL OF RIGHTS

Although prisons even with rights would still be punitive, we feel strongly that the Bill of Rights for Prisoners offers a method of working for change in the justice system that would begin to lessen the human costs of penal coercion. The movement for prisoners' rights runs directly counter to the growth of unfettered discretionary powers; it calls for shifting power from administrators towards those who are on the receiving end.

—AFSC 1971, 169

Following the publication of *Struggle for Justice,* some states did enact different versions of a "Bill of Rights," but most have been repealed at this writing. What remains is considered "civil death." Only constitutional rights are retained, and those can only be guaranteed through lengthy court battles. The AFSC again calls for a Prisoners' Bill of Rights that would guarantee that a person whose freedom was taken away would still retain full due-process and legal rights, as well as recognition of his or her basic human rights.

Many of the rights required by prisoners are those affecting imprisonment itself, such as the rights to receive mail, visit with friends and family, have access to a law library, and have procedural due process in disciplinary hearings. Other rights are seriously curtailed by imprisonment, such as freedom to worship in the church/synagogue/mosque/temple of one's choice; or the rights to health care, psychiatric care, dental care, and prescription medications. Prisoners should have the rights to sign contracts, marry, and inherit property. If democratic processes are important to us as a culture, prisoners should retain the right to vote. In all cases, prisoners have the right to be free from retaliation for exercising these rights and must have the unrestricted ability—including state-paid, competent, appointed counsel—to petition for redress of grievances.

The prison should bear the burden of proving why any of these rights cannot be granted based on a compelling state interest. Such is the standard established in the Religious Freedom Restoration Act. It is not a sure test, because prisons, like the military, have a tendency to justify almost all their actions on "security" grounds. "Security" has kept families apart, restricted spiritual directors from ministering to condemned prisoners, limited telephone calls, and required certain haircuts. The real goal must be full human rights—that is, the right of each of us to be fully human.

7. Rights upon Release

The problems with the parole system do not lend themselves to easy solutions. Abolishing all parole boards immediately is an attractive option, but it could be difficult to determine a fair method for converting the indeterminate sentences of those already in the system to determinate ones. Furthermore, given current punitive attitudes, merely implementing definite sentences is not guaranteed to create a more humane and effective criminal justice system. In addition, most prisoners continue to favor the concept of parole. Given that parole boards will continue to wield great power over the lives of prisoners and their families in the foreseeable future, AFSC criminal justice staff favors several specific changes that would at least start the movement toward a more just system:

- Parole boards should not be permitted to use hearsay evidence, arrest records, and charges that did not lead to convictions in their deliberations.

- People should not be returned to prison for technical parole violations. Parolees found guilty of technical violations should be subject to sanctions in the community rather than being reincarcerated.

- Parolees' free speech should not be curtailed as a condition of parole.

- Support services should be equally available to all persons leaving prison. Participation in these programs should not be coerced or mandated.

- Parole officers' main function should be to help parolees in their transition rather than to monitor and enforce parole rules, and their caseloads should be much smaller than current practice. Intensive supervision parole programs, staffed by social workers—many of whom develop caring relationships with parolees and facilitate multidisciplinary interventions based on the needs of the parolees—should be available for released prisoners needing special assistance in making the transition.

- Even if a person on parole is charged with a crime, he or she must have a trial, with full due process, before being sent back to prison.

Survivors should not be permitted to testify at any parole hearings, and survivors should not be appointed to the parole board simply because they are survivors. The purpose of this recommendation is not to silence survivors. On the contrary, survivors must be encouraged to tell their stories and grieve their losses. Opportunities to do this must be established. However, parole hearings should focus on the future, not on the original crime.

8. AMEND THE THIRTEENTH AMENDMENT OF THE U.S. CONSTITUTION

The AFSC National Board also calls for revision of the Thirteenth Amendment to the U.S. Constitution, which reads:

> Neither slavery nor involuntary servitude, *except as a punishment for crime whereof the party shall have been duly convicted* shall exist within the United States, or any place subject to their jurisdiction. (Emphasis added.)

The exception clause should be deleted so that the Thirteenth Amendment prohibits all slavery and involuntary servitude within the United States and its jurisdictions. Work may be seen by some as a legitimate sanction—a way for people to "give back" if they have caused harm. However, permitting slavery as an exception to the Thirteenth

Amendment makes the prison system the direct heir to the chattel system. The fact that the United States incarcerates people of color at an alarmingly higher rate than whites makes this heritage all too clear. Rather than legitimizing a permanent underclass, the Constitution should establish minimum standards for everyone, consistently.

Similarly, the AFSC Criminal Justice Task Force calls for the end of the disenfranchisement of released prisoners. Many states permanently bar anyone convicted of a felony from voting. Other states allow ex-prisoners to vote under certain circumstances—for instance, once they have completed parole, and if they have not committed an offense that involved voter fraud. The core of democratic principles is violated, however, when any population is prevented from full participation. If the goal is wholeness, for both individuals and the community, we must be prepared to bring people to the table where their contributions are honored.

9. Implementation of International Law

The Charter of the United Nations is based on the principles of the dignity and equality inherent in all human beings, and that all Member States have pledged themselves to take joint and separate action, in cooperation with the Organization, for the achievement of one of the purposes of the United Nations, which is to promote and encourage universal respect for and observance of human rights and fundamental freedoms for all, without distinction as to race, sex, language or religion.

—International Convention on the Elimination
of All Forms of Racial Discrimination

United States laws and court processes have not provided adequate protection against cruel and unusual punishment, torture, human rights abuses, or abuses of political rights. Increasingly, the AFSC is turning to United Nations instruments to challenge prison practices and conditions. The three instruments that the United States has signed and is a party to are the International Covenant of Civil and Political Rights; the Convention on the Elimination of All Forms of Racial Discrimination; and the Convention Against Torture and Other Cruel, Inhuman, or Degrading Treatment or Punishment.

The AFSC offices in Newark, New Jersey, and Oakland, California, have documented violations of specific provisions of all three treaties and forwarded the information to the appropriate U.N. committees. Education and dissemination of information about treaty compliance are an integral part of enforcement. Although the U.S. courts often do not recognize the authority of international law, we believe that these instruments and tribunals are essential to world peace and justice.

In addition to these valuable documentation and education efforts, advocates of social justice must mount an active campaign for the United States' ratification of the United Nations Convention on the Rights of the Child. The United States is one of only two countries (Somalia is the other) that have not ratified this convention. One provision that has heretofore inhibited ratification is the prohibition against execution of any person who committed the crime before the age of eighteen. Yet, there are a number of other provisions that would guarantee rights to children that are not protected by law or practice within the United States.

10. LET CHILDREN BE CHILDREN

The idea that youthful offenders should be treated differently from adults is more than one hundred years old and is based on the scientific knowledge that children are developmentally different from adults. It is now known that the brain is not fully developed in human beings until they reach their early twenties. Youth should not be tried and punished as adults if they are not fully capable of making mature decisions. The AFSC Criminal Justice Task Force vigorously opposes recent changes in laws across the country that treat juveniles as if they were adults.

Neither can we embrace "zero tolerance" policies where children are concerned. Children sometimes learn by making mistakes. If their mistakes are punished with permanent sanctions—school expulsion, life sentences in prison (even life sentences without the possibility of parole, as are being imposed on children in some jurisdictions)—no room is left for them to change or grow or correct their mistakes.

Instead, we should invest in our children and in our own future. In particular, there is need to fully fund education, from preschool to after-school, to public schools and universities. Children must be cared for in loving environments. Children should be a community priority, not a private matter between individuals.

11. RECLAIMING FAMILIES AND COMMUNITIES

There is no way to move beyond the penal system without serious investment in families and communities. Rather than dismantling welfare programs, the United States should be finding ways to offer families the support they need to become viable. The United States should adequately fund public schools so that children learn in an environment that builds them up and prepares them to be full participants in a democratic society. In order to accomplish this at the level that will be necessary, tax structures cannot favor the wealthy. Rather, they must redistribute wealth to those most in need. Living-wage laws must be passed in every jurisdiction, and a full-scale reexamination of our nation's priorities must begin.

James Gilligan, in his book *Preventing Violence,* demonstrates that western European countries devastated at the end of World War II, as well as Japan, adopted new social policies to recover from the effects of the war and the high homicide rates that preceded the war.

> They all took two steps which have been empirically demonstrated throughout the world to prevent violence. They instituted social democracy (or "welfare states," as they are sometimes called), and achieved an unprecedented decrease in the inequities in wealth and income between the richest and poorest groups in the population, one effect of which is to reduce the frequency of interpersonal or "criminal" violence. And Germany, Japan and Italy adopted political democracy as well, the effect of which is to reduce the frequency of international violence, or warfare (including "war crimes"). While the United States adopted political democracy at its inception, it is the only developed nation on earth that . . . does not provide universal health insurance for all its citizens; it has the highest rate of relative poverty among both children and adults, and largest gap between the rich and the poor, of any of the major economies; . . . Thus it is not surprising that it also has murder rates that have been five to ten times as high as those of any other developed nation, year after year. (Gilligan 2001, 83–84)

Social policies that guarantee a minimum income, as well as provide for basic needs, do not require dramatic sacrifices from even the wealthiest 1 percent of the population. But they will literally save lives, reduce violence, and build community. According to the United Nations Human Development Report of 1998:

It is estimated that the additional cost of achieving and maintaining universal access to basic education for all, basic health care for all, reproductive health care for all women, adequate food for all, and safe water and sanitation for all is roughly $40 billion a year. This is less than 4 percent of the combined wealth of the 225 richest people in the world. (Cited in Gilligan 2001, 82)

12. CAMPAIGN FOR REPARATIONS

One of the best places to start on a road to peace-building justice would be to work for reparations for a wide range of injustices perpetrated, especially against people of color. Whether it addressed the legacy of slavery; the extermination, relocation, and robbery of First Nations people; or any number of other social injustices, such a program would provide a forum for practicing the principles of healing justice, while creatively exploring options for reparations. Because true justice must be placed squarely within a context of social and economic justice, a campaign for reparations could address these issues head on.

An inspiring contemporary example of a process of this kind is currently under way in Greensboro, North Carolina. On November 3, 1979, members of the Ku Klux Klan and American Nazi Party opened fire on a peaceful labor demonstration, comprised largely of African Americans. Five people were killed, ten were wounded, and the police were conspicuously absent. Although four TV crews captured the killings on film, the perpetrators were twice acquitted in criminal court of any wrongdoing. Eventually, in a federal civil suit, Klan members, Nazis, and Greensboro police were found jointly liable for one of the deaths. Although the city paid a $385,000 settlement, it has never apologized or acknowledged any wrongdoing.

In 2004, under the leadership of a number of African American pastors, a commission was appointed to hear testimony about the November 3 incident. The mandate of the commission reads in part: "The passage of time alone cannot bring closure, nor resolve feelings of guilt and lingering trauma for those impacted by the events of November 3rd, 1979. Nor can there be any genuine healing for the city of Greensboro, unless the truth surrounding these events is honestly confronted, the suffering fully acknowledged, accountability established, and forgiveness and reconciliation facilitated." Though local government officials have tried to discredit the commission, it represents a first vital step in healing justice—truth telling. Whether this process leads to public apologies or any form of compensation remains to be seen. At the very least it is empowering participants and establishing an historical record—making it much more difficult for the official record to omit details of this traumatic occurrence.[3]

Reparations must have at their core the concept of self-determination. This is particularly important in addressing such horrific practices as enslavement and racial extermination. How could such wounds be healed? Is there any compensation commensurate with the harm done?

Following the healing-justice principles that survivors must be central to the healing process and that systemic issues must be addressed, real engagement with the concept of reparations could be a significant step. Because healing justice is a process, not a specific solution or outcome, it is difficult to make specific recommendations here. Possible scenarios might include restitution to descendants of slaves or other oppressed peoples, repatriation away from the United States for those who desire it, housing, medical care, job training, culturally centered educational programs, and economic development. To adequately address the harms that have been done, and ongoing white supremacist practices, realistic economic development would have to involve a redistribution of wealth from the top to the bottom.

The practice of building organizational consensus within AFSC is itself a step in the reparations process by openly acknowledging and engaging on some of the deepest wounds the United States faces. This engagement must then be duplicated in the wider public arena as the work moves toward building a national consensus.

Conclusion

While there is a lower class I am in it;
While there is a criminal element I am of it;
While there is a soul in prison I am not free.

—Debs 1983, 48

For AFSC, the criminal justice issue is the domestic equivalent of the international peace issue. Just as Friends have refused to go to war because they believe in that of God in everyone and will not engage in the hatred and demonization that allow killing in wartime, so must we resist the creation of enemies at home.

George Bernard Shaw, in his essay "Imprisonment" (1925), said:

> We must get out of the habit of painting human character in soot and whitewash. . . . From the people who tell white lies about their ages, social positions, and incomes, to those who grind the faces of the poor . . . buy valuable properties from inexperienced owners for a tenth of their value . . . or obtain vast sums on false pretenses held forth by lying advertisements . . . you could at any moment find dozens of people who have never been imprisoned and never will be, and yet are worse citizens than any but the very worst of our convicts. (Shaw 1925, 45–46)

Although we work diligently to remove the injustices that result in crime, we recognize our responsibility to stand with the imprisoned, as well as the survivors of crime, as long as social policy results in their abandonment and isolation. Official sanction of cruelty will not produce positive change in individual lives or in social structures. Official sanction of cruelty is not justice. Rather, it leads to abuse and deeper violence.

As long as prisons exist, it is our duty to shine a critical light on them and to walk with those most affected. As we work for penal abolition, we also work in solidarity with the imprisoned, their families, and survivors. We recognize that we all do harm, and we have all been harmed. In working cooperatively toward justice, we are redefining ourselves within our communities. When the captives are finally set free, we will recognize that we and they are one.

> *Under a government which imprisons any unjustly, the true place for the just man [sic] is also a prison. . . . It is there that the fugitive slave and the Mexican prisoner on parole, and the Indian come to plead the wrongs of his race should find them; on that separate, but more free and honorable ground, where the State places those who are not with her, but against her—the only house in a slave State in which a free man can abide in honor.*
>
> —Henry David Thoreau, cited in Soelle 2001, 264

NOTES

Introduction

1. In this book, the AFSC Criminal Justice Task Force revisits the positions taken in its 1971 publication *Struggle for Justice,* its 1978 *Perspectives on Criminal Justice,* and a number of other AFSC publications (see bibliography).

2. The poor are portrayed by the corporate media, political demagogues, and many in the law enforcement and prosecution arms of our criminal justice system as the cause of most of our crime problems. See Jeffrey Reiman, *The Rich Get Richer and the Poor Get Prison,* 7th edition (Boston: Allyn and Bacon, 2004) for an extended discussion of the way the media and the criminal justice system work to target the poor.

3. Ched Myers, *The Biblical Vision of Sabbath Economics* (Washington, D.C.: The Church of the Savior, 2002), 22. For a fuller treatment of jubilee and Sabbath understandings of justice, especially economic justice, see Richard Lowery, for the Hebrew Bible, *Sabbath and Jubilee* (Atlanta: Chalice, 2000), and Sharon Ringe for the Gospels, *Jesus, Liberation, and the Biblical Jubilee* (Philadelphia: Fortress Press, 1985). In addition, for use in study groups, consult Ross and Gloria Kinsler, *The Biblical Jubilee and the Struggle for Life* (Maryknoll, N.Y.: Orbis, 1999).

Chapter 2

1. Judge Leon Higginbotham, quoted in "Is Yesterday's Racism Relevant to Today's Correction?" Law Enforcement Assistance Administration, *Outside Looking In* (Department of Criminal Justice, April 11, 1970). (As quoted in AFSC, *Struggle for Justice,* 101. Original no longer available.) See also other works by Judge Leon Higginbotham, *In the Matter of Color* (New York: Oxford University Press, 1976), and also a carefully researched and impressively documented book that contains thoughtful sections on the Supreme Court's legitimization of racism, *Shades of Freedom: Racial Politics and Presumptions of the American Legal Process* (New York: Oxford University Press, 1996).

2. For a good overview of the history of the southern convict lease system, see Alex Lichtenstein, *Twice the Work for Free Labor: The Political Economy of Free Labor in the New South* (New York: Verso, 1996).

Chapter 3

1. Since September 11, 2001, racial profiling has been seen as a "necessary" strategy for curbing "terrorism," instead of shocking the public as a blatant form of racism. The United States is rapidly moving toward a new form of apartheid, where legal immigrants will be required to carry papers to show their legitimacy, and constitutional protections will be available only to citizens. Though such racially-driven law enforcement has appeared in the past (for example, toward the Japanese after the bombing of Pearl Harbor), it has usually been more narrowly applied to smaller groups of people. The post-9/11 atmosphere has resulted in racist law enforcement that is much broader in scope and has already led to massive detentions and deportations.

Chapter 4

1. The Sentencing Reform Act of 1984, 18 USC 3551; The Anti-Drug Abuse Act, 1986; Federal Sentencing Guidelines, 1987.

2. Gary Webb, "Dark Alliance: The Story behind the Crack Explosion," *San Jose Mercury News*, August 18–20, 1996. See also http://www.narconews.com/darkalliance/drugs.

3. California Department of Corrections, Data Analysis Unit.

4. Craig Haney, *Death by Design: Capital Punishment as a Social Psychological System* (Oxford, Eng.: Oxford University Press, 2005); Benjamin D. Fleury-Steiner, *Jurors' Stories of Death: How America's Death Penalty Invests in Inequality* (Ann Arbor, Mich.: University of Michigan Press, 2004); Robert L. Young, "Guilty until Proven Innocent: Conviction Orientation, Racial Attitudes, and Support for Capital Punishment," *Deviant Behavior* 25, no. 2 (March-April 2004): 151–67; Center for Jury Studies at the National Center for State Courts in Williamsburg, Va.; Capital Jury Project, Northeastern University, William Bowers et al., http://www.cjp.neu.edu/.

5. See http://www.deathpenaltyinfo.org.

6. For more on this topic, read Joan Petersilia, "When Prisoners Return to the Community: Political, Economic and Social Consequences, Research in Brief, *Sentencing & Corrections: Issues for the 21ˢᵗ Century,* (Washington, D.C.: U.S. Department of Justice, National Institute of Justice, November 2000), NCJ 184253.

7. *Billiteri v. United States Parole Board*, 541 F. 2d 938 (2d Cir. 1976); *Bistram v. United States Parole Board*, 535 F.2d 329 (5th Cir. 1976).

8. See Safer Society Foundation, http://www.safersociety.org/.
9. See R. Karl Hanson et al., *Study in Sexual Abuse: A Journal of Research and Treatment* 14, no. 2 (2002), for a definitive meta-analysis of many studies on the effectiveness of treatment for sex offenders.
10. Intensive Parole for Sex Offenders, a program of the Framingham office of the Parole Board in the Commonwealth of Massachusetts, begun in 1998.
11. Ibid.

Chapter 5

1. In recent years several U.S. Christian denominational bodies have taken a formal position in opposition to private, for-profit prisons and jails. See http://www.flpba.org/private/religion.html for statements by The United Methodist Church, the Presbyterian Church (U.S.A.), and the Catholic Bishops of the South.
2. *Estate of Preston Tate, William Tate, and Vivian Mosely v. James Gomez,* CV-F-95-5239DLB.
3. Many government reports remain unpublished. In this case the New Jersey office of the AFSC obtained a copy of the survey, which documents policies of departments of corrections across the country with regard to gang designations. Too often such reports, gathered at taxpayers' expense, are either classified or suppressed because their content may reflect negatively on a particular administration. Whatever the reason for not publishing this survey, the information gathered is consistent with the experiences AFSC has had in investigating circumstances under which prisoners are assigned to security housing units.
4. See also http://www.stopgatekeeper.org.

Chapter 6

1. OJJDP Statistical Briefing book, February 28, 2005.
2. Children's Defense Fund, 1998. For more information see *Doe v. Burwell,* 537 F. Supp. 186 (S.D. Ohio 1982); *Yellen v. Ada County,* Civil No. 83-1026 (U.S.D.C., D. Idaho 1985); Kristen Del Guzzi, "Prison Security Went Away," *Cincinnati Enquirer,* April 30, 1996, p. B1; Gretchen Schuldt and Mary Beth Murphy, "Suicide Prompts Copycat Attempts," *Milwaukee Journal Sentinel,* May 29, 1997, p. 1.

Chapter 7

1. For the most part this document uses the term *survivor* rather than *victim* in keeping with what we have learned from survivors themselves—that they do not wish to define themselves in terms of victimization. However, there are places where this did not seem appropriate, or where we used "victim/survivor" to denote possible ambiguity.

2. Testimony at a hearing, observed by AFSC Cambridge staff, March 8, 1999.

3. "This Life We Take," pamphlet published by the California Friends Committee on Legislation, 2002.

Chapter 8

1. The most common term for this new form of justice is *restorative justice*. However, the term has already been co-opted and corrupted by some players in the retributive justice field—or restorative justice has been understood too narrowly. This paper will use the terms *peace-building* or *healing* justice interchangeably with *restorative*, understanding them all to represent a new paradigm.

2. Howard Zehr, author of *Changing Lenses* and a pioneer in restorative justice, believes this model of justice is outcome-driven, in the sense that it requires the offender to take responsibility to "make it right"—the outcome should include repentance, some sort of restitution, and changed behavior, perhaps reconciliation. Zehr argues that it is the retributive model of justice that is driven by legalistic procedures rather than by the goals of problem-solving, fairness, and change of behavior.

3. See the Web sites of the Greensboro Truth and Community Reconciliation Project (http://www.gtcrp.org) and the Greensboro Truth and Reconciliation Commission (http://www.greensborotrc.org).

BIBLIOGRAPHY

Abbreviations in brackets indicate how the citation appears in the text. Unless otherwise noted, all Web addresses were accessed and active on January 25, 2006.

Abu-Jamal, Mumia. 2003. *Death Blossoms: Reflections from a Prisoner of Conscience.* Farmington, Pa.: Plough Publishing House.

The Advancement Project and The Civil Rights Project of Harvard University [AP/CRP]. 2000. "Opportunities Suspended: The Devastating Consequences of Zero Tolerance and School Discipline Policies." Cambridge, Mass.: Harvard University. Available online at http://www.civilrightsproject.harvard.edu/research/discipline/opport_suspended.php

Alexander, John. 1980. *Render Them Submissive: Responses to Poverty in Philadelphia, 1760–1800.* Amherst: University of Massachusetts Press.

Alexander, M. A. 1999. "Sexual Offender Treatment Efficacy Revisited." *Sexual Abuse: A Journal of Research and Treatment,* 11, no 2., 101-117.

Allegretto, Sylvia A. 2004. "Economic Snapshots: Social Expenditures and Child Poverty." Washington, D.C.: Economic Policy Institute. Available online at http://www.epi.org/content.cfm/web features_snapshots_06232004.

Alonso, Karen. 1998. *Korematsu v. United States: Japanese-American Internment Camps.* Landmark Supreme Court Cases. Springfield, N.J.: Enslow.

American Friends Service Committee [AFSC]. 1971. *Struggle for Justice: A Report on Crime and Punishment in America.* New York: Hill and Wang.

———. 1978. *Perspectives on Criminal Justice.* Criminal Justice Committee Statement. Philadelphia: AFSC.

———. 1981. *Perspectives on Nonviolence in Relation to Groups Struggling for Social Justice.* Philadelphia: AFSC.

———. 2001. *Torture in U.S. Prisons: Evidence of U.S. Human Rights Violations.* New York Metropolitan Region Criminal Justice Program. New York: AFSC (Fall 2001). Available online at http://www.afsc.org/nymetro/criminalJustice/prisonwatch.htm.

———. 2004. *Beliefs and Practices of the American Friends Service Committee.* Philadelphia: AFSC. Available online at http://www.afsc.org/jobs/aabelief.htm.

Atkins v. Virginia. 536 US 304, June 20, 2002.

Bazelon, Lara. 2000. "Exploding the Superpredator Theory: Why Infancy Is the Preadolescent's Best Defense in Juvenile Court." *New York University Law Review* 75 (1): 159–98.

De Beaumont, Gustave, and Alexis de Tocqueville. 1833. "On the Penitentiary System in the United States and Its Application in France." Available online at http://www.law.du.edu/sterling/content/alh/tocqueville_pen.pdf.

Beck, Allen J. 2000. "Prisoners in 1999." August 2000, NCJ 183476. Washington, D.C.: United States Department of Justice, Office of Justice Programs, Bureau of Justice Statistics Bulletin. Available online at http://www.ojp.usdoj.gov/bjs/abstract/p99.htm.

Beck, Allen J., Jennifer C. Karberg, and Paige M. Harrison. 2002. "Prison and Jail Inmates at Midyear 2001." April 2002, NCJ 191702. Washington, D.C.: United States Department of Justice, Office of Justice Programs, Bureau of Justice Statistics Bulletin. Available online at http://www.ojp.usdoj.gov/bjs/abstract/pjim01.htm.

Becker, Elizabeth. 2001. "As Ex-Theorist on Young 'Superpredators,' Bush Aide Has Regrets." *New York Times*, February 9, 2001, A19.

Bennett, William J., John J. DiIulio, and John P. Walters. 1996. *Body Count: Moral Poverty . . . And How to Win America's War Against Crime and Drugs.* New York: Simon & Schuster.

Bergner, Daniel. 2003. "When Forever Is Far Too Long." *New York Times*, June 17, 2003, A27.

Bureau of Justice Statistics [BJS]. 2002. "What Is the Sequence of Events in the Criminal Justice System?" United States Department of Justice, Office of Justice Programs, Bureau of Justice Statistics, Washington, D.C. Available online at http://www.ojp.usdoj.gov/bjs/flowchart.htm.

Butterfield, Fox. 1995. *All God's Children: The Bosket Family and the American Tradition of Violence.* New York: Knopf.

Callins v. Collins. February 22, 1994. 510 U.S. 1141.

Coyle, Andrew, Allison Campbell, and Rodney Neufeld, eds. 2003. *Capitalist Punishment: Prison Privatization and Human Rights.* Athens, Ga.: Clarity Press.

CURE [Citizens United for the Rehabilitation of Errants]. 1996. Ohio newsletter, "Against All Odds." 11 (2): 1. Available online at http://www.cureohio.org/.

Currie, Elliott. 1998. *Crime and Punishment in America.* New York: Metropolitan Books.

Debs, Eugene V. 1983. *Walls and Bars.* Chicago: Charles H. Kerr.

Defoe, Daniel. 1722 (1991). *Moll Flanders.* New York: Knopf; David Campbell Publishers Ltd.

DeFrances, Carol J. 2001. "State Court Prosecutors in Large Districts, 2001." December 2001, NCJ 191206. Washington, D.C.: United States Department of Justice, Office of Justice Programs, Bureau of Justice Statistics Special Report. Available online at http://www.ojp. usdoj.gov/bjs/abstract/scpld01.htm.

———. 2002. "Prosecutors in State Courts, 2001." May 2002, NCJ 193441. Washington, D.C.: United States Department of Justice, Office of Justice Programs, Bureau of Justice Statistics Bulletin. Available online at http://www.ojp.usdoj.gov/bjs/abstract/psc01.htm.

Dickens, Charles. 1996. *American Notes and Pictures from Italy.* London: Chapman and Hall.

Durose, Matthew R., David J. Levin, and Patrick A. Langan. 2001. "Felony Sentences in State Courts, 1998." October 2001, NCJ 190103. Washington, D.C.: United States Department of Justice, Office of Justice Programs, Bureau of Justice Statistics Bulletin. Available online at http://www.ojp.usdoj.gov/bjs/abstract/fssc98.htm.

Easwaran, Eknath (transl.). 1985. *The Dhammapada.* Petaluma, Calif.: Nilgiri Press.

Feinstein, R., A. Greenblatt, L. Hass, S. Kohn, and J. Rana. 2001. "Justice for All? A Report on Lesbian, Gay, Bisexual, and Transgendered Youth in the New York Juvenile Justice System." New York: Lesbian and Gay Project of the Urban Justice Center.

Fellner, Jamie, and Marc Mauer. 1998. "Losing the Vote: The Impact of Felony Disenfranchisement Laws in the U.S." Washington, D.C.: The Sentencing Project; New York: Human Rights Watch. Available online at http://www.hrw.org/reports98/vote/.

Fins, Deborah. 2004. "Death Row U.S.A.: Summer 2004." A quarterly report by the Criminal Justice Project of the NAACP Legal Defense and Educational Fund, Inc. Available online at http://www.naacpldf. org/content.aspx?article=297.

Flaherty, Michael G. 1980. "An Assessment of the National Incidence of Juvenile Suicide in Adult Jails, Lockups, and Juvenile Detention Centers." Champaign, Ill.: Community Research Forum.

Foucault, Michel. 1995. *Discipline and Punish: The Birth of the Prison.* Trans. Alan Sheridan. New York: Random House.

Friedman, Lawrence. 1993. *Crime and Punishment in American History.* New York: HarperCollins.

Frist, Michael, ed. 1984. *Diagnostic and Statistical Manual of Mental Disorders IV.* Washington, D.C.: American Psychiatric Association.

Gifford, Sidra Lea. 2002. "Justice Expenditure and Employment in the United States, 1999." February 2002, NCJ 191746. Washington, D.C.: United States Department of Justice, Office of Justice Programs, Bureau of Justice Statistics Bulletin. Available online at http://www.ojp.usdoj.gov/bjs/abstract/jeeus99.htm; updated stats are available at http://www.ojp.usdoj.gov/bjs/abstract/jeeus01.htm.

Gilligan, James. 2001. *Preventing Violence.* New York: Thames & Hudson.

Griffith, Lee. 1993. *The Fall of the Prison: Biblical Perspectives on Prison Abolition.* Grand Rapids, Mich.: Wm. B. Eerdmans.

Halifax, Joan. 1993. *The Fruitful Darkness.* San Francisco: HarperSanFrancisco.

Harrison, Paige M., and Allen J. Beck. 2002. "Prisoners in 2001." July 2002, NCJ 195189. Washington, D.C.: United States Department of Justice, Office of Justice Programs, Bureau of Justice Statistics Bulletin. Available online at http://www.ojp.usdoj.gov/bjs/abstract/p01.htm; updated stats are available at http://www.ojp.usdoj.gov/bjs/abstract/p02.htm.

————. 2005. "Prisoners in 2004." October 2005, NCJ 210677. Washington, D.C.: United States Department of Justice, Office of Justice Programs, Bureau of Justice Statistics Bulletin. Available online at http://www.ojp.usdoj.gov/bjs/abstract/p04.htm.

Haverty et al. v. Commissioner of Corrections. 437 Mass. 737, 2002.

Herrera v. Collins. 1993. 506 US 390.

HIV PLUS Magazine. 1999–2000. "HIV in Prison: A Special Report." Issue 6 (December 1999–January 2000). Available online at http://www.aidsinfonyc.org/hivplus/issue6/report/picture.html.

Hollow Water Report. 1995. "Seeds of a Community Healing Process." Appendix 3, Interim Report of the Hollow Water First Nations Community Holistic Circle Healing. Originally published in *Justice as Healing,* Winter 1995. Available online at http://www.usask.ca/nativelaw/publications/jah/seeds.html.

Hood, Roger. 2002. *The Death Penalty: A Worldwide Perspective.* 3rd ed. New York: Oxford University Press.

Horigan, Damien. 1999. "Buddhist Perspectives on the Death Penalty." *Turning Wheel* (Winter): 16–19.

Human Rights Watch [HRW]. 2000. "Out of Sight: Super-Maximum Security Confinement in the United States." New York: Human

Rights Watch. Available online at http://www.hrw.org/reports/2000/supermax/.

———. 2001. "No Escape: Male Rape in U.S. Prisons." New York: Human Rights Watch. Available online at http://www.hrw.org/reports/2001/prison/report.html.

Immarigeon, Russ. 1999. "Restorative Justice, Juvenile Offenders and Crime Victims: A Review of the Literature." In *Restorative Juvenile Justice: Repairing the Harm of Youth Crime*, ed. Gordon Bazemore and Lode Walgrave. Monsey, N.Y.: Criminal Justice Press.

Jensen, Derrick. 2001. "A Weakened World Cannot Forgive Us: An Interview with Kathleen Dean Moore." *The Sun Magazine*. March 2001. Available online at http://www.thesunmagazine.org/dean-moore.html.

Juvenile Justice Project of Louisiana [JJPL]. 2004. "And Justice for Some." Available online at http://www.jjpl.org/Publications_JJ_InTheNews/JuvenileJusticeSpecialReports/BBY/justiceforsome/jfs.pdf.

Kairos Theologians. 1986. *Kairos Document: Challenge to the Church, A Theological Comment on the Political Crisis in South Africa*. Grand Rapids, Mich.: Wm. B. Eerdmans.

Kassel, Phillip. 1998. "The Gang Crackdown in Massachusetts' Prisons: Arbitrary and Harsh Treatment Can Only Make Matters Worse." *New England Journal of Criminal and Civil Confinement* 24 (37): 40.

Kerness, Bonnie. 1996. "History of Control Units." Northeast Regional Hearings on Control Units, April 27, 1996. Available online at http://www.afsc.org/nymetro/criminalJustice/resources/CJhistoryCU19960427.pdf.

Kicenski, Karyl K. 2002. "The Corporate Prison: The Production of Crime and the Sale of Discipline: A Proposal to Study the Drive to Privatize the Prison System in the State of California." Available online at http://www.csun.edu/~hfspc002/karyl.prison.pdf.

Knight, Barbara B. 1984. "Religion in Prison: Balancing the Free Exercise, No Establishment and Equal Protection Clauses." *Journal of Church and State* 26:437–54.

Krog, Antjie. 1999. *Country of My Skull: Guilt, Sorrow, and the Limits of Forgiveness in the New South Africa*. New York: Three Rivers Press.

Lichtenstein, Alex, and Michael Kroll. 1990. *The Fortress Economy: The Economic Role of the U.S. Prison System*. Philadelphia: American Friends Service Committee.

LIS, Inc. February 2002. "Services for Families of Prison Inmates, Special Issue in Corrections." Longmont, Colo.: National Institute of Corrections, U.S. Department of Justice.

Logan, Enid. 1999. "The Wrong Race, Committing Crime, Doing Drugs, and Maladjusted for Motherhood: The Nation's Fury over 'Crack Babies.'" *Social Justice* 26 (1):115–38.

Mackey, Virginia. 1981. *Punishment in the Scriptures and Traditions of Judaism, Christianity, and Islam.* A paper presented to the national religious leaders consultation on criminal justice, convened by the National Council on Crime and Delinquency, Claremont, Calif.

Magnani, Laura. 1990. *America's First Penitentiary: A Two Hundred Year Old Failure.* San Francisco: American Friends Service Committee.

Malone, Kobutsu. 2000. "On Punishment." Available online at http://www.engaged-zen.org/articles/Kobutsu-Punish.html.

Maruschak, Laura. 2005. "HIV in Prisons, 2003." September 2005, NCJ 210344. Washington, D.C.: United States Department of Justice, Office of Justice Programs, Bureau of Justice Statistics Bulletin. Available online at http://www.ojp.usdoj.gov/bjs/pub/pdf/hivp03.pdf.

Mennonite Central Committee [MCC]. 2003. "MCC Washington Office Guide to Juvenile Justice." Available online at http://www.mcc.org/us/washington/juvenilejustice_guide.pdf.

Mohr, Renate. 1987. "A Feminist's Analysis of the Objectives and Alternatives Regarding Punishment." Unpublished paper presented to the Conference on Feminist Perspectives on Criminal Law Reform. Ottawa: Canada. The quotation is from Howard Zehr, *Changing Lenses* (Scottdale, Pa.: Herald Press, 1990), 74n6.

Moynihan, Daniel Patrick. 1965. "The Negro Family: The Case for National Action." Washington, D.C.: Office of Policy Planning and Research, United States Department of Labor. Available online at http://www.dol.gov/asp/programs/history/webid-meynihan.htm.

National Center on Institutions and Alternatives [NCIA]. 2004. "What Every American Should Know about the Criminal Justice System." Available online at http://web.archive.org/web/20030218060503/http://www.ncianet.org/ncia/facts.html.

National Institute of Corrections [NIC]. 1991. "Management Strategies in Disturbances and with Gangs/Disruptive Groups." Washington, D.C.: U.S. Department of Justice. Available online at http://www.nicic.org/Library/016993.

National Interreligious Task Force on Criminal Justice [NITFCJ]. 1980. Consensus Paper. Unpublished.

National Survey Results. 1997. "Security Threat Groups in Prison." Washington, D.C.: U.S. Department of Justice, Bureau of Justice Assistance.

Nicholl, Caroline G. 1999. "Community Policing, Community Justice, and Restorative Justice: Exploring the Links for the Delivery of a Balanced Approach to Public Safety." Washington, D.C.: U.S. Department of Justice, Office of Community Oriented Policing Services. Available online at http://www.cops.usdoj.gov/default. asp?Item=290.

Owen, Barbara, and Barbara Bloom. 1995. "Profiling the Needs of California's Female Prisoners–A Needs Assessment." Washington, D.C.: U.S. Department of Justice, National Institute of Corrections. Available online at http://www.nicic.org/Library/012451.

Parenti, Christian. 2000. *Lockdown America: Police and Prisons in the Age of Crisis*. New York: Verso.

Pastore, Ann, and Kathleen Maguire. 2002. *Sourcebook of Criminal Justice Statistics 2001*. Washington, D.C.: U.S. Department of Justice, Office of Justice Programs, Bureau of Justice Statistics.

Pranis, Kay, Barry Sutart, and Mark Wedge. 2003. *Peacemaking Circles: From Crime to Community*. St. Paul: Living Justice Press.

Prison Policy Initiative [PPI]. 2004. "U.S. Incarceration Rates by Race." Available online at http://www.prisonpolicy.org/graphs/raceinc. shtml.

Reiman, Jeffrey. 2004. *The Rich Get Richer and the Poor Get Prison: Ideology Class, and Criminal Justice*. 7th ed. Boston: Allyn and Bacon.

Rennison, Callie Marie. 2002. "Criminal Victimization 2001: Changes 2000–2001 with Trends 1993–2001." September 2002, NCJ 194610. Washington, D.C.: U.S. Department of Justice, Office of Justice Programs, Bureau of Justice Statistics, National Crime Victimization Survey. Available online at http://www.ojp.usdoj.gov/ bjs/abstract/cv01.htm.

Richardson, Don, et al. 2001. "California Mental Health Master Plan." Sacramento: AB 904 Planning Council.

Roper v. Simmons. 543 US 551, March 1, 2005.

Rothman, David. 1971. *The Discovery of the Asylum: Social Order and Disorder in the New Republic*. Boston: Little, Brown.

Russell, Marta, and Jean Stewart. 2001. "Disablement, Prison, and Historical Segregation." *Monthly Review* 53 (3): 61.

Schiraldi, Vincent. 1999. "Testimony of Vincent Schiraldi Executive Director Center on Juvenile and Criminal Justice before the Committee on Education and the Workforce's Subcommittee on Early Childhood, Youth, and Families." Available online at http:// edworkforce.house.gov/hearings/106th/ecyf/juv31899/schiraldi.htm.

Seiber, Lones B. Jr. 1984. "Churches Without God." *Liberty*, 8-10.

Sentencing Project. 2002. "Prison Privatization and the Use of Incarceration." Washington, D.C.: The Sentencing Project. Available online at http://www.sentencingproject.org/pubs_02.cfm.

———. 2005. "Incarceration and Crime: A Complex Relationship." Washington, D.C.: The Sentencing Project. Available online at http://www.sentencingproject.org/pubs_06.cfm.

Shaw, George Bernard. 1925. *Imprisonment*. New York: Brentanos.

Shepherd, Robert E., Jr. 2000. "Sentencing a Child for Murder in a 'Get Tough' Era." *Criminal Justice Magazine* 15 (1). Available online at http://www.abanet.org/crimjust/juvjus/cjmag/15-1shep.html.

Sherman, Arloc. 1997. *Poverty Matters: The Cost of Child Poverty in America*. Washington, D.C.: Children's Defense Fund.

Singleton, Laura, and Heather Boushey. 2002. "Economic Snapshots: Bringing the Jobs Back Home to Prisons." Washington, D.C.: Economic Policy Institute. Available online at http://www.epinet.org/content.cfm/webfeatures_snapshots_archive_2002_0821_snap08212002.

Snell, Tracy L., and Laura M. Maruschak. 2002. "Capital Punishment 2001." December 2002, NCJ 197020. Washington, D.C.: U.S. Department of Justice, Bureau of Justice Statistics, Bulletin. Available online at http://www.ojp.usdoj.gov/bjs/abstract/cp01.htm.

Soelle, Dorothee. 2001. *The Silent Cry: Mysticism and Resistance*. Minneapolis: Fortress Press.

Stahl, Anne L. 1999. "Delinquency Cases in Juvenile Courts, 1996." OJJDP Fact Sheet #109. Washington, D.C.: U.S. Department of Justice, Office of Justice Programs, Office of Juvenile Justice and Delinquency Prevention. Available online at http://www.ncjrs.gov/txtfiles1/fs99109.txt.

Sterling, Eric E. 1999. "The War on Drugs in Context: The Legal System, the Need for Social Change, and Personal Responsibility. " *The Drug Policy Letter*. Washington, D.C.: Drug Policy Foundation. Available online at http://www.pro-control.net/drug/drugsandpolitics.html.

Trowbridge, Alina. 1997. "Haunting Voices from a Divided Table." Quaker Service, Summer. AFSC publication.

Tutu, Desmond. 2000. *No Future Without Forgiveness*. New York: Doubleday.

United Nations Convention Against Torture and Other Cruel, Inhuman or Degrading Treatment or Punishment. 1984. Article I. New York: United Nations.

United Nations Human Development Report. 1998. U.N. Development Programme. New York: United Nations.

United Nations International Convention on the Prevention and Punishment of the Crime of Genocide. 1948. Article II. New York: United Nations.

Wagner, Peter. 2003. "The Prison Index: Taking the Pulse of the Crime Control Industry." Portland, Oreg.: The Western Prison Project; Northampton, Ma.: The Prison Policy Initiative. Available online at http://www.prisonpolicy.org/prisonindex.shtml.

Whitlock, Kay. 2003. Personal communication.

Williams, Glanville. 1957. *Salmond on Jurisprudence*. 11th ed. London: Sweet & Maxwell.

Wilson, James Q. 1983. *Thinking about Crime*. Rev. ed. New York: Basic Books.

Yazzie, Robert. 2000. "Navajo Justice." *Yes* (Fall). Available online at http://www.yesmagazine.org/article.asp?ID=382.

Yoder, John Howard. 1984. *The Priestly Kingdom*. Notre Dame, Ind.: University of Notre Dame Press.

Zehr, Howard. 1995. *Changing Lenses*. Scottdale, Pa.: Herald Press.

Zimring, Franklin, and Gordon Hawkins. 1995. *Incapacitation: Penal Confinement and the Restraint of Crime*. New York: Oxford University Press.

Zinn, Howard. *A People's History of the United States*. 1980. New York: Harper & Row.

INDEX

Abu-Jamal, Mumia, 16
African Americans. *See also* Blacks
    and the death penalty, 73
    incarceration rates, 32, 35–36, 141
    and reparations, 169, 185
    youth, 141, 145
Alexander, John, 19–21
Asian Americans, 35
Atkins v. Virginia, 74

bail, 53, 55, 89, 163
Bentham, Jeremy, 24–25, 28
Blackmun, Harry, 70–71
Blacks. *See also* African Americans, 32,
    33, 54, 62, 81, 85
    Black children and racism, 138,145
    The Black Codes, 39
    Black women and sexism, 113–14,
    116
    and the death penalty, 73
    and disenfranchisement, 36
    and isolation units, 102
    legal system as extension of slavery
    system, 34
    and The Philadelphia Experiment,
    19–21
    and prison gang policies, 102–4
Bosket, Willie, 97–98
Buddhism, 15–17, 72

capital punishment. *See also* death
    penalty, 69–76
    and Buddhism, 72
    Gregg v. Georgia, 70–75
    and homicide rates, 152
    and racism, 73
    and "special circumstances," 75
Catholic, 23, 191
chain gangs, 38–39
chaplains, 132–36
Children's Defense Fund, 137
class, 9, 37–42, 46, 51, 53, 78

and Criminal Offender Records
    Information, 87
and "Criminal Type," 10
intersection of race and class, 33
and the penitentiary movement,
    22–23
and sexism, 114
convict lease system, 39, 89–90, 189
Corrections Corporation of America,
    89, 112

De Beaumont, Gustave, 27
De Tocqueville, Alexis, 27
death penalty, 69–76
    and Buddhism, 16
    and the "deterrence" argument,
    151–53
    and life sentence without possibility
    of parole, 76–77
    and penal abolition, 175
    and survivors, 150
Debs, Eugene V., 186
Declaration of Charles I, 5
Defoe, Daniel, 24
deterrence, 78, 151–52, 155
Dickens, Charles, 27–28, 177
DiIulio, John, 140
disabilities, 120–22, 177
    civil disability, 33, 86
disenfranchisement, 33, 36, 86, 131,
    182
drugs, 52, 65, 74, 83, 138, 176
    drug policy/"War on Drugs," 65–66
    and the mentally ill, 125
    and sexism, 114–16
    and Three Strikes, 67–68

Executive Order #9066, 168–69

First Nations. *See also* Native Americans,
    170–71

forgiveness, 15, 50, 150, 135, 154–55, 185
  and restorative justice, 166
Foucault, Michel, 18, 24–25, 27
Franklin, Benjamin, 24
Friedman, Lawrence M., 6, 8–9, 11, 19, 27, 28
Furman v. Georgia, 70

gay/lesbian
  female defendants in court, 74
  incarcerated gay/lesbian youth, 132, 141–42
  and "sex offenses," 86–87
  sexual relations and prison rape, 117–18
gender
  and criminal records, 87
  gender-variant and transgender prisoners, 119–20
  and sexism, 113–15
genocide, 16, 34, 36
Gilligan, James, 184–85
Gregg v. Georgia, 70–75
Griffith, Lee, 8, 13, 14, 161

Haverty v. Commissioner of Corrections, 105
health care, 127–28, 176, 185
  and disability, 120
  mental health care and transgender prisoners, 119
  and the mentally ill, 126
  privatization of prisoner health care, 126
Hebrew, 13, 72, 175, 189
Hepatitis C, 127–28
Herrera v. Collins, 74
Higginbotham, Leon, 32, 189
HIV, 16, 121, 127–28
Hollow Water, 155–56, 168, 170–71
Holmes, Oliver Wendell, 153
Human Rights Watch, 100
human rights, 14–15, 46, 98, 122, 143
  and control units, 101
  and criminal records, 86

and international law, 182
  and political prisoners, 106–7
  and Prisoners' Bill of Rights, 179–80
immigrants, 28, 108–12
  and education, 145
  and The Philadelphia Experiment, 19, 21
  and racial profiling, 190
incapacitation, 78, 152, 175
incarceration rates, 35–36, 54, 93, 115
insanity, 8, 123, 152
Islam, 104, 154
Israel, 23

Japanese-American Evacuation Claims Act, 169
Jewish, 17, 72
Jubilee. *See also* Sabbath Year, 12, 189
justice
  definition of, 11–16
  peace-building justice, 13–14, 153, 164–69, 171, 185
  restorative justice, 47, 58–60, 164–68, 174–75, 192
Juvenile Justice and Delinquency Prevention Act, 139

Kairos Document, 10–11
King, Martin Luther Jr., 109
Knopp, Faye Honey, 82
Korematsu, Fred, 168–69
Krog, Antjie, 148

Lord Acton, 48

maximum security. *See also* super-max, 99, 102
McClary, Tonya, 74
Mead, Ed, 81
mentally ill, 28, 31, 55, 80, 120–21, 123–27, 176–77
  deinstitutionalization of, 30
  and sexual abuse, 118
  violation of rights, 102
Mexican Americans, 35–36

Miller, Jerome, 59–60, 92
Mills, Reverend Clara, 172
Moore, Kathleen Dean, 166
Myers, Ched, 12

National Interreligious Task Force on
    Criminal Justice, 136, 191
Native Americans. *See also* First Nations,
    17, 34, 167

Panopticon, 24–26
Parenti, Christian, 9
Peltier, Leonard, 108
Prison Industrial Complex (PIC), 4, 8,
    88–95
Protestant, 3, 4, 20, 22, 24

racial profiling, 46, 104, 116, 190
rehabilitation, 16, 28, 78, 134, 159–60,
    178
    and juvenile justice, 139
    and sentencing, 63
retribution, 50, 78, 109, 152–53
    and death penalty, 71
    and restorative justice, 164
revenge, 3, 15–17, 51, 76, 150–54, 166,
    175
    and death penalty, 72
Rothman, David, 123
Rush, Benjamin, 20, 24

Sabbath Year, 13
Security Threat Groups (STGs), 102–6,
    173
Sentencing Project, 89, 91, 92, 95, 124,
    162
sexism, 51, 87, 113–15
Shaw, George Bernard, 187
slavery, 34–35, 39, 42, 90, 113

legacy of, 163
and reparations, 169, 185
and the Thirteenth Amendment,
    42, 181
South Africa, 1, 10, 15, 32, 34, 153–54
Sterling, Eric, 67–68
suicide, 27, 143
super-max, 31, 97–102
survivors. *See also* victims, 2, 3, 14
    and adversary system, 52, 71–72,
        79–80
    and the new paradigm, 141,
        148–49, 154–55, 161–65, 167,
        169, 171, 174
    and the Twelve-point Plan, 177,
        181, 186–87

Thoreau, Henry David, 187
torture, 4, 22, 36, 107, 161
    and international law, 182
    solitary confinement as, 97–98,
        100–102, 177
Toure, Kazi Ajugun, 108
transgender, 86–87, 119–20
    youth, 132, 141–42
Tutu, Desmond, 155

victims. *See also* survivors, 2, 17, 50–53,
    70–73, 75, 95, 97, 171–72, 192
    and adversary system, 79, 148–49
    as lobbyists, 97
    restitution to, 58, 88

Wilson, James Q., 64
Wink, Walter, 178

Yasuda, Jun, 178

Zehr, Howard, 50, 192